The Perfection of Military Discipline

The Plug Bayonet and the English Army 1660–1705

Mark W. Shearwood

Helion & Company

Helion & Company Limited
Unit 8 Amherst Business Centre
Budbrooke Road
Warwick
CV34 5WE
England
Tel. 01926 499 619
Fax 0121 711 4075
Email: info@helion.co.uk
Website: www.helion.co.uk
Twitter: @helionbooks
blog.helion.co.uk

Published by Helion & Company 2020
Designed and typeset by Mach 3 Solutions Ltd (www.mach3solutions.co.uk)
Cover designed by Paul Hewitt, Battlefield Design (www.battlefield-design.co.uk)

Text © Mark Shearwood 2020
Illustrations © as individually credited
Colour artwork by Patrice Courcelle © Helion & Company 2020
Maps drawn by Alan Turton © Helion & Company 2020

ISBN 978-1-913118-87-7

British Library Cataloguing-in-Publication Data.
A catalogue record for this book is available from the British Library.

For details of other military history titles published by Helion & Company Limited
contact the above address or visit our website: http://www.helion.co.uk.

We always welcome receiving book proposals from prospective authors.

Contents

List of Illustrations

List of Tables

Abbreviations

BL	British Library, London
NA	National Archives, Kew
NAM	National Army Museum, London
RA	Royal Armouries, Leeds
SR	Stafford Record Office, Stafford

Conventions

Dates will be recorded in the old-style Julian calendar, with the exception of the start of the year which will be recorded as 1 January and not 25 March.

During the seventeenth century, infantry was commonly referred to as 'foot', cavalry as 'horse' and mounted infantry as 'dragoons'. Grenadiers refer to infantry elite or assault troops armed with grenades.

Prior to the Act of Union in 1707, although England, Scotland and Ireland were ruled by the same monarch, each country's army was a separate entity and funded through the individual parliaments.

Wherever possible the modern spelling will be used to avoid any confusion, including the modern spelling of bayonet instead of the numerous seventeenth-century variations.

The Board of Ordnance was a government agency responsible for the Crown's fortresses, armouries and siege trains to the army, later becoming responsible for the supply of small arms and equipment to the navy and army.

During this period military discipline refers to the drill of arms as well as the rules and regulations which govern the army.

Evolutions refer to individual motions when performing a complex drill such as loading a musket.

During the seventeenth century, flintlock muskets were also known as fusils, firelocks, doglocks, and snaphance muskets.

Plug Bayonet Terminology

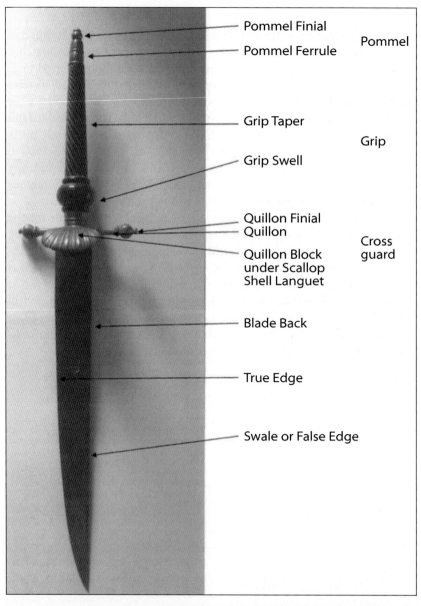

Pommel Finial

Pommel Ferrule

Pommel

Grip Taper

Grip

Grip Swell

Quillon Finial
Quillon

Cross guard

Quillon Block under Scallop Shell Languet

Blade Back

True Edge

Swale or False Edge

Plug Bayonet Terminology, late seventeenth-century plug bayonet. (Author's collection)

Acknowledgements

It would not have been possible to conduct this research without the help and support of a great number of people, I would first like to thank Professor Kevin Linch for his help and enthusiasm for this project. I am most grateful to the following people for giving their time so freely and for access to their individual archives: His Grace The 10th Duke of Buccleugh and 12th Duke of Queensberry, and Scott Macdonald for access to the armoury at Boughton House, Northamptonshire. The Right Hon. The 10th Earl of Dartmouth for allowing me access to his family's papers. Lisa Traynor, Curator of Firearms, Royal Armouries, Leeds for two unfettered days of access to the reference collection at Leeds. Stuart Ivinson, Librarian, Royal Armouries, Leeds for your encyclopaedic knowledge and for finding obscure articles for my research. David Packer, Historic Royal Palaces, for your help with my research at Hampton Court Palace. Alan Larsen for his enthusiasm and for helping me with photographing bayonet drill and to Stuart Makin who gave up his time to stand for the photographs and go through the drill. This project would not have been possible without the support of Charles Singleton of Helion & Company for his support and enthusiasm.

Lastly, but not least I would like to thank my beautiful wife for all her support and putting up with numerous road trips

1

An Introduction

Technological change is often considered, in both coverage and analysis, only selectively, in that solely the successes are considered, while unsuccessful or less successful ideas, inventions and developments, such as the plug bayonet are overlooked or neglected.[1]

General Background and Historical Context

Rather than looking at the development and expansion of the English army from the post-Reformation army inherited by Charles II to the professional army of the Duke of Marlborough independently and in isolation from the development of weapons it uses, this book proposes that the development of the army is intrinsically linked. That the development of the structure, formations and tactics of the army shared a symbiotic relationship with the technological developments of the weapons it used and specifically during the time period in question, with the development of the plug bayonet. The plug bayonet, rather than being the limited technological advancement, it was the right weapon for the manufacturing and technological abilities available to the Board of Ordnance and was the keystone that enabled further advances in bayonet design and technology to follow and succeed.

Our impression of weapons understandably changes over time and can on occasions be considered outdated when viewed against contemporary weapons and advances in military technology. During the seventeenth century the pike was regarded as the queen of weapons and vastly superior in the eyes of the senior officers to the musket, which at best must have been due to a romanticised view of martial combat. When Colonel Clifford Walton wrote his seminal work on the *History of the British Standing Army*, published in 1894, his opening text on the bayonet states that:[2]

---

1   J. Black, *Rethinking Military History* (London: Routledge, 2004), pp.123–124.
2   C. Walton, *History of the British Standing Army. A.D. 1660 to 1700* (London: Harrison and Sons, 1894), p.304.

> There is probably no weapon that has, at least in this country, been so loudly extolled as the Bayonet. For a century and a half, the bayonet has been to us what the bow was of old, our special weapon, the piece de resistance of every British army.

What Clifford had in mind when he wrote is quote would have been a socket bayonet that had not substantially changed from the early socket bayonets associated with the 'Brown Bess' used by the Duke of Marlborough's men during the War of the Spanish Succession.

The bayonet and its use by British forces is deeply engrained within Britain's cultural memory, becoming indicative of the British army. It is so ingrained in our collective culture from images of Grenadier Guards on parade at the annual trooping the colour, to the BBC show 'Dad's Army',[3] Where Lance Corporal Jones' catchphrase, 'they don't like it up 'em!' refers to the bayonet and his service in the Sudan; while the plug bayonet has been forgotten or deemed insignificant within both the British historical memory and as an innovation of military technology.

Overlooked in current historiography as nothing more than a semi-interesting sideline of military technology, which is well postulated in Black's quotation at the start of this chapter, this book is my attempt to re-establish the plug bayonet within its true historical context and examine the impact this simple weapon had on the English army. While the focus of this book is primarily on the English army, the impact from the introduction of the plug bayonet was felt throughout all the European armies to one extent or another. While proposing any date for the removal of the pike from constant use within most European armies, a general date of post 1705 is probably an acceptable point, although there are exceptions. Sweden maintained the pike as its primary offensive weapon until the 1720s, which forced Russia and Denmark to reintroduce the pike within its own forces to counteract the Carolean army's *Gå På* battle tactic.[4] There were still proponents of the pike as late at 1779, with General Henry Lloyd proposing the reintroduction of a fourth rank of foot 'being composed of the tallest and strongest men' and armed with 'a pike, eleven or twelve feet long, two feet being made out of steel'.[5] The original focus of my research looked at the development of the plug bayonet, and to answer the primary research question – to what extent did the English Army replace the pike with the plug bayonet during the second half of the seventeenth century? Contrastingly Childs and Hughes when describing advances in military technology move directly from the pike to the socket bayonet.[6]

---

3   *Dad's Army*, created by Jimmy Perry and David Croft, was first shown on 31 July 1968 and finally finished production on 13 November 1977.

4   The *Gå På* tactics used by the Carolean army was centred around contacting the enemy at the first available opportunity. Swedish units would only fire one or twice only prior to charging home with pike and bayonet.

5   P. Speelman, *War, Society and Enlightenment: The Works of General Lloyd* (Leiden: Brill, 2005), p.364.

6   J. Childs, *Warfare in the Seventeenth Century* (London: Cassell, 2001), p.211, and M. Hughes, 'Technology, Science and War' in *Palgrave Advances in Modern Military History*, ed. by M.

Prior to answering the primary research question, the plug bayonet will need to be placed within its correct historical context, both in terms of the historical environment and its physical presence. The military plug bayonet is in essence a piece of civilian technology that was developed and adapted for military use. The origins of the bayonet can be found in boar hunting during the late sixteenth century in France and Spain. Historically a huntsman would be armed with a musket and a heavy (boar) spear with a cross-guard to stop the boar from fully impaling itself. The hunting bayonet was a short-bladed dagger, where the conical handle of the weapon would fit inside the barrel of the musket, allowing the user to defend himself against the boar, replacing the boar spear. This version of the bayonet was in use for nearly 300 years, with Spanish bayonets still being made in the 1850s.[7] It would be almost 100 years later that a military version of this weapon would appear. The basic design did not change and the military used it to transform a musket into a shorter version of a pike, thereby giving the infantryman a defensive weapon primarily against cavalry, but also against foot.[8] Prior to this, the non-pike armed troops would resort to using their muskets as clubs when defending themselves at close quarters, although as we shall see later, this tactic was still used into the early 1700s as a prescribed method for infantry to engage enemy foot.

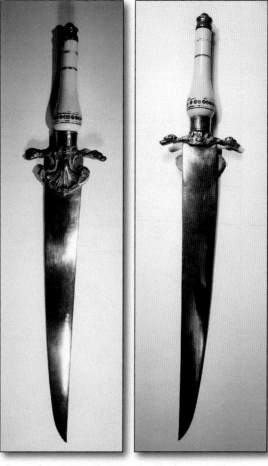

German late eighteenth-century hunting bayonet with an ivory grip and brass cross guard and pommel. (Author's collection)

From the late fifteenth century until the introduction of the plug bayonet, troops were categorised as being offensively armed with a firearm, or defensively armed with a pike. The pike were made of ash or oak and originally were between 15–18 feet long, later being cut down to between 11–12 long for ease of use. Tactics evolved from the arquebus-armed troops protecting large blocks of pikemen, to the late 1600s when the pikemen protected the musket-armed troops.[9] As we shall see later in the book, the number of pikemen in each company was reduced to around 14 men, giving a battalion with 10 companies a maximum of 140, this number of men would leave the vast majority of the battalion unable to defend themselves against enemy horse. The invention of the plug bayonet resulted in a paradigm

Hughes and W. Philpott (Basingstoke: Palgrave Macmillan, 2006), pp.231–57 (p.236).

7   R. Evans, *The Plug Bayonet: An Identification Guide for Collectors* (Shipley: R. Evans, 2002), p.94.

8   G. Hayes-McCoy, 'The Battle of Aughrim 1691', *Journal of the Galway Archaeological and History Society,* 20 (1942), pp.1–30 (p.8) <https://www.jstor.org/stable/25535200>.

9   Hughes 'Technology, Science and War', p.236.

Seventeenth-century print of army marching, unknown artist. (Author's collection)

shift to all infantry, having both offensive and defensive capability, with the first reference to the plug bayonet within the English army appearing in 1662.[10] This reference relates to a contract awarded to Samuel Law and Robert Steadman of the London Cutlers Company, for the repair of bayonets belonging to English troops returning from Dunkirk.[11]

During the seventeenth century, a colonel would be commissioned by the Crown to raise a regiment of foot or horse, or by Parliament from the start of the English Civil War to the end of the Commonwealth (1642 to 1660), and would have been allowed a large amount of latitude regarding clothing and equipping the battalion along with the types of musket being used. In 1706 the Board of Ordnance still complained that 'few … officers agree in the sort of bayonet to be used or the manner of fixing them'.[12] Following the English Civil War, the gentry and by default Parliament, found the idea of a standing army odious, they instead believed the defence of England should be kept in the hands of the militia. According to Manning, the rationale for this belief resulted from the political leadership's 'beliefs and prejudices being acquitted from the writings of Machiavelli and Harrington'.[13] The landed gentry and political classes believed that the country's militia was a more loyal body than any standing army, 'because the officers of the militia were of a higher social standing and would fight for religion, King and Country'.[14]

The only permanent institutions surrounding the army were the Board of Ordnance, and the Royal Military hospital built in Chelsea by King Charles II in 1682.[15] Without a permanent standing army and the corresponding ability to train officers within the English army, soldiers' training was left up to individual officers. This lack of central control produced a profusion of privately published military manuals, this area will be further explored in chapter 4. Although the primary focus of this manuscript is on the English army of the late seventeenth century, due to the close relationship between the English establishment and the colonies, documentary evidence will be included from these areas to help show the development of technology and battlefield theory.

Historiography

Due to the limited amount of literature available regarding plug bayonets, the relevant historiography will be included within each individual chapter, rather than in a chapter of its own. Historians, both amateur and professional

---

10 J. Black, *A Military Revolution? Military Change and European Society 1550–1800* (Basingstoke: Macmillan Education, 1991), p.20.

11 R. Evans, 'The Plug Bayonet', *New Zealand Antique Arms Gazette* (1999), pp.19–22 (p.19).

12 M. Anderson, *War and Society in Europe of the Old Regime 1618–1789* (Stroud: Sutton Publishing, 1988) p.105.

13 R. Manning, *An Apprenticeship in Arms: The Origins of the British Army 1585–1702* (Oxford: Oxford University Press, 2008), pp.290–91.

14 Manning, *An Apprenticeship in Arms*, pp.290–91.

15 J. Childs, *Armies and warfare in Europe 1648–1789* (Manchester: Manchester University Press, 1982), p.66.

tend to overlook the plug bayonet within their individual spheres of military research, while historians researching military technology relegate the plug bayonet to a mere technological dead end prior to the invention of the socket bayonet. Their colleagues studying battlefield accounts tend to focus on its faults and common myths: Stuart Reid's latest research on the Battle of Killiecrankie (2018) is indicative of this mindset. Here, he regurgitates General Mackay's famous statement that 'his men were defeated by an unforeseen technical flaw in their weaponry [plug bayonet]', however, without giving any analysis this just perpetuates the urban myths relating to the plug bayonet.[16]

Texts relating to the history and use of plug bayonets can be divided into three areas. First, works on the English army where technology and equipment is not the primary focus; Black when discussing changes in weapon and tactical changes from 1660–1760 fails to mention the plug bayonet, only stating that Britain adopted the bayonet in 1704.[17] The second area includes works on specific military technologies including bayonets and muskets, where plug bayonets only receive slight attention. Norris' book on bayonets (2016) claims to trace the development of the bayonet and 'challenge many myths and misconceptions'. Although the plug bayonet features in a number of chapters, he makes a number of common unsubstantiated statements without offering up any sources or evidence.[18] This area also includes non-academic texts written primarily for collectors, which are very detailed regarding the physical characteristics, but short on context and lack academic rigour. The exception to this rule is Evans' book *The Plug Bayonet: An Identification Guide for Collectors*, which is the seminal work on the topic.[19] The incorporation of non-academic texts into my research can have specific issues, for as Black states 'books published for the popular market often offer no new insights or analysis, and their conclusions will not always stand up to the accepted standards of academic works'.[20] The third category comprises works on the 'military revolution' of the seventeenth century, which tend to overlook the impact of plug bayonets and concentrate on the later socket bayonet.

Characteristics of the Plug Bayonet

The first question to be resolved is what constitutes a plug bayonet and perhaps more importantly, was the plug bayonet a universal fit, or was it matched to a specific musket? Chapter 2 looks at the physical aspects of the plug bayonet. As previously stated, there are a number of myths and general theories surrounding plug bayonets that are being taken as fact. These

---

16 S. Reid, *Battle of Killiecrankie 1689: The Last Act of the Killing Times* (Barnsley: Frontline Books, 2018), p.84, and J. Childs, *Armies and Warfare in Europe 1648–1789* (Manchester: Manchester University Press, 1982), p.107.

17 Black, *Military Revolution*, p.20.

18 J. Norris, *Fix Bayonets!* (Barnsley: Pen and Sword Military, 2016), p.9.

19 Evans, *The Plug Bayonet*.

20 Jeremy Black, *Rethinking Military History* (Abingdon: Routledge, 2004), pp.26–29.

include two theories that are perpetuated by Norris in his book *Fix Bayonets!* in that they are a universal fit, and that the grip swell was designed to stop the bayonet being stuck within the musket.[21], [22] The research has drawn on data from the reference collection at the Royal Armouries Leeds, as well as bayonets held in a number of private collections including the Boughton House collections. Additional data on muskets and their accuracy has been obtained from the Littlecote House collection and works on the East India Company.

Previous data gathered on the plug bayonet has taken standardised measurements for a bladed weapon, the overall length, the dimensions of the blade, and the length of the handle or grip; however, no one has previously looked at the dimensions of the grip. This measurement is essential to understanding the relationship between the bayonet and the musket, for without this data no clear picture can be revealed regarding the universality of plug bayonets.

This chapter will also look into the issues surrounding standardisation. Warrants in the Board of Ordnance minutes books for 1682–83 show a contract issued for 1,000 snaphance muskets which were divided between 29 individual gunsmiths.[23] The minute book for 1695–96 shows another warrant issued to a John Hawgood for 2,626 'reasonably ordinary bayonets'. Hawgood was in charge of a consortium of sword and bayonet cutlers.[24] Both these warrants show the issues confronting any attempt to standardise production, with multiple manufactures working without a universal specification. In conclusion, this chapter with examining the purported universality of the plug bayonet and if this impacted on the development and distribution of plug bayonets within the English army.

Weapons and Equipment

Previous academic works have failed to consider the impact resulting from the fragmented procurement systems of the late seventeenth century. Chapter 3 will look at the weapons of the English army and the challenges of the procurement system operated by the Board of Ordnance. By taking a revisionary view combining the latest research and utilising and re-interpreting contemporary drill books, myths and misconceptions regarding weapons such as matchlock and flintlock muskets can corrected; in addition using contemporary records to show both the increase in popularity of the bayonet, and the limitations of the procurement system for the English army, and its effect on the development and distribution of plug bayonets. The first part of the chapter focuses on the changes to infantry weapons and the difficulty in assigning clear dates for change, while the second half looks at the procurement systems used by both the Board of Ordnance and individual

---

21 Norris, *Fix Bayonets!*, p.9.

22 See p.10 for the definition of the grip swell.

23 NAM, WO47/13 *Book of Minutes 1682–83*, Folio 93, 3 April 1683.

24 NAM, WO47/18 *Book of Minutes 1695–96*, Folio 194, 29 February 169⅚.

battalions. Specifically, this chapter will try to answer the following questions – who, if anyone was responsible for the introduction of the bayonet? – did any increase in bayonet use correspond to a decrease in the use of the pike? During the later years of the seventeenth century the Board of Ordnance became more responsible for the ordering and distribution of small arms and bladed weapons.

Records from the Board of Ordnance provide a substantial amount of information regarding plug bayonets, from yearly records of the amount of supplies held within the state armouries, to records of the despatch of equipment for individual regiments and campaigns. The yearly 'state of the Ordnance' records provide a snapshot of the numbers of weapons held at each fortress and armoury, and together they can provide details of the change in infantry equipment over time.

Chapter 3 will also incorporate the limited archaeological records available into the research to help to gain a complete picture regarding the influence and disbursement of the plug bayonet within the English army. Evidence from the battlefield sites of Sedgemoor (1685), and Killiecrankie (1689) will help to identify the spread of bayonets during the late 1680s. While the documents within chapter 3 could be seen as incontrovertible evidence for the change from pike to bayonet, to paraphrase David Chandler – historians reliance on primary sources as an absolute truth can be problematic without collaborating evidence that any given item is indeed true, or that orders or warrants were actually acted on in full.[25] However, when this data is used in conjunction with the information from both the preceding and following chapters, this will help to build a balanced picture of the development and distribution of the plug bayonet.

Tactical Changes and Variations

Chapters 4 and 5 will deal with the change in infantry tactics resulting from the increased use of the plug bayonet within the English army. Due to the nature of English army during this period, there was not any uniformity of tactics or training, with regimental colonels and officers being responsible for deciding which drills would be used. The historical evidence for this chapter will be provided by the numerous drill manuals and guides to infantry discipline published during the latter half of the seventeenth century. Without a centralised system for officer training within the English army, officers had to rely on a number of privately printed treaties and manuals, including works by the Duke of Monmouth and the Duke of Marlborough.[26]

The appearance of a number of these manuals suggests that they were intended for the general military education of junior officers, and not for operations on the field of battle. The number of individual evolutions can

---

25 David Chandler, *Blenheim Preparations: The English Army on the March to the Danube, Collective Essays* (Staplehurst: Spellmount Publishing, 2004), p.192.

26 J. Morphew, *The New Exercise of Firelocks & Bayonets; Appointed by his Grace the Duke of Marlborough to be used by all the British Forces* (London: John Morphew, 1708).

Raising of the army, print by Jacques Callot, 1633. (Courtesy of the Rijksmuseum, Netherlands)

amount to 55 separate and consecutive commands for use in the parade ground, as described in *The New Exercise of Firelocks & Bayonets* published in 1708.[27] The inconsistencies in musket drills was a concern to officers, as noted by Richard Kane who stated that 'Great pains have been taken to bring our troops under one method of discipline, but most officers preferring to have some trifling motions performed after their own whims.'[28] With drill manuals during this period being privately published, there is unfortunately no certain way of confirming how many were actually used, and how many were just treated as curiosities.[29] Another evolution of drill manuals included other matters considered important for a junior officer's education, including fortifications, mathematics and how to set up a camp as seen in the published work by Capt. J Storey in 1688.[30] Even with these caveats, contemporary drill manuals still offer an excellent insight into the changes in drill and the transition from the pike to the bayonet and can be used to chart the development of tactical theory as well as practice.

English Army

Chapter 6 looks at the organisation and structure of the English army, along with those regiments that were attached to the English establishment during times of conflict. It details the care and pay of soldiers over the time period in question. It shows the Crown's tactics with dealing with a parliament and population that were opposed to having a large standing army in times of peace. It confirms that in times of contraction of the army, independent companies were formed to garrison the nations strategic towns, forts, and

---

27 Morphew, *The New Exercise of Firelocks & Bayonets*, pp.25–31.

28 R. Kane, *Campaigns of King William and Queen Anne; From 1689 to 1712, also a New System of Military Discipline for a Battalion of Foot on Action* [facsimile], p.109.

29 Chandler, *Blenheim Preparation*, p.95.

30 J. Storey, *Fortification and Military Discipline 1688* [Facsimile] (London: Robert Morden. 1688).

Map of Great Britain and Ireland battlefields. (Map drawn by Alan Turton © Helion & Company)

castles. In times of growth, the Crown incorporated these independent companies into either new or existing regiments. The Crown's other strategy was to increase the numbers both of companies within a regiment and men within each company during times of potential conflict, then reduce the numbers in times of peace.

Conclusion

As demonstrated in the following chapters, there is a systemic misunderstanding about the original purpose and role the bayonet was meant to play within the English army. The leading texts on the equipment and operations of the army during the period in question, both from academic and non-academic authors, tend to place the emphasis on the negative aspects of the plug bayonet. Leading works by Childs, Chandler, Norris, and Reid, for example focus on General Hugh Mackay's description of his defeat at the battle of Killiecrankie.[31] Losing the battle due to his troops either not being able to fit their plug bayonets in time to receive the Highlander's charge, or fitting them too early, resulting in them not being able to continue to give fire.

What Mackay's contemporary account, and the above-mentioned authors fail to articulate clearly, is that the bayonet was never originally intended as the soldier's main means of self defence against enemy infantry. The plug bayonet was originally intended as a replacement for the pike, as an anti-cavalry defence for an infantry regiment. Indeed, the first recipients of the plug bayonet were units that were historically equipped without pikes, dragoon regiments, marine regiments, and grenadiers. The infantry's primary close combat weapon had not changed from the English Civil War, which was either an upturned musket, the sword, or hangar. One further piece of information generally overlooked, is that if muskets and bayonets replaced the pike, the firepower of any unit would be increased proportionally.

---

31 J. Childs, *Armies and Warfare in Europe, 1648–1789* (Manchester: Manchester University Press, 1982), pp.106–107; S. Reid, *Killiecrankie*, p.84; Norris, *Fix Bayonets!*, p.84.

2

Plug Bayonets

Introduction

The following chapter will concentrate on the physical features of the plug bayonet, with the aim to answer part of the main research question. While the primary question looks at 'to what extent does the bayonet replace the pike', this chapter looks at, was the plug bayonet a universal fit with all muskets? And did this have an impact on the general acceptance of the weapon? To answer these questions, a detailed evaluation of surviving plug bayonets is necessary, with the primary research focus being on the bayonet grip. This is the first time that any academic research has looked into this aspect of the plug bayonet and in context with contemporary muskets. As previously stated in chapter 1, the universality of the plug bayonet has always been assumed by academic and non-academic authors alike, without offering any evidence to substantiate their claims.[1]

This chapter will use statistical analysis to enable a better understanding of the relationship between the plug bayonet and its host, in this case seventeenth-century matchlock and flintlock muskets. While no previous work has used statistical analysis regarding plug bayonet research, Ballard had some success when using statistical analysis as an adjunct to aid historical research into the identity of the manufacturers of British pattern 1907 bayonets.[2]

Prior to a detailed examination of the physical characteristics of plug bayonets, a brief explanation regarding the difference between colonels' or non-Ordnance pattern bayonets, and Ordnance pattern bayonets is required. Colonels' bayonets encompass all bayonets not directly purchased by the Board of Ordnance. These include the original bayonets acquired by the English army and continued to be produced until their complete replacement by socket bayonets in the early part of the eighteenth century. This type of

---

1 Norris, *Fix Bayonets!,* p.9
2 J. Ballard, 'Statistical Analysis as an Adjunct to Historical Research: Identification of the Likely Manufacturers of British Pattern 1907 Bayonets Supplied by the Birmingham Small Arms Company to the Siamese Government in 1920', *Arms and Armour*, 15.1 (2018), 83–95 (p.93) <DOI 10.1080/17416124.2018.1436491> [accessed 10 July 2018].

High quality non-Ordnance pattern bayonet 1691, inscribed with 'God save King William and Queen Mary, Anno Domini 1691 WMR'. (Photo courtesy of the private owner)

Ordnance pattern plug bayonet, brass fittings. (Author's collection)

bayonet has either iron or brass fittings, and generally will have greater decoration especially on the quillons and pommel with officer bayonets being very ornate, including grips made of carved ivory. R. Evans, in his book *The Plug Bayonet* identifies 89 designs within this category and the author has identified an additional 12 designs.

The bayonet in image 6 is an excellent example of a high-quality non-Ordnance bayonet with dark wood grip with iron quillons, with a small shell-guard. Dated to 1691 and inscribed with 'God save King William and Queen Mary, Anno Domini 1691 WMR'. Ordnance pattern bayonets on the other hand, tend to be more simplistic or utilitarian, and exclusively found with brass fittings and cheaper oak grips. This philosophy is exemplified by a warrant dated 29 February 1685, addressed to Master Hawgood for 2,626 'reasonably ordinary bayonets'.[3],[4] A large number of Ordnance bayonets can be found with replacement soft wood grips following a fire at the Tower of London in 1841, where approximately 2,000 bayonets had been in storage. These bayonets have been excluded from the research as the dimensions of the grips are suspect and would invalidate the data collected.

The Board of Ordnance either issued contracts or warrants directly to artisans, or to middlemen such as Hawgood, who would then distribute the work to a stable of artisan cutlers. These blades tend to be straight, single-edged, unfurled and with a spear point, and logic would dictate that they were of a more uniform size. When looking at a universal fit, as stated in the introduction, it is clear that a brief

3   NA, WO47/18, *Board of Ordnance Minute Book 1695–6*, Folio 194.

4   John Hawgood was the master of the London Cutler Company in 1687, and was the head of a collective of cutlers, trading from 'The Sign of the Kings Head' in Charing Cross, London.

discussion regarding the production and specifications of contemporary muskets is required.

The research into universality is based on the detailed examination of 47 bayonets and encompasses the complete reference collection at the Royal Armouries Leeds, and the largest contemporary collection in England, belonging to the Duke of Buccleuch and Queensbury located at Broughton House. The bayonets studied originated from 19 different cutlers, with a further five bayonets with Kings Head marks too faded to identify the maker, with the consensus of opinion that these are from the stable of cutlers working for the Hawgoods.[5] The identification of the bore size of contemporary matchlock and flintlock muskets is of critical importance to the research in this section of this work. The author was able to take advantage of the work carried out by Richardson and Rimer in their cataloguing of the Littlecote collection which is an excellent source of information, with additional primary research carried out at the Royal Armouries Leeds.[6]

Ordnance Pattern Plug Bayonets

As previously stated in the introduction to this chapter, Ordnance pattern bayonets tend to be of a more standardised design, however the generic term of bayonet can be problematic at best and can easily lead to misidentification. Unfortunately for historians, clerks and authors in the seventeenth century tend to describe bayonets as just that, so a clerk in 1662 will describe a plug bayonet generally as just a bayonet. The same can be said for a clerk in 1720 when he describes a socket bayonet as simply a 'bayonet'. This will be expanded on in further detail in chapters 3 and 4 but this can be the cause of misunderstandings and assumptions by modern-day historians. Professor John Childs in his work *The Nine Years' War and the British Army* states that:

> This suggests that the socket bayonet was steadily ousting both the pike and the plug bayonet in the middle years of the war. The train of artillery in 1693 conveyed 3,960 spare pikes but also 1,500 replacement 'sword bayonets'.[7]

This assumption by Childs, is however, not backed up by the evidence, there is one design of Ordnance pattern sword plug bayonet in existence, which changes our understanding and interpretation of the extent that plug bayonets were used. The evidence is further enhanced by records from the Ordnance Board that show the numbers of bayonets purchased during the period in question.

These figures clearly show that the one example held in the reference collection at the Royal Armouries Leeds is not a unique item, sword bayonets

---

5   Evans, *The Plug Bayonet*, p.57.
6   Thomas Richardson and Graeme Rimer, *Littlecote, the English Civil War Armoury* (Leeds: Royal Armouries, 2012), pp.194–287.
7   J. Childs, *The Nine Years' War and the British Army 1688–97: The Operations in the Low Countries* (Manchester: Manchester University Press), p.76.

are also mentioned in a guide to the Tower of London printed in 1767.[8] The figures in Table 1 are for bayonets purchased directly by the Board of Ordnance and do not include bayonets purchased by colonels of regiments directly from cutlers or their agents.

Table 1 Plug Bayonets Purchased by the Board of Ordnance Per Year[9]

Year	Plug	Socket	Sword	Sea
1689–90	32,500		6,000	5,000
1691			1,500	
1692	6,000			
1695	1,000			
1697	1,000			
1702	225		450	

The Ordnance pattern plug bayonets in this study are all from the reference collection of the Royal Armouries Leeds, and could readily be described as a utilitarian design bereft of any excessive ornamentation. The sword bayonet in image 4 has a knuckle guard formed from one of its brass quillon, the rear of the knuckle guard is not fixed to the pommel allowing its insertion into a musket barrel. There are 18 Ordnance pattern bayonets within this study, all with the standard feature of a brass pommel, quillon and finials (although some examples have these missing). All have a straight blade with a spear point. The sample includes blades from nine identified cutlers, with a further six bearing the probable mark of the Hawgoods, one blade is unadorned without a cutler's mark. With the obvious exception of the sword bayonet, these bayonets have an overall length of between 357mm and 480mm. The important measurements for this study as previously stated revolve around the dimensions of the grip, with four measurements being taken on each bayonet. Measurements were taken at the base of the grip, the top of the grip where it met the swell, halfway between these two points, and the diameter of the swell.

The relevant information regarding grip diameters is shown in full information in appendix I. When looking at the reputation of the plug bayonet, one aspect regarding the design is the function of the swell, *Norris* states that the swell was designed to stop the bayonet from getting stuck in the barrel of the musket.[10] If this theory is correct there should be a comparison between the dimensions of the musket barrel (see section 2.2 above), and the data stated in appendix I, specifically the measurement taken at the top section of the bayonet grip.

The data set of Ordnance pattern bayonets gives an arithmetic mean measurement of 27.2mm where the grip meets the swell and of 21.32mm at the midpoint of the grip, the median measurements are 28.4mm and 20.7mm respectively. The full results and their implications will be discussed in the conclusion to this chapter.

---

8   Anon., *A Companion to Every Place of Curiosity and Entertainment in and about London and Westminster*, (London: J. Lawrence, 1767), p.19.
9   E. Goldstein, *The Socket Bayonet*, p.8.
10 Norris, *Fix Bayonets!*, p.9.

When the research data is taken into consideration, it is clear that the generalisations of previous works on the subject are problematic at best, the average bore of all four categories of muskets is between 19.64mm and 20.28mm, with 66.3 percent of the musket samples having a bore in the 20–21mm range. When these results are compared with the grip data, 38 percent of the sample has a middle grip measurement greater that the standard range of musket bore. In all cases the largest grip diameter of every bayonet is greater that the musket bore, thus discounting Norris' theory regarding the grip for Ordnance pattern bayonets.

Non-Ordnance Plug Bayonets

While Ordnance pattern bayonets can be described as having a uniform utilitarian design, the same cannot be said regarding non-Ordnance pattern bayonets. The first plug bayonets purchased by the English army had steel fittings giving way to cast brass in 1683.[11] After 1683, brass becomes the predominant metal, but steel mounts can occasionally be found along with bronze, gilt and silver mounts used for officers' bayonets.[12] These bayonets will often be found with grips of horn, ivory, or expensive woods such as walnut.

By definition, the non-Ordnance bayonets encompass all designs of bayonets outside of the standard design of Ordnance bayonets. Officers bayonets in the collection of the Royal Armouries Leeds can be identified to the reign of Queen Anne (8 March 1702 to 1 August 1714), which puts the plug bayonet still in use far later that commonly thought. Chandler gives one date of 1698 in an early work and a later date of 1704 (in a subsequent work) for when the majority of English troops were equipped with the new socket bayonet.[13] Chapters 3 and 4 will go into greater depth regarding both the lifespan of the plug bayonet and the transition to the later socket version.

The non-Ordnance pattern bayonets used for this survey are predominantly from the reference collection at the Royal Armouries, and the Boughton House collection. This study includes 17 examples from the Royal Armouries and a further 12 examples from other specified sources. The data obtained from this sample of bayonets is shown in appendix II and is generally consistent with the findings for the Ordnance pattern bayonets in section 2.3. When comparing this data against the 63 percent of muskets which fall within the 20–21mm bore range, the majority of non-Ordnance bayonets middle or median measurement are contrastingly smaller than those from the Ordnance samples. In this sample only three, or 12 percent, of the bayonets surveyed have a median measurement within the 20–21mm range,

Non-Ordnance Pattern Officer's bayonet c.1686, bone fluted grip, steel berry quillons and scallop shell languet. Rose and crown cutlers mark on reverse, made by William Hoy. (Author's collection)

11   R. Evans, 'The Plug Bayonet', *The Armourer: The Militaria Magazine* (1999), pp.19–22.

12   Evans, 'Plug Bayonets', pp.47–53

13   Chandler, *Age of Marlborough*, pp.83–84 and Chandler, *Blenheim*, p.100. John Childs puts the date as 1697, by when 'virtually of the British line musketeers were wielding socket bayonets'. J. Childs, *The Nine Years' War and the British Army 1688–97: The Operations in the Low Countries* (Manchester: Manchester University Press, 1991), p.76.

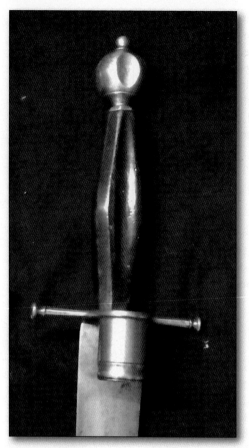

Close-up of socket and cut-out of the grip and pommel to allow musket barrel to fit. (Courtesy of His Grace, The 10th Duke of Buccleugh and 12th Duke of Queensbury)

with an additional two, or eight percent, just outside this range at 21.1mm. Probably more importantly, four of the bayonets in question have their largest diameter of the grip measuring smaller than the average musket bore, the fact that it is only non-Ordnance pattern bayonets that make up this category does suggest a standardisation in design parameters.

The most consistent grip sizes are found in the bayonets belonging to the samples from Broughton House which consist of nine plug bayonets and one early ring bayonet which was an unsuccessful hybrid design between a plug and the later socket bayonet. The armoury in the house is recorded on 27 November 1718 to contain 530 muskets, 530 bayonets, 100 carbines and 282 cases of pistols, with another 367 muskets and 367 bayonets within an 'Old Wardrobe'.[14] Another possibility is that the collection may have been assembled by His Grace the 2nd Duke, John Montagu, who was Master of Ordnance between 1742 and 1749. Without written records it is impossible to know whether any of these nine bayonets were part of the above inventory, but their uniformity of grip sizes, if not of grip styles does suggest a specific standardisation being obtained.

These bayonets are described in appendix II, with references prefixed by 'N', and shown in illustration 5 on the following page. As shown in the photograph five of the bayonets are inside their original scabbard, unfortunately due to the condition of four of these scabbards it was impossible to locate the makers' marks. It was possible to remove the scabbard of one bayonet (N116) which revealed a previously unidentified maker's mark of a shooting star, two of the bayonets with visible marks can be attributed to the cutler Hawgood or his associates. The bayonet on the far right of the Broughton House collection photograph is an early type of ring/socket bayonet.

Plug Bayonet Supply and Demand

The following chapter will look at how plug bayonets were ordered and the evidence relating to the disbursement of bayonets within the English army, and to lesser extent the state sponsored trading companies.[15] The aim of this chapter is to try to answer the following questions: to what extent were plug bayonets ordered in conjunction with muskets, or were they ordered separately? Does the information show an increase in requests for bayonets and a decrease in the need for pikes?

---

14 P. Wilcock, 'The Armoury of His Grace the Duke of Buccleuch and Queensberry', *Arms and Armour*, 9, (2012), pp.181–205 (pp.192–92).

15 These include the Honourable East India Company and the Hudson Bay Company.

Collection of 8 plug bayonets and 1 ring/socket bayonet from Broughton House, Northamptonshire. (Courtesy of His Grace, The 10th Duke of Buccleugh and 12th Duke of Queensbury)

If plug bayonets did in fact supersede the pike within the English army, the records should help to form a picture of plug bayonet availability within the stores and fortresses of the British Isles. This information when added to the answers obtained in chapter 2 will provide a substantial foundation for the fourth chapter which will look at the changes in drill of the English army during the seventeenth century. The Board of Ordnance was under the control of the Master of Ordnance, this position was appointed by the King and during the period in question changed hands numerous times:

Table 2 Holders of the Position of Master of Ordnance Musket Barrel, Internal Measurements

Sir Thomas Chicheley	Master of Ordnance	1670–79
Sir John Chicheley Sir William Hickman Sir Christopher Musgrave	Commission	1679–82
Frederick Schomberg, 1st Duke of Schomberg	Master of Ordnance	1689–90
Vacant		1690–93
Henry Sidney	Master of Ordnance	1693–1702

Whereas the previous chapter relied on physical evidence, the following chapter relies exclusively on contemporary written evidence predominately obtained from the Dartmouth papers with additional information obtained from the Blenheim papers, and the Egerton papers. Further research is required to examine the records of the 1st Duke of Schomberg and Henry Sidney and to obtain evidence regarding the purchasing of non-Ordnance bayonets.

Section 3.2 will look at the surviving documentation which relates to the demand for plug bayonets. Section 3.3 will investigate and examine the records of the fortresses, armouries, and stores, thus giving a picture of the supply and availability of plug bayonets. While these two sections show the paper records of the plug bayonets process of superseding the pike, while section 3.4 will look at archaeological records to try to identify the plug bayonet's use on the battlefields of England and Scotland. The final part of this chapter will correlate and summarise the findings and relate them to the research questions stated at the start of the chapter.

Plug Bayonet Demand

The evidence for the procurement and issue of plug bayonets will be obtained from a variety of written contemporary papers, with the majority of evidence being derived from Royal Warrants and Board of Ordnance records. Prior to looking at the available evidence one has to be aware of the possible limitations in using primary sources; for, without corroboration, it is impossible to understand if any given order or instruction was carried through. As Chandler states in every age – not least our own – it is necessary to regard official contemporary government pronouncements with the traditional 'pinch of salt'.[16] Previous studies into the operation of the English army during the seventeenth century including those by Childs and Chandler, have used the Board of Ordnance records individually to make a particular point, either directly or through secondary sources.[17] This work however, is the first study to systematically use these records to produce a historical picture of the progression of the plug bayonet into everyday use within the English army. The official practice of the Board of Ordnance only being responsible for supplying the original arms to newly raised regiments, with further issues being the responsibility of the said regiment, hampered the modernisation of the English army.[18]

As explained in chapter 1, bayonets were first issued to grenadiers and dragoons, troops that were deployed without the protection of pikes. In 1669–70 King Charles II issued instructions for a regiment of dragoons to be raised, to consist of 12 troops of 80 men and to be armed with matchlock muskets, bandoliers, and to carry one bayonet or great knife.[19] Records show

16 Chandler, *Blenheim*, p.95.

17 Chandler, *Blenheim*, p.100; Chandler, *Age of Marlborough*, pp.79–80; Childs, *Army of William III*, p.172; C. Walton, *History of the British Standing Army A.D. 1660 to 1700* (Pall Mall: Harrison and Son, 1894), pp.349, 423–27, 438; D. Blackmore, *Destructive & Formidable: British Infantry Firepower 1642–1765* (London: Frontline Books, 2014), pp.62–63.

18 NA, WO 55/334, *Entry Book of Warrants*, 4 August 1686, NA, NA, WO 55/345, *Entry Book of Warrants*, pp.156–7 17 October 1710.

19 J. Scott, *The British Army: its Origin, Progress, and Equipment, Volume 1* (San Bernadino: Ulan Press, 2012), p.295.

that an order was places for 10,000 plug bayonets on 12 March 1678.[20] Twelve days later on 20 March 1678 a Ordnance document was raised proposing arms and ammunition for 12,978 foot, armed with 8,820 musket and 4,158 pike, the document specifies 8,820 bayonets for the muskets.[21] Although there is no evidence that all musketeers were in fact armed with bayonets in 1678, this critically shows an intent to modernise infantry tactical theory some 10 years earlier than previously thought. In July 1683 a warrant for the delivery of 66 fusils with bayonets to the third troop of [horse] grenadiers confirms the increased use of the bayonet.[22] King Charles II issues another warrant dated 27 November 1683 to establish an additional regiment of dragoons under the command of John, Lord Churchill. This regiment was to comprise of two troops consisting of 50 soldiers, and to be equipped with 106 fusils with slings and bayonets:[23] The regiment was expanded to six troops, each of 50 troopers by a later order of King Charles II on 6 October 1684.[24]

In some cases the absence of bayonets is an important indicator of the contemporary view regarding the issuing of the weapon, as it could be indicative of bayonets only being deemed necessary as a defence against horse.[25] This is confirmed by the minutes of the Hudson Bay company showing receipts for the outbound vessels *John & Thomas* (1684), *Happy Return* (1685), and *Lucey* (1685) showing large numbers of muskets, granados [grenades], bundles of match, belts and swords, but no bayonets.[26] Records of Ordnance sent to the plantations and colonies where there was the possibility of conflict with other European powers show that snaphance muskets were sent to Jamaica as early as April 1662, with quantities of bayonets being despatched in December 1679. The number of bayonets and ancillary stores suggest they were for the companies of grenadiers and a further two companies of dragoons already in Jamaica.[27] Virginia gets a shipment of 100 bayonets and cartouche boxes on 2 December 1679, with New England receiving 220 bayonets and snaphance muskets in August 1686.[28] The East India company records show the first shipment of bayonets from England in 1685, comprising of one shipment of 30 bayonets to Surat and another 20 to Priaman; the following year Sir John Child, Governor of Bombay, requested that 550 bayonets and 250 muskets be sent to him.[29]

20 SR, D(W)1778/V/13, *Dartmouth Papers*, folio 15.
21 SR, D(W)1778/V/71A, Folio 170, Armes and Amunicon Proposed for 12,978 foot. 20 March 1678.
22 NA, WO 55/470, *Entry Book of Warrants*, p.167, Warrant for the delivery into His Grace Christopher Duke of Abbormach.
23 NA, WO 55/470, *Warrants*, p.189.
24 NA, WO 55/470, *Warrants*, p.195. The increase to six troops is confirmed in C. Dalton, *English Army Lists and Commission Registers, 1661–1714, Vol. 2* (London: Eyre & Spottiswoode, 1894), p.10; NA, WO 55/470, *Warrants*, p.212 dated 2 May 1684 confirms the order to the Ordnance board to supply the additional 310 muskets, 310 bayonets etc.
25 This field of research will be covered in depth in chapter 4.
26 NA, 55/470, *Warrants*, p.238, warrant authorising the shipment of snaphance muskets to His Majesties Governor of New York, but no bayonets.
27 NA, CO 323/4, *Account of the Ordnance sent to the Plantations between the Restoration of Charles II and the Accession of William in 1688*, pp.7–8.
28 NA, CO 323/4, *Ordnance sent to the Plantations*, p.15.
29 D. Harding, *Small Arms of the East India Company 1600–1856*, Volume 2 (London: Foresight Books, 1997) pp.15–19.

It is possible to follow the development of infantry equipment through the example of two regiments, in this case the two regiments of foot guards. A royal warrant from King Charles II dated 29 January 1683 states that:

> His majesty has thought it fit for his service your twelve companies of foot guards called [the] Coldstream Guards to be supplied with new arms … each company with forty-one snaphance muskets (latest style), twenty pikes, two halberds, and two drums.[30]

Four months later on 28 April 1684 the King issues a second warrant affecting his foot guards and states:

> Having thought fit to establish two companies of grenadiers on foot to be added to his majesties regiments of foot guards … Out of his majesties stores to be delivered … Fifty-three light fusils with slings, fifty-three cartouche boxes with girdles, fifty-three grenade pouches, fifty-three bayonets, fifty-three hatchets, 3 halberds, and two partizans [per company].[31]

Following his accession to the throne, King James II on 22 February 1685 requested that 'all the musketeers in our two regiments of guards … Be furnished with bayonets' and that 'numbers of such bayonets as our said stores afford, proportionately to the said musketeers in each of them etc.'[32] On 2 May 1685, a further royal warrant was received stating that 'his [Majesties] regiments of guards to be supplied with new snaphance muskets.[33] A royal warrant issued by King William III at Kensington on 30 December 1695 states that 'each company of Our foot-guards have likewise a proportionable number of pikes [14 pikemen in each company of 60]'.[34]

While the musketeers of the King's foot guards received bayonets, five other regiments with the exception of their grenadier company were to be equipped only slightly better than their forefathers who had served in the English Civil War.[35] Board of Ordnance records show that His Majesty's Scotch Regiment consisted of 20 companies of 50 foot and one company of 50 grenadiers, to be equipped, see Table 3.

The Holland Regiment was equipped as above, the evidence is the same for Kirk's and Trelawny's regiments with the exception of only having 10 companies of foot and one grenadier company each. Finally, the Duke of York's Regiment was to have 12 companies, one of 80 men and 11 of 50 men, equipped as above, the 80-man company was to be equipped with 40 matchlock and 15 snaphance muskets and 28 pikes. King James II sent new

---

30 NA, WO 55/470, *Warrants*, p.197.
31 NA, WO 55/470, *Warrants*, p.206.
32 NA, WO55/339, *Ordnance Office: Miscellaneous Entry Book, 22 Feb 1685*, f.60, and Scott, *British Army*, p.542.
33 NA, WO 55/470, *Warrants*, p.212.
34 Walton, *British Standing Army*, p.786.
35 NA, WO 55/470, *Warrants*, pp.215–17.

arms for the Irish army on 24 March 1686, consisting of 2,600 matchlocks, 1,000 snaphance muskets with bayonets and 2,050 pikes.[36]

Table 3 Equipment of His Majesty's Scotch Regiment by Company

Companies of Foot		Grenadier Company	
Matchlock Muskets	26	Fusils	53
Snaphance Muskets	9	Partizans	2
Pikes	19	Halberds	3
Partizans	2	Cartouche Boxes	53
Halberds	3	Grenade Pouches	53
Drums	2	Hatchets and Girdles	50
		Bayonets	50
		Drums	2

The evidence from the aforementioned royal warrants shows that in 1684–85 the pike was still the primary defence against enemy horse and concurs with previous works by Childs and others. However, due to either the need for generalisation or as a result of less systematic research they failed to identify the split between musket types allocated to individual companies.[37] There is contradictory documentation that suggests that warrants adding a company of grenadiers to the eight oldest regiments were issued in April 1678, and again in 1684, this suggests that the warrant of 1678 was never acted upon.[38] Five royal warrants were issued between 15 March 1688 and 3 April 1689 issuing between 290 and 685 bayonets to seven regiments: the Coldstream Guards, Bath's, Montgomery's, Lichfield's, Huntingdon's, Hales', and Monmouth's regiments of foot, these numbers clearly indicate that they were for musketeer companies and not grenadier companies. The 13th and 15th regiments also received 240 and 340 bayonets respectively. This evidence from the royal warrants issued in 1688 and 1689 indicates that bayonets were now being issued to all regiments in addition to pikes, confirming that the bayonet was ingrained in current military theory and practice.[39]

What can clearly be seen in Board of Ordnance pay books and warrants for posts of storekeepers is the increasing importance and numbers of plug bayonets within the English establishment. When Benjamin Banbury was appointed sword cutler to King Charles II on 15 June 1682, he was responsible for all the swords and hangars belonging to His Majesty. Following his death, in July 1683, his replacement was Michael Richardson who was responsible 'to this office in all swords, hangars and bayonets'. Due to the death of Benjamin Banbury we are able to show a documented change in the job description of the King's sword cutler, emphasising the growing importance of plug bayonets.[40] Confirmation of this change in the importance and availability of

---

36 SR, D(W)1778/V/68 Ordnance Papers M, Folio 16,17, 20, 21, consisting of a formal proposal, estimate of costs, confirmation of charges and details of equipment sent.
37 Chandler, *Art of War*, p.79 and Childs, *Nine Years' War*, p.76.
38 Walton, *British Standing Army*, p.788.
39 Walton, *British Standing Army*, p.436.
40 NA, WO 55/470, *Warrants*, pp.28 and 177.

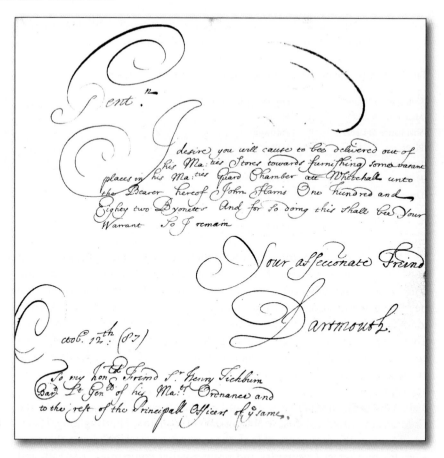

Copy of letter from Lord Dartmouth to Sir Henry Tichburn 1687. (Photo author's collection)

bayonets is also found in the warrants for the employment of a storekeeper in Portsmouth. Warrants dated prior to 12 December 1685 state '[storekeeper] shall be responsible for muskets, carbines, pistols, swords, halberds, and all manner of other arms', while in contrast warrants dated from the last day of December 1686 state:

> Whereas there is as in his maj[esty's] stores in the office of the ordnance a considerable quantity of swords, hangars, and bayonets which for a want of a skilled person to take care of keeping them oiled and cleaning and oiling those are subject to corruption and decay.[41]

On 12 October 1687 we see a further request for 182 bayonets for His Majesty's guard chamber at Whitehall, from Lord Dartmouth addressed to Sir Henry Tichburn [Tichborne], Lieutenant General of the Ordnance.[42] This is confirmed to a degree by a survey of small arms completed on 21 July 1688, which confirms that the yeoman of his Majesty's foot guard at Whitehall were issued with the following;[43]

---

41 NA, WO 55/472, *Entry Book of Warrants*,1681–82 folio 45 and folios 56–7.
42 NA, WO 55/474, *Entry Book of Warrants*, p.1, Request to John Starms for 182 bayonets.
43 NA, WO 55/474, *Warrants*, p.32, Survey of Small Arms at Whitehall.

Short Carbines with their Swords [bayonets]	100
Cartouche boxes	100
Powder chest	1

The prospective invasion by William of Orange produced a large number of royal warrants from enquiring about the status of regiments, or the ordering of new equipment for regiments. These include a request by King James II for 'My Lord Lichfield's regiment to be furnished with your best snaphance muskets and bayonets, in lew of [as] many long carbines as they bring into stores'.[44] Further evidence of bayonets becoming the standard armament of foot troops can be found in a letter sent during the Glorious Revolution from Sir John Lowther requesting that 150 muskets be sent forthwith to Whitehaven [Cumbria] 'and what bandoleers and bayonets could be got in an hour's time'.[45] Evidence that the pike's favour was waning can be found in a letter from the Duke of Schomberg to the Board of Ordnance dated 6 December 1689, written during King William III's campaign against James II in Ireland. This states: 'Firelocks will be the arms we shall have most occasion for here, there need be … few long pikes, intending to make use of Chevaux de frise'.[46]

Two new regiments of marines were raised by Royal Warrant, Pembroke's on 14 April and Torrington's 22 April 1690, they were equipped with Dutch snaphance muskets and bayonets. Marine regiments were never historically armed with pikes, so the issuing of bayonets shows a paradigm shift, from being issued as an addition to pikes to now being a general defensive weapon.[47] Further evidence of this shift is recorded in the minute book for 1695–96 which shows a warrant issued for 224 bayonets for a train of artillery.[48] When the Earl of Nottingham submitted a demand for supplies in relation to his upcoming expedition to Portugal in 1703, it included arms for 5,500 foot:[49]

Table 4 Arms and Equipment for the Expedition to Portugal in 1703

Item	Number	Cost*
Snaphance Muskets	3,736	3,736.00.00
Snaphance Musket with sling	384	425.12.00
Long Pike	925	196.11.03
Cartouche Boxes	736	435.17.04
Grenade Pouches	384	67.04.00
Hammer Hatchet	384	40.00.00
Bayonets	384	24.00.00

* Indicated in Pounds, Shillings, and Pence

44 NA, WO 55/465, *Entry Book of Warrants*, pp.79–80.
45 Historical Manuscript Commission, *The manuscript of S.H.L.E Flemming Esq of Rydal Hall* (London: HMSO, 1890), p.231.
46 NAM, 6807.211. Letters from the Duke of Schomberg, 16 December 1689, p.1.
47 Walton, *British Standing Army*, p.854.
48 NA, *Entry Book of Warrants*, WO47/18, p.62, 21 December 1695.
49 BL, Add MS 61165 *Blenheim Papers Vol. LXV*, pp.24–25, 15 June 1703.

This is evidence that as late as June 1703, some senior officers still favoured the pike over bayonets. The number of bayonets requested is significant, as are the numbers of grenade pouches and muskets with slings, this signifies that as far as the Earl of Nottingham was concerned, only the grenadier companies were to be armed with bayonets. Additional evidence of the continued use of the pike comes from a notation on an undated list of supplies of firelock muskets to the Princess Anne of Denmark's Regiment, stating they have enough pikes fit for service. This document must have been written between 1695 and 1715, as it states that the commander of the regiment was Colonel John Webb.[50]

A 1704 letter states that the King of Portugal received 6,500 snaphance muskets with socket bayonets fitted to them, with an additional 2,166 spare snaphance muskets [without bayonets].[51] Interestingly, a request for stores to be transported to Gibraltar was answered on 11 November 1704 by the Office of Ordnance stating they could supply:

> 3,000 Firelock Muskets, and also the like number of the ordinary short bayonets with wooden handles to put into the muzzle of the musket, But of the Socket bayonets such as were furnished lately to Portugal, there are none in store … And to supply such a number of that sort will take up at least six weeks' time, and be also very chargeable.[52]

Unfortunately, the research failed to find documentary evidence as to whether the garrison at Gibraltar was ever issued with the plug bayonets or waited for the socket bayonets. In addition to the 3,000 muskets the proposal also included 1,000 short pikes.[53] This evidence challenges the commonly held belief that the 'majority of Marlborough's men were re-equipped with flintlock muskets and socket bayonets by 1704'.[54] Having looked at the demand for plug bayonets and the transition to the new socket bayonet, the following section will take a more in-depth look at the supplies available to the Board of Ordnance.

Plug Bayonet Supply

Plug bayonets supplied to the English army during the seventeenth century were supplied indirectly through the London Cutlers Company (L.C.C), their tradesmen worked either independently or as loose consortiums such as the one Thomas Hawgood operated. Unfortunately for historians, what records the L.C.C. held were destroyed during the Blitz.[55] This leaves just the Board

---

50 BL Add MS 61355 Blenheim Papers Vol. CCXXXV, p.64.
51 NA SP41/34 pp.38, 40.
52 NA SP41/34, p.38.
53 BL Add MS 61165 *Blenheim Papers Vol. LXV*, pp.73–77, and NA, SP41/41/11 11 November 1704.
54 Chandler, *Blenheim*, p.100.
55 The L.C.C. became part of the Worshipful Company of Cutlers; their clerk confirmed the lack of archives.

of Ordnance records, as the primary records available for use. These include the yearly state of ordnance reports and additional letters giving details of supplies held at the various fortresses, arsenals and stores. Invoices for the ordering of plug bayonets from their suppliers are very rare, a list of stores and provisions of war for His Majesty's Ordnance dated 3 June 1678, records the following contracts being issued:

Joseph Andley 12 March 1678	10,000 Bayonets
W. Gladwin 16 March 1678	10,000 Belts for bayonets

These contracts were confirmed in a second document showing accounts received.[56] Further evidence confirming contracts for the supply of bayonets to the Ordnance Board can be found in receipts issued for work completed by Joseph Andley for 900 bayonets in 1672, Thomas Elliott in 1676, John Hawgood in 1685, Thomas Hawgood in 1688–89 and again in 1696.[57]

Table 5 includes information collated from *General State of Ordnance* documentation and has been compiled from a number of sources discovered during this research.[58] Due to the dislocated nature of Board of Ordnance archives, it is unlikely that a complete picture will ever be produced, however, this research gives a good understanding of both the amounts of ordnance stored and how it changed over time. The implication of these findings will be discussed further in the conclusion to this chapter. A survey of eight northern garrisons conducted in the spring of 1682 only found bayonets in one location: Tinmouth (Teignmouth) Castle, which held 257 bayonets and 1,371 pike.[59]

Table 5 Supplies of Bayonets and Pikes Available to the Board of Ordnance

	1677	1678	1679	1680	1684	1686	1687	1688	1689	1695
No of Ordinary Bayonets	300		6,500	6,159	7,442*	5,272	3,462	1,198	686	7,119
No Extraordinary Bayonets[60]						878	165		43	
Bayonets with sockets for Muskets							60		60	
No of Pike		14,778	10,715	12,291	14,717		17,733			

*A document dated 'May Last 1684' puts the number of bayonets with belts at 8,200.[61]

56 SR, D(W)1778/V/13, *Dartmouth Papers*, folio 16.

57 R. Evans, 'The Early British Plug Bayonet: Early Iron Mount Pattern', *The Armourer (The Militaria Magazine)*, 5 (1994), BL, Add MS 61346 Blenheim Papers Vol. CCXLVI, p.129B, and Add MS 61331 Blenheim Papers Vol. CCXXXI, pp.29, 47–48B.

58 BL, Add MS 61332 *Blenheim* Papers Vol. CCXXXII; SR, D(W)1778/V/1377, *Dartmouth Papers, State of Stores 1687, Ireland*, p.19; SR, D(W)1778/V/1375/A, *Dartmouth Papers. The General State of the Ordnance 1684*, p.12, 69; SR, D(W)1778/V/1376, *Dartmouth Papers. Ordnance: General State of Stores 1686*; SR, D(W)1778/V/1380, *Dartmouth Papers*; SR, D(W)1778/V/1373, *Dartmouth Papers. The General State of the Ordnance 1679*; SR, D(W)1778/V/48, folios 19–20, 24, State of Small Arms in his Majesties Store house for Small Arms; SR, D(W)1778/V/68 Ordnance Papers M, State of Small Arms in the Tower 1684/5; SR, D(W)1778/V/39 State of Small Arms in His Majesties Store House for Small Arms January 19 1689.

59 SR, D(W)1778/V/1374, *Dartmouth Papers, A Survey and Remains of Northern Garrisons 1 May 1682* and SR, (W)1778/V/71a, folio 166, Tinmouth Castle Stores.

60 Extraordinary are weapons fit for sea service according to D. Chandler, *Art of Warfare*, p.79.

61 SR, D(W)1778/V/48, Folio 10, State of Small Guns at Ye Tower.

A survey of ordnance conducted within the Kingdom of Ireland at the end of 1685, summarised that there were no bayonets in any of the garrisons, however the Dublin garrison was in possession of 94 bayonet belts.[62] Two years later a survey dated 1 January 1687, states that a total of 1,053 bayonets and 13,247 pikes were stored in Irish garrisons and in good condition.[63] Fort James, New York, is recorded as having 87 bayonets in storage along with 119 pikes in January 1687, with the same number recorded on 11 August 1688.[64] In the months following the Glorious Revolution a memorandum shows that on 26 January 1689, 301 bayonets were recovered on behalf of the new king [presumably from private hands], indicating that bayonets were in wide circulation.[65]

As late as 1706 there is some evidence that bayonets were still considered as ancillary weapons and not as a standard issue. Documents dating from the 6 July 1704 and 10 July 1704 show that the Board of Ordnance was being asked to supply 3,000 muskets but only 1,000 bayonets.[66] In addition when a shipment of supplies for the islands of Nevis and St Christopher were ready to load onto the ship, the Board of Ordnance sent a request to Secretary Hedges [16 November 1706] to see if bayonets and swords were to be dispatched.[67]

Plug Bayonets on the Battlefield

Examples of plug bayonets on British battlefield are extremely rare, although we know that bayonets of all types are lost in great numbers during battle. A letter to the Duke of Marlborough dated 10 December 1704, gives us an insight into just how many arms and accoutrements were claimed as lost; although the letter unfortunately fails to mention the action concerned, it probably included the Siege of Trarbach, Germany (3 November–25 November 1704).[68] The report covers 13 battalions, who are claiming a total of 3,669 bayonets lost and requiring replacement.[69]

There are two main battles on British soil during the period covered, Sedgemoor, Somerset (6 July 1685) and Killiecrankie, Scotland (27 July 1689), as well as a number of smaller actions including Phillips Norton, Somerset (27 June 1685) and Dunkeld, Scotland (21 August 1689).[70] Surviving examples of plug bayonets on British battlefields of the seventeenth century are almost

62 SR, D(W)1778/V/1378 13 March 168⅘, SR, D(W)1778/V/70 *Survey Book Ireland.* 3 February 168⅘.
63 SR, D(W)1778/V/1377, *Dartmouth Papers*, p.56.
64 SR, D(W)1778/V/68, folio 124, An account of Stores in Fort James in New York August 11 1688.
65 SR, D(W)1778/V/2, *Dartmouth Papers,* and SR, D(W)1778/V/2, folio 4, Account for Arms and Armour and Stores Collected from several parts of ye Country.
66 NA, SP41/34/5 *State papers Domestic*, and NA, SP41/3/7 *State Papers Domestic.*
67 NA, SP41/34/78 *State Papers Domestic.*
68 J. Falkner, *Marlborough's Sieges* (Stroud: Spellmount Ltd, 2007), pp.77–78.
69 BL, Add MS 61335, *Blenheim Papers CCXXXV*, p.74.
70 J. Tincey, *Sedgemoor 1685: Marlborough's First Victory* (Barnsley: Pen & Sword Books, 2005), pp.67–69, 84; D. Chandler, *Sedgemoor 1685: from Monmouth's Invasion to the Bloody Assizes* (Staplehurst: Spellmount Ltd, 1995), pp.37, 43; S. Reid, *Battle of Killiecrankie 1689: The Last Act of the Killing Times* (Barnsley: Frontline Books, 2018), pp.57, 94.

IV — The Battaile att Bridgwater

V — The Rout of a 1000 of the Rebells horse Comanded by ẙ Ld: Gray

Copies of propaganda playing cards depicting the skirmish at Bridgewater and the Battle of Sedgemoor 6th July 1685. Printed after the Monmouth Rebellion. (Author's collection)

non-existent; archaeological surveys of the Sedgemoor battlefield conducted by GUARD archaeology for the 'Two Men in a Trench' television series only uncovered musket balls and a piece of musket trigger guard.[71] The Blake Museum in Bridgwater has the remains of two plug bayonets believed to have been found on the battlefield during the early nineteenth century.[72] Due to the Board of Ordnance being a separate entity to the army, they have left us with financial evidence relating to the Monmouth Rebellion. An account of stores despatched and received following the rebellion in the West Country was compiled on the last [day] of June 1686 and recorded that:

> Bayonets extra for muskets and carbines, received [by the army] 1,600, brought in [to ordnance stores] 538, remaining to be brought in 1,062 chargeable at 18d each.[73]

71 T. Pollard and N. Oliver, *Two Men in a Trench: Uncovering the Secrets of British Battlefields* (London: Penguin, 2002), pp.152–173; G. Foard & R. Morris, *The Archaeology of English Battlefields: Conflict in the Pre-Industrial Landscape* (York Council for British Archaeology, 2012), pp.114–120.

72 S. Ede-Borrett, 'A Walk Around the Battle of Sedgemoor Museums', *Arquebusier: Journal of the Pike and Shot Society*, XXXV/V (2018), pp.15–19 (p.18).

73 SR, D(W)1778/V/13, *Dartmouth Papers*, folio 68, 30 June 1686.

QUEEN ♣

The Defeat of the Rebells
2000 Slayn & their Canon taken

Defeat of the rebels at the Battle of Sedgemoor. Copy of Monmouth Rebellion propaganda playing card. (Author's collection)

This figure is consistent with the numbers of troops at Sedgemoor, Tincey places 292 matchlock armed and 746 flintlock armed troops, in addition to 250 grenadiers, who were already armed with bayonets.[74]

The battlefield site of Killiecrankie has been subject to a number of archaeological surveys due to a project to widen the A9, which runs through the site. Recorded finds number 245, including numerous musket balls and other battlefield detritus but no plug bayonets have been found.[75] The research conducted for this present work only found evidence for one other plug bayonet, found in an archaeological dig. This was a Canadian excavation of the ship *Elizabeth and Mary* in 1997, which sank in 1690 and was part of Sir William Phips' failed expedition against Quebec City. The dive team uncovered the definite remains of one plug bayonet with a brass ferrule.[76] As to why so few plug bayonets have been recovered from British battlefields is a matter of conjecture, one possible hypothesis is the utilitarian nature of the plug bayonet meant that it was readily adaptable for civilian use, whereas the latter socket bayonet had only a military use.

Conclusion

There have been a number of generalisations in the historiography regarding both muskets and plug bayonets, specifically in works where the plug bayonet is not the primary focus of the research. These conclusions are understandable when the authors are looking for clarity, in most cases caveats are noted in the footnotes. Where Chandler cites English matchlocks having a calibre of 0.8 inch, this research tends to agree regarding the general calibre of matchlocks, however where Chandler states that William III flintlocks have a calibre of 0.85 inch, this research finds that they also show a calibre of 0.8 inch or smaller.[77]

My research has identified that Ordnance pattern bayonets grips statistically are a match for the average musket bore of all the Littlecote

---

74 Tincey, *Sedgemoor*, p.27.
75 M. Kilpatrick and W. Bailie, *A9 Dualling Programme Killiecrankie to Pitagowan: Archaeological Metal detecting Survey at Killiecrankie Battlefield* (Glasgow: Guard Archaeology, 2015), pp.21–32.
76 E. Baker, and others, *L'épave du Elizabeth and Mary (1690): Fouilles Archéologiques: Rapport d'Activités 1997* (Ontario: Service d'Archéologie, 2008), pp.29–30.
77 Chandler, *Age of Marlborough*, p.137.

collection of muskets.[78] The results are identical for the samples of muskets, both matchlock and flintlock from within the reference collection of the Royal Armouries, including the four 1690 service type William III muskets. While the non-Ordnance pattern bayonets show a more diverse range of grips, the results of the research into the grip dimensions show the same trend, in that the majority of bayonets will fit muskets within the average bore range of 20–21mm. There are specific exceptions: bayonet (X.207) from the Royal Armouries has a maximum grip diameter of 16.8mm, this bayonet is compatible with a flintlock carbine (XII.5470) and a flintlock musket (XII.5363). Overall, there are only four bayonets that would not achieve a fit with the 63 percent of muskets within the 20–21mm range, this data confirms the hypothesis that while the majority of bayonets could be described as a universal weapon that would confidently fit any musket, a small percentage of bayonets were made for a specific musket or carbine design. Chapter 3 will take this argument further by looking at how muskets and bayonets were ordered by the Board of Ordnance and requested by individual battalions.

Critics may argue that the numbers involved within this study would make any conclusion inconclusive. Statistically however, due to the number of designs and manufacturers incorporated into this study, the author is confident that his hypothesis has a sound academic basis, additional data from further collections of bayonets would always increase the statistical reliability of this report.

However, that said, the numbers involved combined along with the standing and provenance of the collections used, ensure that the figures and conclusions of this report add a new dimension into the research of bayonets within the English army of the seventeenth century.

At the start of this chapter the following questions were asked in relation to the primary research question: was the plug bayonet a universal fit with all muskets? And did this have an impact on the general uptake of the weapon? The data proves that the answer to the first question is yes, plug bayonets are universal. The inference gained from section 3.2 is that the decision regarding the adoption of the bayonet was in the hands of the King alone, and not necessarily in the control of the colonels of English regiments. The King's warrants for the arming of his foot guards with

Duke of Grafton at the Battle of Philip's Norton, copy of Monmouth Rebellion propaganda playing card. (Author's collection)

---

78 Professor John Childs previous research suggested that the bore of flintlock or snaphance muskets were smaller than the previous matchlocks allowing soldiers to carry more rounds, the data gathered for this manuscript tends to show that the majority of flintlock muskets had the same bore as matchlocks.

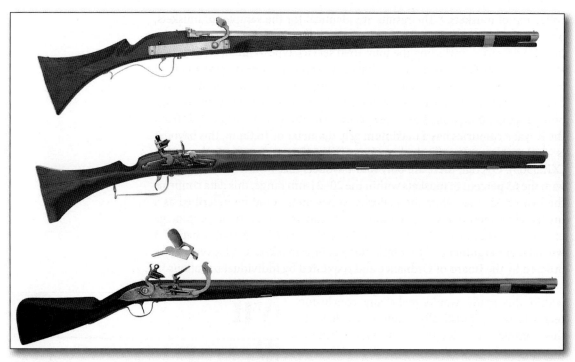

Three muskets – top to bottom these are Matchlock, Flintlock, Doublelock. (Jacques le Roux)

bayonets, but not the eight other regiments, evidences this fact.[79] While King William III issued bayonets to six regiments including the Coldstream Guards in 1689, these were in addition to pikes. While bayonets started to appear more often in Ordnance paperwork from the early to mid 1680s, there is not a corresponding reduction in the mentioning of the pike. The uncovering of the Board of Ordnance document from 1678 showing the intent to arm all musketeers with the bayonet, changes our understanding of the English establishment's relationship with the bayonet. This does leave an unanswered question as to why this did not happen, as the Ordnance board obviously had both the intent and the means to supply bayonets. While the figures shown in table 5 do show an increase in the bayonets held within Ordnance stores, the corresponding increase in numbers of pike is problematic. This increase could be as a result of pikes being returned to stores, rather than any stockpiling for a potential need. Records for the supply of bayonets to the Board of Ordnance prove that bayonets were ordered separately from muskets.

Additionally, the information from the Board of Ordnance confirms that in 1685 the musketeers of the five government battalions of foot engaged at the Battle of Sedgemoor were equipped with bayonets. The fact that we have four documents dating from 21 November 1687 to 25 February 1689, stipulating that His Majesty's small arms stores hold 60 'bayonets with sockets for muskets' gives us a confirmed date for the socket bayonets.[80] One

79 Walton, *British Standing Army*, p.786; NA WO 55/470, *Warrants*, pp.215–17.
80 SR, D(W)1778/V/39, Folio 19, *State of Small Arms in His Majesties Store House for Small Arms*, 18 January 1689, folio 20, *State of Small Arms*, 5 February 1689, folio 24, *State of Small Arms*, 21 November 1687, folio 25, *State of Small Arms*, 25 February 1689.

of the possible reasons for the longevity of the plug bayonet is exemplified by what happened to the French du Roi Regiment during the Nine Years' War. The whole regiment had been issued with socket bayonets, but due to the difference in the external diameters of their muskets, the bayonets either were too loose and therefore unusable, or to tight and would not fit at all.[81]

The fact that the numbers in store stayed static suggests that these were never issued to regiments, and as such must be treated as only a curiosity. This information when added to the data from chapter 2 increases our understanding regarding the plug bayonet. Chapter 4 will address the impact that the bayonet had on battlefield tactics and how the regulations surrounding musket drill changed over time.

The following chapter will look at both the procurement process that surrounded the purchase and supply of muskets and bayonets within the English establishment of the seventeenth century. This chapter will also look at the material evidence of the disbursement of the bayonet, specifically the disbursement of bayonets found in English and Scottish battlefield of the seventeenth century.

81 B. Nosworthy, *Anatomy of Victory, Battle Tactics 1689–1783* (New York: Hippocrene Books, 1992), pp.43–44.

3

Weapons and Equipment

Introduction

A lot of ink has been previously spent on the subject of matchlock muskets vs flintlock muskets, with several assumptions being made regarding the changeover from one to another. One of this chapter's primary intentions is to take a new look at how the English army changed from matchlock muskets to the newer flintlock muskets. By examining new source material as well as re-examining existing documentation, this chapter will show that the changeover was not as straight forward as previously suggested. There has also been quite a debate regarding the difference in bore and universality between matchlock and flintlock muskets, with the current consensus being that matchlocks having a larger bore than the newer flintlocks.

By looking at two of the largest collections of late seventeenth-century muskets, the Littlecote collection and the reference collection of the Royal Armouries at Leeds, the following section will look at the different types of muskets in use within the English army during the latter half of the seventeenth century, along with the dimensions or bore of these weapons. The sample size of muskets used for this research encompasses 13 matchlocks, five flintlocks, and one Dutch combined matchlock and flintlock musket, from the reference collection of the Royal Armouries Leeds. Of these, 13 muskets have a distinct flair in the final aperture of the barrel. This flair, according to Goldstein, facilitates the plug bayonet and 'increases the surface area of the barrel wall gripping the bayonet' and also indicates that the musket was never adapted to receive the later socket bayonet.[1] The Littlecote collection supplied additional data on 35 matchlocks, 42 flintlock muskets, and 17 flintlock carbines. Unfortunately, this data does not include any information on aperture flair on any of the musket barrels.

According to Chandler the English army used muskets with a 14-bore, this correlates to 14 musket balls being made from one pound of lead. One of the issues with a standard generalisation such as this is that it fails to consider the number of muskets imported from the Continent. Chandler

---

1   E. Goldstein, *The Socket Bayonet: In the British Army 1687–1783* (Rhode Island: Andrew Mowbray Publishing, 2000), p.7.

also confirms that after the Glorious Revolution of 1688, and the accession to the throne of King William III, William imported large quantities of muskets from Holland.[2]

Table 6 Musket Barrel, Internal Measurements (Millimetres)

Data Set Description	Min	Max	Mean	Median	Mode
Littlecote Matchlock Muskets	19.0	22.6	20.12	20.1	20.3
Littlecote Flintlock Muskets	17.0	21.0	19.64	20.0	20.0
Littlecote Flintlock Carbines	16.5	22.0	20.28	21.0	21.0
Leeds Armouries Reference Collection	18.4	21.1	19.80	19.8	19.9

The Littlecote data is divided into three main parts: matchlock muskets dating from 1645, flintlock muskets, and flintlock carbines, with the majority from the last two categories undated. Of the 35 matchlock muskets, 32 are described as being of 9-bore with a 0.8 inch internal diameter. At first glance, this would seem to suggest a standardised size, however, when you measure the internal diameter of these weapons in millimetres you arrive at a very different picture. The smallest diameter was measured (XII.5395) at 19.1mm, just 0.1mm greater than the one musket described as 14-bore or 0.7 inch diameter, with the largest bore (XII.5375) at 20.9mm.[3] Overall the muskets in this sample have an arithmetic mean of 20.12mm, with a median of 20.1mm and a mode of 20.3mm. The three other matchlocks comprise of two 7-bore, and one 14-bore musket.

The data for the 42 flintlock muskets shows a similar result with 33 muskets being categorised at 9-bore or 0.8 inch, with an additional seven described as 14-bore or 0.7 inch, the last two muskets are described as 13-bore or 0.7 inch and 21-bore or 0.6 inch. In-depth analysis of this tranche of data is hampered by the original published data using whole numbers, but it still is worth analysis. Of the 33 muskets described as 9-bore, 30 have an internal diameter of 20mm with the other three having an internal diameter of 21mm.[4] The 14-bore musket's internal diameter ranges from 17mm to 19mm. The muskets in this sample have an arithmetic mean of 19.64mm, with a median and mode of 20mm.

The third tranche of information from the Littlecote collections covers 17 flintlock carbines, 15 are undated with two being dated between 1690 and 1710. Thirteen of these are described as 9-bore or 0.8 inch, one 12-bore

---

2   D. Chandler, *The Art of Warfare in the Age of Marlborough* (London: B.T. Batsford, 1976), pp.78–79. Chandler also quotes the *Summary of Arms, 1687–1691* that reveals 14 different types of long arm in existence within the English army, p.79; Chandler, *Blenheim*, p.100; J. Childs, *The British Army of William III, 1689–1702* (Manchester: Manchester University Press, 1987), p.172. The Calendar of Treasury Papers shows that between 22 May 1689 and 1 June 1689, the Customs commissioners were instructed to deliver, customs free two shipments of Dutch muskets for three Huguenot regiments in English pay, A. Shaw, *Calendar of Treasury Books: 1689–1692*, Volume 2 (London: HMSO, 1931), pp.136, 145.

3   Richardson, *Littlecote*, pp.194–218.

4   Richardson, *Littlecote,* pp.224–67.

or 0.68 inch, two 14-bore or 0.7 inch, and one 21-bore at 0.6 inch. Further analysis of this data set produces internal diameters for the 9-bore carbines between 21.0mm and 22.0mm, with the other four carbines varying in diameter between 16.5mm and 18.1mm.[5] The final tranche of musket data is derived from examination of the reference collection of the Royal Armouries Leeds, this data is displayed in full in appendix III. This sample contains 19 muskets, which includes 13 matchlocks, six flintlocks and one Dutch matchlock/flintlock combination. This is the only section where a flare diameter was recorded, unfortunately the researchers behind the Littlecote records did not look at this aspect, or one can assume that all the muskets had straight barrels. The 13 matchlocks have an internal diameter of between 19.2mm and 20.4mm, with the five flintlocks recording diameters of between 18.4mm and 21.1mm. The Dutch combined flintlock/matchlock has an internal diameter of 20.8mm.

This combined data indicates the lack of standardisation in the manufacture and internal diameters of English muskets and carbines, which as we shall see in the conclusion of this chapter has an impact on the suitability of plug bayonets to gain a tight fit.[6] As a side note, it also highlights an issue with the suitability of musket balls fitting without an excess of windage, or the possibility of musket balls to fit correctly within the barrel of any musket. Interestingly, five of the Leeds Armouries matchlock muskets which can be positively identified as William III 1690 service muskets, have an internal diameter of between 19.2mm and 20.4mm which is well within the statistical range of the Littlecote 1645 matchlock muskets. Chandler's argument that old weapons were still in use 20 to 30 years after manufacture confirms the validity of including the Littlecote matchlocks data within this survey.[7] A matchlock stock re-fitted with a flintlock firing mechanism illustrating the use of older equipment is exhibited at the Royal Armouries Leeds.[8] The complete data for the average musket barrel dimensions from the preceding four data sets is located in appendices III and IV.

Matchlock or Flintlock: A Question of Perspective?

The date of the transition from matchlock to flintlock in armies of the European nations has long been subject of much conjecture and a great deal of ink! Depending on your given source you get a great deal of variation

---

5   Richardson, *Littlecote*, pp.273–87.

6   There was an attempt at standardisation musket design as early as 1688, as the Board of Ordnance sent Sir Richard Newdigate MP of Arbury two flintlock muskets on the 10 January 1688 and asked him to sound out Birmingham gunmakers on the supply of complete guns, B. De Witt, 'The Board of Ordnance and Small Arms Supply: The Ordnance System 1714–1783', unpublished Ph.D. thesis (London: King's College, 1988), p.30. WO47/13 *Board of Ordnance Minute* Book 1682/83, folio 193 shows a contract for the production of 1,000 snaphance muskets given to 29 gunsmiths, to be brought into stores in 10 weeks in accordance to the pattern in the Ordnance office. H. Thomlinson, *Guns and Government: The Ordnance Office under the Late Stuarts* (London: Royal Historical Society, 1979) p.110; Anderson, *War and Society*, p.105.

7   Chandler, *Blenheim*, p.95.

8   RA, XII.72 Flintlock Musket, located in the Littlecote room, Royal Armouries, Leeds.

and confusing dates, William Urban's *Matchlocks to Flintlocks* tells us that the Saxon army was the most modern army in Europe and the first flintlocks to be used in their army were introduced in 1687; but at first they were only assigned to grenadier companies.[9] John Childs adds a different perspective, giving details of James II's regiment of fusiliers which was formed in 1685 and equipped with flintlocks, or more specifically fusils.[10] The regiment of fusiliers was raised to guard trains of ordnance, and as such not having to rely on a constantly lit match was obviously advantageous around the abundant supply of black powder which was a necessity of any artillery train. Childs puts the dates for the implementation of the flintlock as Brandenburg–Prussia 1689, Russia 1700, and France from between 1693 and 1707. The dates become confusing as it is not always clear whether they relate to the flintlock being introduced to specific regiments with an army, specialised regiments (fusiliers or dragoons), specific companies such as grenadier companies, or the re-equipping of the entire army. The dates given by Childs for France are more specific with his date of 1693, being for the French army 'halfway through its modernization' program, with it fully complete by 1707. Experience tells us that any modernisation program either in the late seventeenth century or even in the twenty-first century will be a slow and piecemeal process, with new equipment being issued to units based on need, location, or convenience. Troops serving in the home countries will be issued with new equipment before those serving overseas.

There has been a general assumption that when regiments were equipped with flintlocks, that the Grenadier company would be equipped first, followed by the whole regiment, this certainly not the case for the English army. Luckily enough we have documentary evidence that shows how and when the English army received new weapons, these documents are held in the National Archives in Kew, London. Snaphance are recorded in the records for the English garrison in Tangiers as early as 1660, these records show that equal quantities of matchlock and firelock muskets were held within the warehouse. A record of all ordnance stored in Tangiers dated 29 March 1660 shows a delivery of 200 matchlocks and 200 snaphance muskets.[11] In addition, there were 400 bandoliers and 400 swords with belts, this clearly indicates that in this case there was clearly a plan for a 50/50 split required between troops armed with snaphance and matchlock muskets.[12] A detailed account of the stores within the Tangiers garrison dated 29 July 1666, reports that there were 292 firelocks in good condition, with an additional 156 requiring repair. Of interest there were some 1,353 pikes in storage, of which 493 were reported as damaged.[13] Further supplies were landed from the merchant vessel *Nathanial Peeter* on 27 January 1667, these included a further 600 matchlocks and 400 snaphance.[14] The Ordnance records enable

---

9 W. Urban, *Matchlocks to Flintlocks: Warfare in Europe and Beyond 1500–1700* (London: Frontline Books, 2011), p.53.

10 J. Childs, *Warfare in the Seventeenth Century* (London: Cassell, 2001), pp. 53, 154–55.

11 BL, Sloane MS 3509, Papers Relating to Tangier, vol.1, F.119.

12 BL, Sloane MS 3509, *Arrival of Stores on the Hoy*, 29 March 1666, f.119.

13 Sloane, MS 3509, *Account of Stores*, ff.180–181.

14 Sloane, MS 3509, *Account of Stores*, f.237.

us to see that the ratio between matchlock muskets to flintlock muskets with individual regiments, is 336 matchlocks to 180 snaphance, this is based on information supplied to the Board of Ordnance by Colonel Beaumont on 22 April 1689. The documents confirm that Beaumont's Regiment of Foot was equipped with 336 matchlocks and only 180 snaphance muskets. As these are records from the regiment, this is further evidence that the prevalence of matchlock muskets is greater than previously stated in much of the historiography. Both Ordnance and regimental records generally state that each of the companies of foot (excluding the grenadier company) would be issued with both types of musket. The author would, however, speculate that where possible regiments would issue whole companies with either matchlock or snaphance muskets, if for no other reason than simplicity and the convenience of the officers when going through the evolution to load their companies' muskets. These records also confirm that the same regiment had 240 men armed with pikes.[15]

Matchlock Muskets

The matchlock musket in use during the 1680s and 1690s was the same weapon used during the Civil War, some 30 years earlier. The musket used a length of match (which had been previously soaked in a solution of potassium nitrate) to ignite the powder in the pan. This 'slow' match would have to kept alight leading up to and during any engagement, and would typically burn at a rate of four inches every hour. Quick match used by grenadiers within their grenades burnt approximately one foot every minute. The match was held in the serpent, which on discharging the weapon would be brought down into the pan, which would have to be open prior to firing. This exposed the black powder to the elements and increased the chances of a misfire. In addition, the presence of a lit match, carried by every musketeer, necessitated that musketeers should be in open order (six foot between files).

Large quantities of matchlock muskets were use in the English army in 1689/90, William of Orange ordered 500 muskets with 'all the match now in stores at Chester' to be sent to James Hamilton in Ireland via Liverpool on 9 February 1688/9. The Board of Ordnance confirmed receipt of this order on the 11th.

One of the primary disadvantages of the matchlock over the flintlock concerns the time it takes to load and fire each type of musket. David Chandler points to the *Exercise of the Foot* (1690), which states that a matchlock musket

Matchlock musket *c.*1650. (Courtesy of the Rijksmuseum, Netherlands)

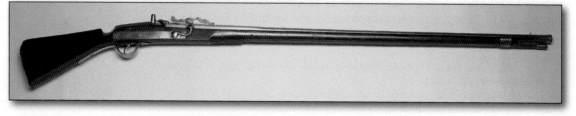

---

15 NA WO55/336 f.84.

has 44 separate evolutions of drill.[16] Stating that the sequence for loading the musket includes: taking a charge from his bandolier, prise open the lid with his teeth, poor the gunpowder down the barrel, 'fumbling in his ball pouch for a bullet', take a wad of paper or cloth, place the ball and wadding in the barrel, draw his ramrod, then ram both down.

Flintlock Muskets

The flintlock in one guise or another had been in existence from the 1620s, and depending on the date and army in question had been called a firelock, snaplock, snaphance, doglock, or flintlock and was a technological successor to the wheellock that was in use from the 1600s. In essence, all the variations of 'flintlocks' used the trigger to release a spring-loaded arm holding a flint to strike a metal plate, with the intention of the sparks igniting a fine black powder in the priming pan, thus setting of the main charge and causing the musket to discharge. This process required a shaped piece of flint to be tightly fitted to jaws and positioned so that it would produce enough sparks to ignite the priming powder; with each action there was the possibility of the flint breaking or coming free from the jaws. Even if these two events were prevented, a flint would wear down and require changing after several uses. Flint sizes and angles were important to ensure that the musket would fire correctly and not misfire; while trying to re-flint five muskets, the author went through almost 20 flints to correctly fit the five muskets and produce sparks every time. Ordnance records show that the standard issue for musketeers going on campaign (Monmouth Rebellion 1685, Flanders 1688/89 and Ireland 1689) was 100 musket balls and 10 flints per man.

Danish pattern 1680 flintlock musket, note the two rings on the obverse side of the musket barrel to take a plug bayonet, still allowing the musket to be fired. (Author's collection)

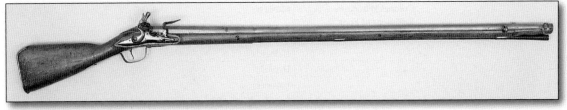

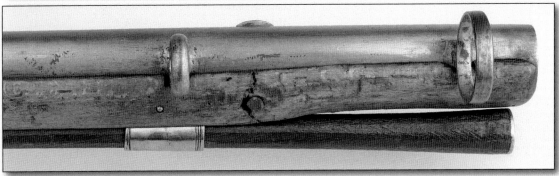

Close-up of rings to facilitate a plug bayonet. (Author's collection)

16 D. Charndler, *the Art of Warfare on the Age of Marlborough* (London: B.T. Batsford, 1976), pp.76–77.

What is seldom mentioned as one of the primary reasons for misfires in flintlocks, is that a good flint will produce a shower of sparks every time. That, and the time it takes to change a flint, although not overly long, is sufficient to interrupt the sequence of firing. Every time a musket is fired, the flint will wear slightly, with a chance of a catastrophic break that will render the flint unserviceable. Accounts for the period in question show large quantities of flints being requested, orders of between 6,000 and 10,000 per battalion are not unusual.

William III inherited a broken English army and found both men and equipment wanting, following its disbandment during December 1688. He instigated a number of audits which then facilitated requests for replacement arms via the Board of Ordnance. One request dated 18 March 1688/9 lists the arms wanting and defective for three regiments of foot:[17]

	Item	Defective	Wanting
Colonel Beveridge's Regiment of Foot	Matchlock Muskets	N/A	250
	Fire Locks (Flintlock Muskets)	N/A	250
	Pikes	N/A	250
	Bayonets	N/A	300
	Drums	N/A	26
	Halberds	N/A	39
	Hatchets	N/A	60
	Flints ready cut	N/A	6,000
Sir John Hanmor's Regiment of Foot	Fire Lock Muskets	N/A	152
	Matchlock Muskets	N/A	103
	Pikes	N/A	33
	Daggers [Bayonets]	Whole Compliment	
Colonel Wharton's Regiment of Foot	Muskets	34	273
	Pikes	34	96
	Halberds	N/A	10
	Drums	N/A	11
	Bayonets	N/A	290
	Pouches [Grenade]	N/A	17
	Cartridge Boxes	N/A	13
	Hatchets	N/A	43

Records show that on 25 May 1689 Colonel Phillip Babington's Regiment of Foot was requested to exchange 14 flintlocks for matchlocks.[18] Unfortunately previous works have tried to solve the complicated problem of the transfer from matchlock to flintlocks by generalisations. Brent Nosworthy in his excellent but perhaps slightly outdated volume *The Anatomy of Victory*, states that the British Guards [presumably the English Guards] and half the regiments of foot were armed with flintlocks in 1690.[19] A more accurate

---

17 NA, WO55/336, f.58.
18 W055/336, King William to Lord Shrewsbury 25 May 1689, f.121.
19 Nosworthy, p.39.

statement would be, that possibly half of the English foot were armed with flintlocks, but divided between all the regiments and battalions. There were always exceptions, the Regiment of Fuziliers were issued flintlocks from the start, as were all the dragoons.

The Best of Both, or only Museum Curiosities

For as long as firearms have existed, there has been a tendency to push the boundaries and produce hybrid weapons. Museums throughout the world are filled with a profusion of exotic combinations, where craftsmen have expertly incorporated a firing mechanism and barrel into every weapon possible. There can be no doubt that some of these capricious and eccentric weapons are no more that master craftsmen showing off their talents – the combination war axe and pistol located within the collection of the Royal Armouries, must surely fall within this category.[20] More convincing articles range from the shield where the central boss contain a pistol, to hidden pistols in swords, walking canes, and umbrellas. One combination weapon that has to be moved from the realms of curiosity to serious military debate is the combination matchlock and flintlock musket. Historians and curators of firearms within English museums have looked at rare examples of these

Saxon combined matchlock and flintlock mechanism. Austrian Military Museum, Vienna. (Author's photograph)

---

20 Combination wheellock axe and pistol (1600–1630), Royal Armouries, Tower of London, ref: XIV.6 containing five barrels in the axe head, one ignited by the wheellock, one by a matchlock mechanism and the remaining three by hand-held matches. A sixth barrel is located within the handle.

weapons often as one-offs or proof-of-concept designs. The Royal Armouries in Leeds holds one such example, a Dutch military pattern musket *c.* 1700 fitted with duel flintlock and matchlock mechanisms.[21]

Only when we look at this type of musket on a European-wide scale and not just at the extremely rare examples held within the United Kingdom, are we able to see the full picture. The Heeresgeschichtliches HGM [military history] museum in Vienna has several examples of this type of combination musket. These include both wheellock–matchlock as well as flintlock–matchlock combinations. These weapons were issued to several Saxon regiments including the Goltz Regiment.[22] The Austrian and Dutch examples both are all based on standard military muskets and show none of the excesses that are characteristically found on exhibition pieces or curiosities. In addition to these examples, there is anecdotal evidence that the French Mousquetaires du Roi and Gardes Françaises were issued with combination matchlock-flintlock muskets in the early 1680s as well as the Dutch Garde te Voet.

Why these combination muskets were so widespread is open to debate. Matchlock muskets as well as flintlock muskets both have disadvantages that are fundamental to their operation. Matchlocks have the obvious disadvantage that the musketeer must have access to a fire source in the form of a glowing match, which is problematic during periods of bad weather or during night attacks. This is in addition to the obvious danger of having a lit match near to the next soldier's powder supply, necessitating a greater distance between files of musketeers. The flintlock, although a more modern design with a reduced misfire rate, still has fundamental design problems. The flintlock by design requires a constant supply of good quality, correctly sized and shaped flints for any useful spark to be generated.

The prevalence of these combinations, may be as a way to mitigate the intrinsic potential problems with both individual locks on their own, allowing for the musketeer to have a second choice should the supply of flints fail.

Bandoliers vs Cartouche Boxes

The primary argument for a slower loading time for matchlocks vs flintlocks is the number of evolutions required to load each musket. This has been based on the assumption that musketeers armed with matchlocks are equipped with bandoliers and those armed with flintlocks have the newer cartouche box. Cartouche boxes were designed to take pre-made cartridges with the musket ball and powder wrapped within a paper cylinder that acted as the wadding. While all accounts for the equipping of grenadiers and dragoons state that they are to be equipped this way, it is not the case for all the regiments of foot. The First Regiment of Foot Guards requested enough bandoliers for the whole regiment to be made available to them from the Ordnance stores

---

21 Royal Armouries, Leeds, ref. XII.2648.
22 A. Querengässer and S. Lunyakov, *Die Armee Augusts des Starken in Nordischen Krieg* (Berlin: Zeughaus Verlag, 2013).

located within the Tower of London on 4 October 1688.[23] Records as late as 1689 show that musketeers were being equipped with bandoliers, the following is an account of 'Armes proper for arming 10 companies & one of Grenadiers in Colonel Trelawnys Regiment of Foot' (Queen Dowager's Regiment of Foot).

Snaphance muskets with walnut stocks & flat hard locks	150
as above but with 'D' strap'd	063
Matchlock muskets	320
Bandoliers	470
Long Pikes	160
Halberds	033
Drums	022
Bayonets (with belts and froggs)	533
Cartouche boxes with belts	063
Grenade pouches	063
Hammer hatchets	063

This order is dated Whitehall 27 August 1689, with a side note that states:

Pray pardon that I cannot send you more snaphances for their Majesties stores can't furnish them at present but shall be changed at demand, I am
    Sir yours
    Goodricke[24]

This order and others with similar quantities of bandoliers and cartouche boxes confirm that troops armed with flintlocks were just a likely to be issued with bandoliers, which would increase the number of evolutions to load the musket and negate some of the suggested advantages.

This use of bandoliers within regiments armed with flintlocks is not limited to the Queen Dowager's Regiment of Foot. Board of Ordnance records from 8 March 1688/9 show that Major General Kirke's Regiment of Foot was re-armed with the following weapons:[25]

Firelocks	433
Collars of Bandoliers	456
Bayonets	536
Hangers for Grenadiers	55
Flints ready cut	6,000

Admiral Herbert sent a request to the Duke of Schomburg on 21 May 1689 requesting that amongst other things, that the bandoliers on board the fleet should be replaced with cartouche boxes and that the muskets be replaces with more serviceable weapons (brass fittings) as soon as possible.[26]

---

23 WO55/335, Sunderland to Dartmouth, 4 October 1688, f.86.
24 Sir Henry Goodricke was Lieutenant General of the Board of Ordnance between 1689 and 1702.
25 WO55/336 Board of Ordnance Records, f.64.
26 WO55/336 Lord Herbert to Duke of Schomburg, f.102.

There is one other cautionary warning that must be observed when discussing the issues of troops being issued with bandoliers, and that is regarding seventeenth-century and eighteenth-century language, or more specifically the definitions of words. The term bandolier can refer to the leather shoulder belt bearing wooden powder charge bottles, worn by musketeers, but equally you can find accounts of pikemen being issued with a bandolier to carry their sword.

Organisation of the Foot

While there is no doubt that during the period between the English Civil War and the Nine Years' War, the English army did not have the same experience of large-scale combat as other European armies. There is evidence that Charles II had made plans for the expansion of the English Army to a comparable size with other European states. In late December 1677, there was correspondence between the King and the Board of Ordnance proposing the

Pikemen and Wagons, print by Jan van de Velde 1632. (Courtesy of the Rijksmuseum, Netherlands)

54

expansion of the army to 30,000 men. The proposal was for 26 regiments of foot consisting of 10 companies of 100 men to each company, four regiments of horse of 600 men in a regiment, two regiments of dragoons of 800 men, together with 700 grenadiers to attend the foot and 200 grenadiers to attend the horse. The detail of the required equipment allows us to see a snapshot of what stores were located within Board of Ordnance stores and armouries.

	Proposed	Out of Stores	Supplies Required
Muskets	17,334	10,334	7,000
Bandoliers	17,334	10,334	7,000
Pikes	8,666	3,000	5,666
Muskets for Dragoons	1,600	1,300	300
Bayonets	1,600	300	1,000

For the 700 grenadiers attached to the foot

	Proposed	Out of Stores	Supplies Required
Long Carbines	700		700
Grenade Pouches with Girdles	700		700
Bayonets	700		700
Hatchets	700		700
Hand Grenades (6 per man)	4,200	4,200	

For the 200 grenadiers attached to the horse, as above but without bayonets, the correspondence also gives us information regarding the proposed supply of ammunition each soldier should be issued with. In this case 100 rounds for each man, foot and horse.[27]

Following the flight of King James II in December 1688, the English army was ordered to disband by the Earl of Faversham. William III, on hearing that the army was disintegrating, quickly rescinded the order on 13 December 1688, and had to reconstitute the English army as quickly as possible. He ordered all the regiments that had received the incorrect orders to submit details of the state of their equipment and what they were missing. The following regiments submitted their requirements for arms wanting and defective which was forwarded to the Duke of Schomberg, head of the Board of Ordnance by Royal Warrant on the 15th day of March 1689.[28]

	Item	Serviceable	Unserviceable	Wanting
Count Beveridge's Foot	Matchlocks			250
	Firelocks			250
	Pikes			250
	Bayonets			300
	Drums			26
	Halberds			39
	Hatchets			60

27 SA, D(W)1778/V/1380, *Earl of Dartmouth, Board of Ordnance Papers*, ff.1–20.
28 NA, WO55/401, *Ordnance Office and War Office: Miscellaneous Entry Book 1689–93*, f.7.

	Item	Serviceable	Unserviceable	Wanting
	Flints pre-cut			6,000
Sir John Hammon's Foot[29]	Muskets		34	273
	Pikes		34	96
	Halberds			10
	Drums			11
	Bayonets			290
	Pouches			17
	Hatchets			43
	Cartridge Boxes			13

Count Beveridge's request for both matchlocks and flintlocks is further confirmation, if any were needed, that both types of muskets were issued and used by English regiments during this period.

	Item	Serviceable	Unserviceable	Wanting
Colonel Beaumont's Foot	Muskets	33	37	470
	Pikes	12	15	217
	Halberds	19	6	14
	Drums	8	2	16
Colonel Hastings' Foot	Muskets	112	179	43
	Pikes	32	108	20
	Halberds	12	9	3
	Bayonets	141	134	69
	Drums	11	1	4
Colonel Lutterell's Foot	Muskets	413	69	19
	Pikes	144	18	108
	Bandoliers	432	N/A	118
	Halberds	24	N/A	15
	Drums		N/A	14
Sir James Leslie's Foot	Muskets	334	187	9
	Pikes	95	78	67
	Halberds	18	N/A	21
	Drums	11	10	5
	Bayonets	121	177	222
	Pouches	50	13	N/A
	Bandoliers	133	N/A	407
	Cartridge Boxes	N/A	63	N/A
	Hatchets	48	15	N/A
Colonel Hales' Foot	Muskets	80	420	40
	Bandoliers	477	N/A	63
	Pikes	199	N/A	41
	Halberds	34	N/A	5
	Drums	11	12	3

---

29 Previous references refer to Sir John Hanmor, so the name given here could be a clerical error.

The follow confirmation warrant from the Board of Ordnance is dated 29 March 1689. The document provides us with an insight into how these six regiments were composed and equipped, it tells us the ratio of muskets to pikes of 2.25 for Colonel Beaumont's, Colonel Hastings', and Sir James Leslie's regiments down to 1.8 muskets for every pike for Colonel Lutterell's Regiment. It is interesting to note that Sir James Leslie's Regiment is the only regiment requesting weapons for a grenadier company, which suggests that the other five regiments have had their grenadier companies dispersed.[30]

On 12 April 1689, an order from King William III instructs Marshal Schomberg, Master of Ordnance to Supply one of four newly raised regiments under the command of Sir John Guys (Guise) with the following equipment:[31]

	Whole Want	Supplied from Portsmouth	Supplied from Tower of London
Snaphance Muskets	62	62	
Matchlock Muskets	122	122	
Pikes	252	252	
Bandoliers	144	144	
Bayonets	504	218	286
Halberds	22	22	
Drums	12	12	
Grenadiers			
Snaphance Muskets	63	63	
Cartouche Boxes	63	63	
Grenade Pouches	63	63	
Bayonets	63		63
Halberds	3	3	
Drums	2	2	
Hammer Hatchets	63		63

On 25 April 1689, a further warrant is issued for the creation and arming of a grenadier company for Colonel Beaumont's Regiment of Foot. The organisation and equipment of grenadier companies for each regiment of foot has now been settled on, amounting to 63 soldiers, three non-commissioned officers and two drummers.

Misfires and Accuracy

While there are no definitive figures for marksmanship and misfire rates during the late seventeenth century, we do have some anecdotal evidence from George Story regarding William III's troops during the Irish campaign of 1689. Story states that only one in four of the new men could fire their muskets, and of those, not many could hit their target. This statement has

---

30 NA WO55/401, *Ordnance Office*, f.19.
31 NA WO55/336, *Board of Ordnance Records 1689–90*, f.51.

been used to infer that there was a very high misfire rate for matchlocks of up to one shot in two.[32] This statement however, should not be taken at face value. There is ample evidence confirming that the Williamite army in Ireland under Schomburg's command was badly trained, neglected by its officers, and lacked serviceable weapons.

While out of the period in question, we have an accurate account of both misfire rate and hit rate from an East India Company test during April 1841. During this test 21 units fired a total of 13,771 rounds, with a misfire rate of between 13.37 percent and 15.0 percent. Line infantry firing flintlock smoothbore muskets fired at targets at 100, 150, and 200 yards and achieved the following:

	Shots Fired per Hit[33]		
	100yds	150yds	200yds
Best	2.25	4.75	2.0
Average	3.96	5.2	13.02
Worst	6.75	16.25	43.5

While direct comparisons may seem impossible due to the 150-year time difference. In reality the smoothbore musket issued to troops in the late 1680s was remarkably similar to those issued to the troops of the East India Company in the 1840s.

Grenadiers

Grenadiers, as well as dragoons, were considered shock troops, and were generally formed of the largest soldiers and veterans within the battalion, thereby becoming the elite of the battalion. Over time their placement within each battalion has changed, from the traditional placement on the extreme right of the battalion, the typical position of honour within any regiment or battalion, to being split into either two or three sections. Grenadier companies split into two equal sections were posted on the right and left flanks of the battalion, with the third section (where used) being paced in front of the centre company of the battalion.

The first earliest drill manual mentioning bayonets was published in 1678, *An Abridgment of the English Military Discipline*, which has bayonets drills for both dragoons and grenadiers. This volume is best described as a training manual rather than a field manual, as its authors intent is to educate the officer in the required commands and to teach the troops being drilled by continued repetition of each of the separate revolutions of drill. Each of the separate evolutions is repeated four times, so that the order to charge bayonets for example is given to the right four times, followed by to the left four times. The evolutions for the dragoons and grenadiers are for firelocks,

---

32 Chandler, *The Art of Warfare*, p.75.
33 D. Harding, *Small arms of the East India Company 1600–1856*, vol. 3 (London: Foresight Books, 1997), pp.289–302.

while stipulating matchlocks for the infantry companies. A later edition printed in 1684 stipulates that:

- Those grenadiers on the right and left of the battalion, are to fire as the musketeers fire, that is the last two ranks, to fire with the musketeers, and as soon as fired are to put their daggers into their firelocks.
- The front rank of the grenadiers having their granados ready are to kneel when the first rank of musketeers kneel, and after the two last ranks have fired,
- They are to stand up, and when the first rank of musketeers fire, they are to deliver their granados, and immediately to fix their daggers into their firelocks.
- When the musketeers club their muskets and fall on, they are to charge with their daggers as aforesaid.[34]

These evolutions of drill show us two important points about infantry combat tactics leading up to the engagements following the Duke of Monmouth's rebellion in 1685. First, that musketeers still relied on using their muskets as clubs when it came to close combat, the same as their predecessors during the English Civil War and the Thirty Years' War. The second and far more important point confirms that the grenadiers role played an important part with the battalion during field engagement with the enemy. The general view has been that grenadiers only used their granados [grenades] when assaulting fixed defences and fortifications, has always seemed at odds with the regular issue of grenades to grenadier companies. The drill books confirm that the grenadiers were trained to throw their granados during infantry combats as well as assaulting fixed defences and fortifications. These findings show that the grenadier companies of English regiments had a far greater impact on the fighting abilities of regiments than previously thought and will be expanded upon within chapter 5, 'The Evolution of Infantry Tactics'.

The Pike

The issuing of pikes to infantry battalions and regiments had not seriously changed from the armies of the English Civil War. While the percentage of pikes within each company of the English army did certainly diminish during the period covered by this book, the pikes eventually being consigned to Ordnance stores and fortresses, they still formed an important part of the equipment and therefore the tactics of the army up to 1705. The pike at its height of fashion had a length of up to about 24 feet in length, while there is little corroborating evidence of the lengths of later pikes, the general understanding is that pikes were classified as 'long' or 'short'. Long pikes were often cut down to between 16 and 18 feet, with short pikes anywhere between 10 and 14 feet in length.

---

34 Anon., *An Abridgement of the English Military Discipline* (London: John Bull deceas'd, Thomas Newcomb, and Henry Hills, 1685), pp.128–29.

Above left: Battle of Reading 9 December 1688, copy of propaganda playing cards produced after the Glorious Revolution in 1689. (Author's collection)
Above right: The English Army going over to the Prince of Orange December 1688, copy of propaganda playing cards produced after the Glorious Revolution in 1689. (Author's collection)

A treatise of the English Military Discipline, published in 1682 by Christopher Whitmore, confirms that battalions of foot still formed up in a similar way to their counterparts during the English Civil War. This shows that the pikes from the 10 infantry companies formed up in the centre of the battalion, major's, 1st captain's, captain lieutenant's, 3rd captain's and 7th captains' musketeer companies on the left of the pike; and lieutenant colonel's, 6th captain's, 4th captain's, 5th captain's, and 2nd captain's on the right. Each of the pike companies is to form in six files, with each musketeer company formed in 12 files. This format would be repeated for battalions with eight, 11 or 13 companies. In 1689 pike-armed soldiers were still accounting for one out of every four soldiers.[35]

During March 1689 the Board of Ordnance requested regimental colonels to conduct audits of all their arms, reporting those that serviceable, unserviceable, and wanting. These audits give us a picture of not only the armaments of these regiments at this time, but also what weapons the regimental colonels believed their regiments should be equipped with, along with the proportion of pikes to muskets.[36]

---

35 WO55/336, f.137.
36 WO55/336, f.70.

	Item	Serviceable	Unserviceable	Wanting
Colonel Beaumont's Foot	Muskets	33	77	470
	Pikes	12	11	217
Colonel Hastings' Foot	Muskets	112	279	43
	Pikes	32	108	20
	Bayonets	141	134	69
Colonel Lutterell's Foot	Muskets	413	69	19
	Pikes	144	18	108
Sir James Leslies' Foot	Muskets	344	187	9
	Pikes	95	78	67
	Bayonets	121	177	222
	Bandoliers	133		407
Colonel Hales' Foot	Muskets	80	420	40
	Pikes	199	N/A	41
	Bandoliers	477	N/A	63
Sir John Guise's Foot	Muskets			400

While it is a commonly held belief that the English army had re-armed all infantry battalions with muskets and socket bayonets by 1700, or the start of the War of the Spanish Succession, this was not a universally accepted tactic amongst the officers in command of brigades, or amongst the Board of Ordnance. This point is perhaps explained best by orders from the Earl of Nottingham drawn up on 15 June 1703.[37] These state that the Board of Ordnance is to supply arms for 5,500 soldiers destined for Portugal, and to include:

Snaphance Musket	3,736
Snaphance Musket with sling	384
Long Pike	925
Cartouche Boxes	3,736
Grenade Pouches	384
Hammer Hatchets	384
Bayonets	384

These figures would seem to suggest a force containing six infantry battalions, each of 10 companies of musketeers and one of grenadiers. It would also suggest a pike to musket ratio of one pike for every four muskets, discounting the grenadier companies. It also shows that according to the Earl of Nottingham only grenadiers should be armed with bayonets. These supplies were subsequently changed to include 6,500 snaphance muskets with socket bayonets attached.[38]

In addition, the train of artillery proposed by the Prince of Hesse for offensive operations by the garrison of Gibraltar on 25 February 1702 included provision of:

Snaphance Muskets	3,000
Bayonets	1,000
Short Pike	1,000

37 BL, Add MS 61165, *Blenheim Papers Vol. LXV*, ff.24–27.
38 NA, SP41/34, f.38.

With the addition of arms for 900 dragoons, each armed with a carbine, pistol, and sword, but no grenadiers.[39] Pikes were not considered suitable for all climates: when the Duke of Bolton's Regiment of Foot was ordered to sail for the West Indies, they were instructed to exchange their pikes for muskets, 'pikes being unsuitable for those small islands.'[40] While the pike had ceased to be valued as a necessary weapon by most European armies in the early years of the eighteenth century, there were a number of countries that either continued to equip a percentage of their foot regiments with pike until the mid 1720s (Sweden) or re-introduced the pike to counter pike-armed troops.

Dutch generals were still of the opinion that pikes were an important defence against horse as late as 1706. The Raad van State of 2 March 1706 stipulated that regiments with companies over 50 men should be equipped with 10 pikemen, and those companies with a strength of below 50 men equipped with nine pikes per company. The reintroduction or continuation in the use of pikes was not only time specific, but could also be theatre specific, as in the case of Denmark. When the Danish corps arrived in Ireland in 1689, all the regiments of foot were equipped with muskets and bayonets, with the addition of *chevaux-de-frise* for defence against horse. Their equipment did not change during their campaigning on behalf of William III in Flanders (1692–1691) or during the War of the Spanish Succession (1701–1714). However, when it came for Denmark to re-enter the Great Northern War in 1711 to counter the Swedish aggressive attack, they were forced to re-introduce pikes to each battalion of foot. Russian was another army that had to reintroduce the pike: Peter the Great's crusade to modernise the Russian army resulted in the 'new' army being armed exclusively with muskets. However, the first contact with Swedish troops armed with pikes forced a change in the policy and the return of the pike.[41]

This did not see the end of the pike, or to be more precise the end of the idea that the pike had a relevant and important place to play on the battlefield. In 1779 General Henry Humphrey Evans Lloyd (b.1729–d.1783) published his *An Essay on the Theory of Money*, published in 1771, which proposed that the French regiments of foot should be drawn up into four ranks, with the fourth rank being wholly composed of pikemen.[42] His proposal was that the pikes should be a minimum of 21 feet long, so that they protruded five feet in front of the first man. He goes further in *Continuation of the Histories of the Late War in Germany, Between the King of Prussia, and the Empress of Germany and Her Allies*, published in 1781. He clarifies his argument, stating that the shortest men should be in the first rank, graduating up to the tallest men in the rear rank.

Why the pike's demise from frontline use was so protracted is not a simple question to answer. Certainly, the enemies of Sweden reintroduced the pike

---

39 Add MS 61165, *Blenheim Papers*, ff.77–78.
40 NA, WO55/336, William Brathwaite, 2 September 1689, f.182.
41 For more information on the Russian army, I would suggest Boris Megorsky, *The Russian Army in the Great Northern War 1700–21: Organisation, Materiel, Training and Combat Experience, Uniforms* (Warwick: Helion & Co, 2018)
42 P. Speelman, *War, Society and Enlightenment*, pp.364–66.

to counter the Swedish *Gå På* aggressive attack strategy using the pike as an offensive weapon. Sweden's tactics placing the queen of weapons as the centre of their army's philosophy probably marks the high water mark for the use of this weapon. This explanation does not however explain the reasons why the pike continued in use within western armies for as long as it did, so the question is was this down to operational need (defence against horse), for morale purposes, giving the battalion a stable centre, or just down to the decision of senior officers.

Chevaux-de-Frise

The *cheval-de-frise* or Frisian horse (plural: *chevaux-de-frise*) has been used in one form or another by armies dating back to the Romans as a temporary defence against cavalry, usually used to defend marching camps. It consists of a log with covered with sharp stakes, spears or short pikes to form an intimidating barrier against enemy horse. Thanks to a letter from the Duke of Schomberg to the Board of Ordnance dated 16 November 1689, we know that the English army were using them in Ireland in 1689. It states, 'firelocks will be the arms we shall have the most occasion for here, there need be few long pikes, intending to make use of chevaux de frise'.[43] *Chevaux-de-frise* appear in further correspondence from Sir Henry Goodricke, Master of Ordnance, to the Duke of Schomberg on 9 July 1689, instructing that 120 *chevaux-de-frise* be prepared to be carried on waggons and accompany the train of artillery that should be directed to march on Friday 22 July at 9:00 a.m.[44]

Siege of Londonderry 1689 and Kinsale 1690. Print by Jan Luyken 1690. (Courtesy of the Rijksmuseum, Netherlands)

Artillery

While the artillery was under the auspices of the Board of Ordnance and generally outside of the scope of this book, it does deserve a brief mention as it did have interactions with the army. The gunners were a profession in their own right, and were appointed by the Crown, they were not, however, soldiers. The mattrosses or labourers, along with the waggon drivers have generally been described as civilians. Although they were civilian contractors rather than military personal, they were still expected to defend themselves. An Ordnance dated 27 December 1677 describes the following arms to be issued to the train of artillery. For the conductors of the waggons and carriages of the train:

---

43 NAM, 6807.211, *Letters from the Duke of Schomberg to the Board of Ordnance, Ireland 1689.*
44 NA, WO55/1792, *Miscellaneous Entry Book: House of Commons*, f.2.

Carbines furnished with Belts	200
Swords with Belts	200

For the 80 gunners and 160 mattrosses:

Half Pikes	240
Boar Spears	240
Brown Bills	240
Swords with Belts	240

These numbers suggest that at least some of these weapons, presumably the boar spears or the half pikes, were intended to form *chevaux-de-frise* to be used for the defence of the artillery.[45] Artillery pieces as well as their corresponding equipment were held at the Tower of London and other major armouries including Berwick-upon-Tweed, Hull, and Portsmouth. With the impending invasion by William of Orange, the Board of Ordnance was instructed to construct a train of artillery for the defence of the nation. This train consisted of 20 pieces of ordnance (cannon) and six field mortars, being attended by lieutenant general, 120 men, a company of pioneer company of 69 men.[46] This is compared to the artillery train that William III constructed prior to his landing in Ireland the following year which consisted of 415 men and 1,092 horses.

One aspect of the interaction between artillery and regiments of foot that is generally overlooked within this period, is that of regimental artillery. We know that the English regiments of foot were equipped with 'battalion guns' from as early as 1686, thanks to records of that year's summer camp on Hounslow Heath. Regiments returning two 'small field pieces' in 1686 were the Battalion of Scotch Guards, Dumbarton's Battalion, Queen Dowager's Regiment, Prince George's Regiment, the Holland Regiment, Earl of Bath's Regiment, and the Marquis of Worcester's Regiment.[47] Guns were provided by and generally stored by the Board of Ordnance and only issued as needed to each battalion. However, following the dispersal of the regiments from the summer camp on Hounslow Heath, the directions for the disposal of the [small] field pieces to the regiments' quarters on Tuesday 13 August 1686 were as follows:[48]

Scotch Guards	Hide Park
Royal Regiment	Hide Park
Prince George's Regiment	Kingston [upon Thames]
Marquis of Worcester's Regiment	Uxbridge

Records from the summer camp of 1687 show that at least six regiments were assigned two guns each, these being:[49]

---

45   SA, D(W) 1778/V/1380, f.10.
46   WO55/335, *Middleton to Dartmouth, 15 October 1688*, ff.89–90.
47   WO55/400, *Ordnance office: Miscellaneous Entry Book, Warrants, 8 Aug 1686*, ff.101–03.
48   WO55/400, *Ordnance Office, 9 August 1686*, f.102.
49   WO55/339, *Ordnance Office, 5 June 1687*, f.158.

Ottoman early eighteenth-century pistol and European early eighteenth-century pistol. (Photo author's collection)

Queen's Regiment of Foot	3 Pounders (new)
Princess's Regiment of Foot	3 Pounders (new)
Colonel Cornwall's Regiment of Foot	3 Pounders Drake
Sir Edward Hales' Regiment of Foot	Falconetts
Colonel Tufton's Regiment of Foot	Falconetts
Colonel Bochan's Regiment of Foot	3 Pounders

The battalion guns would have been services by a gunner's assistant or matrosses with additional manpower coming from the battalion, rather than by gunners from the Board of Ordnance.

In 1674 King Charles II directed that a regiment of fusiliers should be raised, with the intention that this regiment's primary role was the protection of the artillery train. The regiment was named after the fusil musket, which had a flintlock firing mechanism rather that a matchlock and was therefore a safer weapon around the artillery's powder supply.

Arms for the Cavalry

Cavalry during this period was armed with carbines, a pair of pistols, and a sword, while dragoons were armed with a carbine, bayonet, pistol, and a sword. It is interesting to note that following the Duke of Monmouth's landing in the South West, King James II instructed the Board of Ordnance to equip Lord Oxford's Regiment of Horse, Lord Sunderland's regiment of horse and the four troops of Horse Guards with three-quarter harquebusier armour from the Supplies located within the Tower of London. In addition, he commissioned two new sets of three-quarter armour for the Earl of Marlborough and Lord Fairfield. James II also issued orders that every regiment of horse should be issued with 30 sets of 'our newest and best-

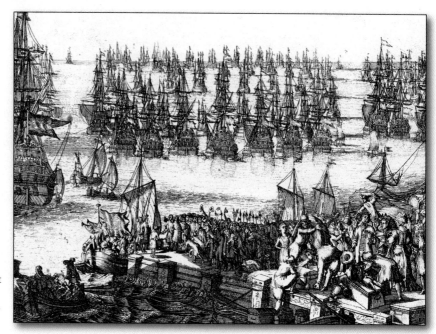

William of Orange landing in England, November 1688. Print dated 1689 by Pieter Pickaert. (Courtesy of the Rijksmuseum, Netherlands)

proofed armour for the use of the officers'.[50] Additionally to this he ordered that every colonel's regiment of horse consisting of nine troops should receive 'thirty sets of Our newest and best proof armour and every colonel of Our regiments of horse consisting of six troops to receive the *pro rata* amounts'. This would equip every officer in each regiment of horse with armour.[51]

On 24 March the Duke of Schomberg received a second warrant to re-equip two other regiments, this time for Colonel John Berkeley's Regiment of Dragoons and Colonel Edward Villiers' Regiment of Horse. The confirmation that the warrant is for replacement equipment is that in both cases they state that all defective arms are to be returned to the Ordnance stores.[52]

Colonel Berkeley's Dragoons	Muskets	170
	Long Daggers	324[53]
	Buckets	324
	Cartouche Boxes	324
	Halberds	6
	Drums	8
	Flints	6,000
Colonel Villiers' Horse	Carbines	152
	Pistols & Holsters	133 pairs

While we can state with certainty that the muskets and carbines for the dragoons and horse will have defiantly been flintlocks, apart from Sir John

---

50 NA WO55/335, Sunderland to the Tower of London, 24 Sept 1688, f.74.
51 NA, Wo55/400 *Ordnance Warrants*, ff.214–15.
52 NA WO55/401, *Ordnance Office*, f.20.
53 Long Daggers refer to plug bayonets.

King Charles Fort, Kinsale, Ireland, subjected to a siege by Marlborough and surrendered on 17 October 1690, after 13 days under siege. (Author's photograph)

King James II landing at Kinsale with French forces on 12 March 1689. James left France on 7 March 1689 with 13 French ships of the line, six frigates and three fireships with English, Irish and Scottish supporters as well as a number of French officers. Print by Pieter Pickaert. (Courtesy of the Rijksmuseum, Netherlands)

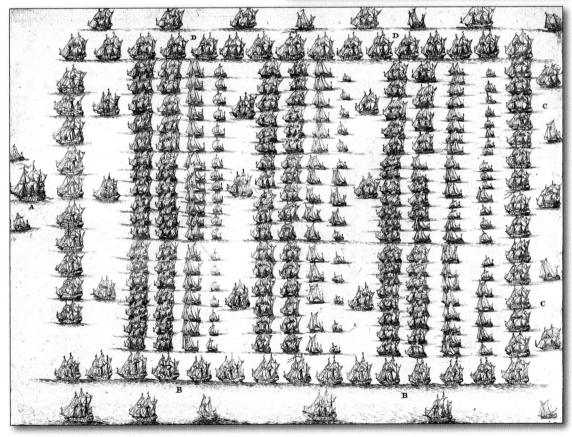

William's fleet in comparison was one of the largest invasion fleets of the time and consisted of over 500 vessels carrying some 20,000 Dutch, Danish, and English troops with an assortment of other small contingents including 200 troops from the Dutch East India Company. Order of the fleet with which William III sailed to England, 1688 print dated 1689 by Pieter Pickaert. (Courtesy of the Rijksmuseum, Netherlands)

Guise's foot, the muskets for the other five regiments of foot would have been a mix of matchlocks and flintlocks. The last warrant also gives an insight into just how many flints were needed with 6,000 flints for 800 dragoons.

Manufacturing and Supply

Although purchasing of weapons and stores as well as artillery was becoming the task of the Board of Ordnance during the period covered by this book, regimental colonels were still able to order arms and specify the design if they so wished, although the Board was attempting to standardise muskets. The main manufacturing base in England prior to 1688 was London. When the Board of Ordnance issued a contract for the manufacture of 1,000 new snaphance muskets in April 1683 the contract stipulated that this would be fulfilled by 28 different tradesmen. Each person listed was responsible for between 15 and 100 muskets at a rate of 15 shillings per gun. In 1688 the MP Sir Richard Newdigate tried to develop the gunmaking trade in Birmingham, and by 1693 five named Birmingham gunmakers were contracted to deliver 200 guns per month to the Tower of London at 17 shillings each.[54] During the expansion of the English army following the Glorious Revolution, the army was reliant on buying guns from Holland to make up the shortfall between what English gunmakers could manufacture and the needs of the army.

The Board does not take over all responsibilities for both the design, manufacture, and delivery of all the necessary supplies of war until 1722. Prior to this date, regimental colonels had a much greater involvement in these aspects of the supply chain.

Conclusion

While there has always been a great deal of debate regarding what particular arms an individual battalion or regiment was issued with during a specific period or event, nothing is ever that simple. The process of arming and re-arming of regiments is a complex and time-consuming process. That statement is as true today as was during the seventeenth century. Regiments with home postings will always receive new equipment before regiments on foreign postings, and regimental colonels will not always be able to receive the quantity or types of equipment needed due to lack of supplies within the stores and warehouses of the Board of Ordnance.

One thing is certain, transitions between existing equipment and new equipment always take longer than expected and therefore it is extremely difficult to give a categoric date when the whole of the army is equipped with the latest equipment. Matchlock muskets were still being ordered by the Board of Ordnance in the last years of the seventeenth century, well after the general introduction of the flintlock musket. As shown by the example in the

---

54 De Witt Bailey, 'The Board of Ordnance and Small Arms Supply: The Ordnance system, 1714–1783', unpublished Ph.D. thesis (London: King's College, 1988), p.30.

Royal Armouries in Leeds, even when transitioning to the newer weapon, old matchlocks were could just be given new locks as an in-service upgrade, rather than being completely replaced. The confirmation that a regiment or battalion was issued with bandoliers or cartouche boxes does not guarantee that they were equipped with a matchlock or a flintlock musket.

Pikes and plug bayonets undoubtedly had longer service lives that has previously been suggested, although as previously stated it is almost impossible to give a date when they were eventually consigned to the forgotten stores within the Tower of London. Wherever possibly multiple sources have been used, in most cases these are the Royal warrants requesting or ordering equipment for regiments and then confirmation from the Board of Ordnance that the warrant is to be enacted upon. There are always issues that will spark controversy and debate, one being if all the troops taking part in the 1703–04 Portugal expedition arrived in country with their pikes, or if they left them in England after being recalled from Flanders.

4

A System of Military Discipline

Introduction

While the preceding chapters have looked at the physical characteristics of the plug bayonet and the issues surrounding the supply and demand, this chapter will address the issue of the changes in military drill during the latter stages of the seventeenth century. This chapter will also address the pivotal issue of: did the drill for foot soldiers change significantly during the latter half of the seventeenth century, and if so, was this to the detriment of the pike?

There are three specific areas of concern regarding the use of contemporary drill manuals. As discussed in chapter one the first area of concern is the nature of the publication of drill manuals during this period, in that they were all published privately. The second is that they were written for training or drill practice and not for battlefield use, this will be dealt with later within the chapter.[1] The final concern was raised by Chandler, who stated that historians needed to be aware that the publication date of any given drill manual did not necessarily correspond with contemporary drill theory.[2] That said, the example he uses of a French manual from 1647 still being used as 'the standard authoritative work … until the 1690s' is both an extreme and specific example. Drill manuals in this chapter are used as additional contemporary evidence and are used to highlight change in military theory as well as battlefield tactics. While historians in the past have viewed drill manuals with scepticism, these same documents are being used by modern historians in cutting edge research including in conflict archaeology.[3] They are being used in this manuscript as an indication of contemporary military theory, in the same way as royal warrants are being used as an indicator of intent in chapter 3.

Drill manuals during this period fall into three general categories. The first being a basic drill manual that just gives the order and wording of the

---

1   Manning, *Apprenticeship in Arms*, p.420.
2   Chandler, *Blenheim Preparation*, p.96.
3   Warwick Louth, *The Arte Militaire: The Application of 17th Century Military Manuals to Conflict Archaeology* (Solihull: Helion & Co., 2016), p.11.

evolutions of drill, as demonstrated by *The General Exercise ordered by his Highness the Prince of Orange*, published in 1689 and running to only 12 pages.[4] The second type includes explanations of each of the evolutions of drill and also can include instructions for how a officer handles a company or battalion. This category includes: *The New Exercise of Firelock & bayonets; appointed by his Grace The Duke of Marlborough*, and *A Treatise of the English Military Discipline both the Old way and the Shortest*.[5] The final category of drill manuals are more of an educational text for young officers and include details of fortification construction, gunpowder, mathematics and geometry as well as musket drill. Examples in this last category are often enriched with detailed diagrams and drawings, but also tend to be volumes with out-of-date information so should be consulted with great care.

As indicated in the previous chapters, plug bayonets were first issued to dragoons and grenadiers, only being issued to general troops later. The theory under investigation is that the drill manuals will provide evidence for when and how this happened by looking at the specific exercises performed by dragoons, grenadiers, and foot. The majority of information for this chapter has been obtained from the National Army Museum in Chelsea, the British Library, and from an ever-expanding source of facsimiles of original texts available through print-on-demand publishing.

Drill manuals were not the only ways for officers to gain an understanding of military matters, it was common practice for officers to serve on the Continent as military observers or as officers with allied armies. One example of this is a royal warrant from King James II giving permission for Edward Clarke to travel with all possible speed to Hungary and to repair to the Emperor's [Leopold I of the Habsburg Empire] army on its next campaign;[6] there to observe and take notes of their methods of marching camps, embattling exercises, ordering their train of artillery, approaching, besieging, and attacking a town, their mines, batteries, lines of circumvallation and contravallation, ways of fortification, their foundries, instruments, and engines of war.

An Exercise in Drill

The *Military Discipline or the Young Artillery-Man* published in 1661, unsurprisingly makes no mention of bayonets.[7] The earliest English volume

---

4 Anon., *The General Exercise ordered by his Highness the Prince of Orange, To be punctually observed of all the Infantry in service of the States General of the United Provinces* (Newgate Street: William Marshall, 1689).

5 Anon., *The New Exercise of Firelocks & bayonets; Appointed by his Grace the Duke pf Marlborough to be used By all the British Forces* (Stationers-Hill: John Morphew, 1708), and Christopher Whitmore, *A Treaty of the English Military Discipline, Both the Old Way, and the Shortest way now in Use* (London: J. Grantham, 1682).

6 NA, WO55/400 Ordnance Miscellaneous Entry Book: Warrants, 29 March 1687, f.127.

7 W. Barriffe, *Military Discipline or the Young Artillery-Man* (London: Gartrude Dawson, 1661, 6th Edition). Also Anon., *The English Military Discipline 1660* (Newgate: John Overton, 1660), and C. Whitmore, *A Treatise of the English Military Discipline: Both the Old Way, and the Shortest way now in Use* (London: J. Grantham, 1682).

that indicated bayonet drill for grenadiers and dragoons is *An Abridgment of the English Military Discipline* printed in 1678, with the first Scottish volume printed in Edinburgh in 1680.[8] The first drawing of a bayonet appears in a volume in 1680 published by Robert Harford, but does not mention any bayonet drills.[9] Volumes printed in England in 1684 and 1685 give more detailed explanations of each evolution and also give a specific phrase which appears in later printed volumes:

> Draw your dagger {Holding it flat before you upright} Screw it into the Muzzle of your firelock {So that the flat side may be towards you when recovered}[10]

This phrase is used again in the 1689 English version of *The general Exercise Ordered by His Highness the Prince of Orange*, indicating that later authors of drill manuals were using previous treaties as guides, if not direct copies. A Scottish version of *An Abridgement of Military Discipline* published in 1686 also used the same phrase in its description of bayonet drill for dragoons and grenadiers.[11]

While Captain J. Stevens' 1688 treatise on *Fortification and Military Discipline* is a book for the general education of officers in the art of geometry, mathematics, and fortifications and includes large number of detailed drawings, it also includes a large section on the art of war and exercises of the pike and musket for horse, foot, grenadiers, and dragoons.[12] While evolutions for the foot include both matchlock and firelock muskets, only grenadiers and dragoons have instructions for the use of daggers [bayonets].[13] The title plate states that the text has been improved and designed by Captain J. Stevens; the first part dealing with fortifications and so on is obviously a reprint, as it uses drawings by the French engineer, Nicolas-Francois Blondel.[14] In addition, Captain Stevens does not appear in the lists of commissioned officers between 9 February 1686 and January 1689, one possible implication of this is that the whole book is a reprint of an earlier text which does compromise the document's value.[15]

---

8 Anon., *An Abridgment of the English Military Discipline: By his Majesties Permission* (London: John Bill, Christopher Barker and Henry Hill), pp.138–150, and Anon., *An Abridgment of the Military Discipline: appointed by His Majesty, to be uses by all His Forces in His Ancient Kingdom of Scotland* (Edinburgh: Andrew Anderson, 1680), pp.106–07.

9 Anon., *English Military Discipline: or the Way and Method of Exercising Horse & Foot* (London: Robert Harford, 1680).

10 Anon., *An Abridgement of the English Military Discipline: Reprinted by His Majesties Special Command* (London: John Bill, Henry Hill and Thomas Newcomb, 1684), pp.126–33; Anon., *An Abridgement of the English Military Discipline* (London: John Bill, Henry Hill and Thomas Newcomb, 1684), pp.80–81, 128–29, 186–87, 204–15.

11 Anon., *An Abridgement of Military Discipline, For the use of His Majesties Forces in the Kingdom of Scotland, By His Majesties Special Command* (Edinburgh: Andrew Anderson, 1686), pp.79–81 and 204–15.

12 J. Stevens, *Fortification and Military Discipline 1688* [Facsimile] (London: Robert Morden. 1688), pp.16–31.

13 Stevens, *Fortifications*, pp.23–30.

14 Nicholas-Francois Blondel, 1618–1686.

15 C. Dalton, *English Army Lists and Commissions Register, 1661–1714*, volume 2 (London: Eyre & Spottiswoode, 1894).

(2)

Commands for the Exercise of the Pikes.

TO the Front : Charge.
  As you were.
To the Right : Charge.
  To the Left, as you were.
To the Left : Charge.
  To the Right, as you were.
To the Right about : Charge.
  To the Left about, as you were.
To the Left about : Charge.
  To the Right about, as you were.

Shoulder your Pikes.
To the Front : Charge.
  As you were.
To the Right : Charge.
  As you were.
To the Left : Charge.
  To the Right, as you were.
To the Right about : Charge.
  To the Left, as you were.
To the Left about : Charge.
  To the Right about, as you were.

Port your Pikes :
  Charge.
Trail with your Spears behind :
  Charge, as you were.
Push your Pikes.

Trail your Pikes the Spears before.
Present your Spears.
To the Front : Charge.
Advance your Pikes.
Order your Pikes.
Lay down your Pikes.
Take up your Pikes.
Plant your Pikes.
Order your Pikes.
Advance your Pikes.

Have a care to present your Arms.

To the Front.
To the Right, Four times.
To the Right about.
To the Left, as you were.
To the Left, Four times.
To the Left about.
To the Right as you were.

Poise your Muskets, and Recover your Pikes.
Shoulder your Muskets, the Pikes to Advance at the same Word.

EVOLUTIONS.

Ranks, to the Right Double your Front. March.
To the Left as you were. March. Halt.
Ranks, to the Left Double your Front. March.
To the Right as you were. March. Halt.

Ranks, to the Right Double your Rere. March. Halt.
As you were. March.
Ranks, to the Left Double your Rere. March. Halt.
As you were. March.
Rere half Files, to the Right Double your Front. March.
To

---

(3)

To the Left as you were. March. Halt.
Rere half Files, to the Left Double your Front. March.
To the Right as you were. March.
Front half Files, to the Right Double your Rere. March. Halt.
As you were. March.
Front half Files, to the Left Double your Rere. March. Halt.
As you were. March.
Files to the Right Double. March. Halt.
To the Left as you were. March.
Files to the Left Double. March. Halt.
As you were. March.
Half Ranks, to the Right Double your Files. March. Halt.
To the left as you were. March. Halt.
Half Ranks, to the Left Double your Files. March. Halt.
To the Right as you were. March. Halt.
Files, to the Right about Counter-march. March.
Files, to the Left about Counter-march. March.
Ranks, to the Right Counter-march. March. Halt.
Ranks, to the Left Counter-march. March. Halt.

Files and Ranks being Closed.

To the Right, Wheel. March. Halt.
To the Right, Wheel. March. Halt.
To the Right about, Wheel. March. Halt.
To the Left, Wheel. March. Halt.
To the Left, Wheel. March. Halt.
To the left about, Wheel. March. Halt.

The Ranks and Files being Opened to their former Distance.

Take heed to lay down your Arms.

Rest your Muskets.
Order your Arms.
Lay down your Arms.

Take care to quit your Arms.

March.
To your Arms. [At beat of Drum.
Put up your Swords.
Take up your Arms.
Rest your Muskets.
Poise your Muskets, and Recover your Pikes.
Shoulder your Muskets.

You are Referr'd for particular Directions to King William's *Exercise.*

F I N I S.

In 1689 the *General Exercise ordered by His Highness the Prince of Orange* was printed in England after the Glorious Revolution, and gives evolutions of drill for matchlock muskets, firelock muskets, and pikes. This is a direct copy of the original Dutch version printed in the Hague in 1688. The English version (1689) stipulated matchlock musket drill for foot, and firelock drill with daggers [bayonets] for grenadiers only.[16, 17] The instruction to 'charge your dagger, the but against the right knee', would indicate that this is for use against enemy horse. For close combat against enemy foot, orders still include 'club your muskets' or 'club your firelocks'.[18]

Anon, Command for the Exercise of Foot, Arm'd with Firelock-Muskets and Pikes; with Evolutions (London: Anon, 1690). (Courtesy of the British Library)

---

16 Anon., *The General Exercise Ordered by His Highness the Prince of Orange, To be Punctually Observed of all the Infantry in the Service of the States General of The United Provences: Being a most Worthy Compendium, Very useful for all Persons Concerned in the Noble Exercise of Arms* (Hague: Jacob Scheltus, 1688) and Anon., *The General Exercise Ordered by His Highness the Prince of Orange, To be Punctually Observed of all the Infantry in the Service of the States General of The United Provences: Being a most Worthy Compendium, Very useful for all Persons Concerned in the Noble Exercise of Arms* (London: William Marshall, 1689), pp.6–7.

17 The original Dutch version states *bajonet* [bayonet], translated as dagger.

18 Anon., *General Exercise 1689*, pp.6–7; BL, Add MS 27892 *Military treaties of General. J. Douglas*, pp.212–224, also J.S., *Military Discipline or the Art of War* (Cornhill: Robert Morton, 1689), pp.31–34.

In 1690 there was an increase in publications exulting the art of war, often claiming to be an officers *Vade Mecum*. An anonymous treatise from 1690 on the commands for troops armed with firelocks and pikes, still has a command for 'club your musket' but no text for bayonets. The copy in the British Library has an annotated back cover stating *fix your bayonets* '+' and to *recover your bayonet* 'Φ' with two sections marked where the two commands should be inserted (see illustration 6).[19] The annotations are not dated, however they illustrate that treaties were updated and continued to be used after the implementation of new drill.

Another volume printed in 1690 by Nicholas Boddington gives similar instructions to the *Prince of Orange* exercise for bayonet drill for grenadiers and dragoons only. It adds some extra evolutions for the parade square – charge to the right and then to the left four times.[20] According to the opening text it was licensed according to an order dated 12 October 1689, therefore it is probably a locally produced copy of the above work. A further work printed in 1690 suggests that:

> … It is also to be observed, that when the grenadiers stand in the body [ranks] with the musketeers, that they must make the same motions as the musketeers, because they do not then meddle with their grenades or bayonets.[21]

This statement if taken at face value questions that even as late as 1690, the general military theory was indicating that all musketeers should not be armed with a bayonet. The drills still dictate that the bayonet is screwed into the muzzle of the musket, and like previous examples is only applicable to drills for grenadiers and dragoons. A drill manual reportedly from 1690 reprinted within a *Compendium of Military Discipline* dated 1726, gives exercises for both foot, dragoons, and grenadiers.[22] This explains the evolutions of drill for firelocks and bayonets and relates to socket rather than plug bayonets. The 39 evolution stating, 'Slip down your bayonet on the barrel, with a quick motion turning your right hand outwards, lock your bayonet.'[23] If the date of 1690 can be believed, this is the first printed instruction for socket bayonet drill for all troops. Later works including those of Nicholas Boddington (1691), and Thomas Axe (1692), still dictate the use of plug bayonets being issued to grenadiers and dragoons only, as does a manual published in 1692, by Captain Lieutenant John Darker for the militia.[24]

---

19 Anon., *Command for the Exercise of Foot, Arm'd with Firelock-Muskets and Pikes; with Evolutions* (London: Anon., 1690), pp.1–4.

20 Anon., *The Perfection of Military Discipline after the new methods, as practiced in England and Ireland etc.* (London: N. Boddington, 1690), pp.33–35.

21 Anon., *The Exercise of the Foot with the Evolutions* (London: Charles Bill and Thomas Newcomb, 1690), p.55.

22 J. Blackwell, *A compendium of Military Discipline* (London: John Blackwell, 1726), p.3.

23 Blackwell, *Military Discipline*, pp.24–28.

24 N. Boddington, *The Perfection of Military Discipline, After the Newest Method; as Practices in England and Ireland, &c* (London: W. Wild, 1691), pp.32–33 & 44–47; T. Axe, *An Epitome of the Whole Art of War: in two parts; the First of Military Discipline. The Second of fortifications and Gunnery* (Warwick Lane: J. Moxon, 1692), pp.63–66; J. Darker, *A Breviary of Military Discipline, Compos'd and Published for the use of the Militia* (London: D. Brown, 1692).

Soldier's Leap, Killiecrankie, where Donald McBane, a Williamite soldier, leapt the 5.5 metre/18ft River Garry. Another exaggeration from the battle of Killiecrankie? (Author's photograph)

Although a lot has been made of General Hugh Mackay's supposed new style of ring bayonet and the plug bayonet causing his defeat at the Battle of Killiecrankie,[25] the evidence in his treatise published in 1693 *The Exercise of the Foot* does not support this view, as it still stipulates the use of plug bayonets.[26] Further evidence of this can be ascertained by the numbers of pike-armed troops in Mackey's army. Out of 3,000 foot, approximately one quarter were armed with pikes – with Kenmure's regiment being issued with 450 bayonets and 150 pikes.[27] This still shows foot armed with matchlock and pike, with dragoons and grenadiers armed with flintlocks with plug bayonets, the phrasing of certain statements indicates it is probably a copy of Bill and Newcomb's edition of 1690.[28]

Two separate volumes published in 1702 both have evolutions of bayonet drill only for dragoons and grenadiers, with evolutions for the foot limited to flintlock, matchlock, pike, and the sword. Both of these volumes include

---

25 Norris, *Fix Bayonets!*, p.26; Mackay, *Memoirs*, p.52.
26 H. Mackay, *The Exercise of the Foot with the Evolutions According to the Words of Command as they are Explained: As also the Forming of Battalions, with Directions to be observed by all Colonels, Captains, and other Officers in Their Majesties Armies* (Edinburgh: John Reid, 1693), pp.31–33.
27 Reid, *Killiecrankie*, p.68.
28 Mackay uses identical sections including the quote from footnote 17.

large sections on military theory including fortifications and other subjects deemed important for an officer's education.[29]

The treatise by an 'Officer in Her Majesties Foot Guards' published in 1708 is specific to firelocks and bayonets. The instructions are clearly for a socket bayonet, as instruction 4, 'fix your bayonet' states:[30]

1. Come up briskly up to the front, entering the socket of your bayonet upon the muzzle of your piece [musket].
2. Shut the bayonet down briskly.
3. Lock your bayonet by giving it a turn from you.

These instructions are also repeated in his 4th edition of *A Military and Sea Dictionary published* in 1711, however his 3rd edition published in 1703 only mentions the plug bayonet.[31]

These documents do not differentiate between foot and grenadiers in their instructions, it is unique in drill manuals as it does not cover any other subject, just explaining the words of command.[32] This edition gives 44 general words of command, these are still intended for the parade square or training. Commands 9–12 dictates, 'draw your bayonet, fix your bayonet, rest your bayonet, and charge your bayonet breast high'. Command 42 of 'club your musket' is indicative of the theory that the musket itself is still usable as a close combat weapon.[33] These instructions for fitting socket bayonets are replicated in Gent's 1717 exercises for *Militia Discipline,* which only has evolutions for flintlocks, indicative of the fact that flintlocks and socket bayonets have replaced matchlocks and pikes even in militia regiments.[34]

Each of the treatises have between 19 and 26 words of command to load and fire a musket, with matchlock drill tending to have a higher number of words of command or evolutions. Comparably the number of commands to either fit or remove a plug bayonet range from three to five. The difference in the number of evolutions needed and time taken to fit or remove a bayonet in comparison to preparing and firing a musket, must remove any direct causality between the plug bayonet and the defeat of government troops

29 N. Boddington, *The perfection of Military Discipline: After the Newest Method; As Practiced in England and Ireland,* 4th edn (London: I. Dawk, 1702) pp.31–44; J.H. *The Complete Gentleman Soldier: or A Treatise of Military Discipline, Fortifications and Gunnery* (London: Thomas Ballard, 1702), pp.42–51.

30 Anon., *The New Exercises of Firelocks & Bayonets; Appointed by His Grace The Duke of Marlborough to be used by all the British Forces: With Instructions to perform every Motion by Body Foot and Horse* (London: John Morphew, 1708), p.5.

31 Anon., *A Military and Sea Dictionary: explaining all difficult terms in martial Discipline, Fortifications, and gunnery, and all Terms of Navigation,* 4th edn (London: J. Morphew, 1711), p.309 and Anon., *A Military and Sea Dictionary: explaining all difficult terms in martial Discipline, Fortifications, and gunnery, and all Terms of Navigation,* 3rd edn (London: J. Morphew, 1703), p.23.

32 J. Morphew, *The New Exercise of Firelocks & Bayonets; Appointed by his Grace the Duke of Marlborough to be used by all the British Forces* (London: John Morphew, 1708), pp.4–5.

33 Morphew, *Firelocks & Bayonets,* pp.26–29.

34 W. Gent, *Militia Discipline: The Words of Command, and the Directions for Exercising the Musket, Bayonet and Cartridges: and the Exercise for the Soldier of Militia Horse,* 2nd edn (London: R. Harbin, 1717), pp.24–25.

Siege of Namen 1695 by Dirk Mass. (Courtesy of the Rijksmuseum, Netherlands)

at Killiecrankie.[35] Mackay states that the government troops opened fire at 100 paces, but that 'Balfour's regiment did not fire a shot and only half of Ramsey's made some little [musket] fire'.[36] This does suggest that it was a lack of training, rather than the equipment that was the reason for his defeat, with Manning stating that Mackay had very little confidence in his troops prior to the battle.[37]

Evolutions of Musket Drill

One of the issues that is constantly raised is the difference in the number of evolutions of drill for matchlock muskets compared to flintlock muskets with matchlocks muskets generally being considered having more evolutions and therefore having a slower rate of fire. Previously historians and authors have just taken the total number of evolutions without looking at which ones are in reality only for the parade ground and not the battlefield. If we have a detailed look at the drill manual brought over by William of Orange for the words of command for a matchlock musket and the 44 words of command:

---

35 Childs, *Armies and Warfare*, p.107.
36 Mackay, *Memoirs*, pp.55–56.
37 Manning, *Apprenticeship in Arms*, pp.378–80.

Image of a soldier loading his musket by Dirk Mass, c.1690.
(Courtesy of the Rijksmuseum, Netherlands)

1. Join your right hand to your Muskets
2. Poise your Musket
3. Join your left hand to your Muskets
4. Take your Matches
5. Blow your Matches
6. Cock your Matches
7. Try your Matches
8. Guard your Pans
9. Blow your Matches
10. Open your Pans in presenting
11. Give Fire
12. Recover your Arms
13. Return your Matches
14. Blow your Pans
15. Handle your Primers
16. Prime
17. Shut your Pans
18. Blow off your loose Corns
19. Cast about to Charge
20. Handle your Chargers
21. Open them with your teeth
22. Charge with Powder
23. Charge with Bullet
24. Wadd from your Hat
25. Draw forth your Scowrers
26. Hold them up
27. Shorten them to your breasts
28. Put them in the Barrels
29. Ram down your Shot
30. Withdraw your Scowrers
31. Hold them up
32. Shorten them to your Breasts
33. Put them up in their places
34. Join your Right hand to your Muskets
35. Poise your Muskets
36. Shoulder your Muskets
37. Rest your Muskets
38. Order your Muskets
39. Lay down your Muskets
40. Take up your Muskets
41. Rest your Muskets
42. Club your Muskets
43. Rest your Muskets
44. Shoulder your Muskets

It is plain that these are evolutions for the parade ground, if the musketeer in question was to continue giving fire, evolution numbers 34 to 44

Jacobite army being defeated at the Battle of Newtowbutler, 31 July 1689 by Pieter Pickaert. (Courtesy of the Rijksmuseum, Netherlands)

would be ignored and the cycle would continue with a total of 33 evolutions. While the corresponding evolutions for a matchlock are:

1. Join your right hand to your Firelocks
2. Poise your Firelocks
3. Join your left hand to your Firelocks
4. Bend your Firelocks
5. [Make Ready]
6. Present
7. Give Fire
8. Recover your Arms
9. Half bend your Firelocks
10. Blow your Pans
11. Handle your Primer
12. Prime
13. Shut your Pans
14. Cast about to Charge
15. Handle your Cartridges
16. Open your Cartridges
17. Charge your Cartridges
18. Draw forth your Cartridges
19. Hold them up
20. Shorten them to your Breath
21. Put them in the Barrels

22. Ram down your Shot
23. Withdraw your Scowrers
24. Hold them up
25. Shorten them to your breaths
26. Put them up in their places
27. Join your right hand to your Firelocks

If the musketeer loading the matchlock was issued with cartridges his evolutions would have been reduced by two, down to 31 evolutions, so in reality there is only a difference of four evolutions between the two types of muskets. In addition, although the evolutions for the matchlock have the musketeer checking his match, there are no such checks incorporated for the musketeer operating a flintlock musket.

Conclusion

While taking Chandler's concerns into account regarding the accurate dating of any specific drill evolution within a published manual, the manuals cannot just be regarded as an unreliable source of information. Even when specific areas of text clearly indicate that they have been copied from earlier works as in the case of Mackay's 1693 *The Exercise of Foot*, these assumptions cannot be extrapolated to the documents as a whole. Approximately 50 percent of the treaties examined contain additional information for the education of officers. Captain Stevens' volume published in 1688 is a prime example covering details on geometry, mathematics and fortifications, while *Military & Maritime Discipline* published in 1672 also includes instructions for artillery and making gunpowder.[38]

As explained in chapter 1, English troops were using bayonets prior to 1662 while in Dunkirk, unfortunately due to the non-official nature of the publication of drill manuals, bayonets do not appear until 1678. This volume is a reprint of one sold by the same publishers Bill and Barker (1676) which does not mention dragoons, grenadiers or bayonets. This gives us a date for the implementation of bayonets into English drill somewhere between 1676 and 1678. One unexpected evolution found in every treatise from the 1661 volume, to 1708 edition covering flintlock muskets and socket bayonets, is the evolution to 'club your musket'.[39] This evolution is associated with using the musket literally as a club, even when the drill manual clearly indicates the use of socket bayonets. This implies that as late as 1708 there is still an institutional lack of trust in the ability and physical construction of the bayonet. Following the Battle of Malplaquet (1709), only two percent of 411 survivors' wounds were found to be from bayonets, indicating that the bayonet was still not prominent in hand-to-hand fighting.[40]

---

38 Stevens, *Fortifications*, pp.1–22 and T. Venn, *Military & Maritime Discipline in Three Books* [Facsimile], book 3 (1672), pp.9–22.
39 Anon., *General Exercise Ordered by His Highness*, pp.6–7.
40 F. Tallett, *War and Society in Early-Modern Europe 1495–1715* (Abingdon: Routledge, 2001), p.45.

The data reported in this chapter appears to indicate that the general consensus of military writers and theorists is that the bayonet was still a specialist weapon up to 1690. This conclusion is backed up by findings from chapter 3 that show the first general issue to musketeers in 1689. One further finding from the examination of these treatise is that evolutions of drill still continue for the pike as late as 1693. The full implication of this and the other findings will be further explored in the final chapter of this manuscript. As previously stated in this chapter, the statement that the plug bayonet was responsible for General Mackay's defeat at the Battle of Killiecrankie (1689), one regurgitated by every historian writing on the subject, is according to this evidence spurious at best. In correspondence sent after the battle no mention is made of the later reported reason, instead cowardly conduct by several regiments is given as the primary cause.[41] Blackwell's compendium highlights the issues of credibility when it comes to using drill manuals as historical evidence. Published in 1726, it includes a reprint of a drill manual reportedly published in 1690, if this date is true, it gives us the earliest date for the inclusion of socket bayonets in drill manuals. It also questions the relevance of all the information within the compendium as the author is using information that is up to 30 years out of date.

Print showing the Battle of Aughrim 1691, unknown artist. (Courtesy of the Rijksmuseum, Netherlands)

---

41 Mackay, *Memoirs*, pp.249–256.

5

The Evolution of Infantry Tactics

Infantry Regiments

English regiments of foot have always varied in size, depending on the year and on operational need. With the exception of the First Foot Guards which always consisted of two battalions, most regiments on the English establishment generally only consisted of one battalion.

By 1689, William III had fixed the number of companies within each of the line regiments to 13, 12 companies of musketeers and one of grenadiers. Each regiment to consist of:

    Regimental Staff of:
        Colonel
        Lieutenant Colonel
        Chaplain
        Major
        Chirurgeon and Chirurgeon's Mate
        Quarter-Master

    1 Grenadier company consisting of:
        Captain
        Two Lieutenants
        Three Sergeants
        Three Corporals
        Two drummers
        Sixty Grenadiers

    12 Companies of Foot
        Captain
        Lieutenants
        Ensign
        Three Sergeants
        Three Corporals

Two drummers
Sixty Private Soldiers

This gives a regimental establishment of 45 officers and 780 soldiers. The company to be made up one captain, one lieutenant, one ensign, three sergeants, three corporals, two drummers, and 60 private soldiers.[1] In addition the regimental staff consisted of a colonel, a lieutenant colonel, major, chaplain, chirurgeon, chirurgeon's mate, and quartermaster.

Officers

Although officers were commissioned by the King, they were normally required to purchase their commission, with the cost of the commission dependant on their new rank and regiment. In general cavalry commissions were more expensive than infantry, and the household regiments of foot and horse guards were more expensive than line regiments. It was not uncommon for a colonel of a foot regiment to hold a commission of a lesser rank in either the foot guards or horse guards. When an officer was promoted, he would sell his old commission, which would then part-fund his promotion. The two exceptions to the purchase rule, were battlefield promotions and upon commissioning new regiments, although these exceptions were at the discretion of the commanding officer. With the size of the army being in almost a constant flux, there had to be a system in place so that seasoned officers were not penalised for taking up commissions in regiments that were later disbanded. In 1679 Charles II made the following order:

> Whereas upon the raising of our late army several officers belonging to the troops and companies of our old forces quit their employment therein for others of a higher degree in the said army, and that the same now being disbanded, their new commissions are determined and maid void. To the end that those persons whom are judged capable of better command & worthy to be preferred in our service may not suffer by what we intended for their encouragement & advantage. We have thought fit to signify to you, and our will and pleasure is that the said officers be forthwith restored to the same commands & in the same troops or companies which they voluntary left upon their taking any other commission on the new raised force. And that those persons who are now in their places be put out to make room for them.[2]

It was recommended that those officers losing their commissions due to this process, were recommissioned as soon as a relevant and appropriate vacancy became available. This procedure was replicated following the army's expansion resulting from the Monmouth Rebellion (June–July 1685).

---

1 NA, WO55/336 Board of Ordnance, f.6.
2 NA, SP44/58 *Military Warrant Book, Duke of Monmouth 1678–79*, ff.21–22.

Musketry Evolution

There has always been a very healthy debate concerning infantry tactics in the late seventeenth century, with the primary focus of these debates circulating around three primary areas:

- The evolution from matchlock to flintlock muskets by individual state armies
- The percentage of pike within certain Western European armies (England, France, and Holland in particular)
- The development and effectiveness of platoon firing in comparison to firing by rank

There has been a general tendency for authors and historians for the sake of neatness and ease of comparison to give specifics for any change in equipment or in infantry tactics. Unfortunately, as even modern-day soldiers know, equipment rollout tends to be more of a drip-feed than a sudden change. British 58 pattern webbing was still in use long after the official role out of the later 90 pattern. The author has personal experience of being issued with a SMG in the early 1980s that had a 1947 War Office stamp, with the weapon simply being re-bored to receive NATO 9mm rounds.

Rank and File

A Treatise of Military Discipline or the Art of War as now Practiced, published in 1688 by Robert Morden and described as being improved and designed

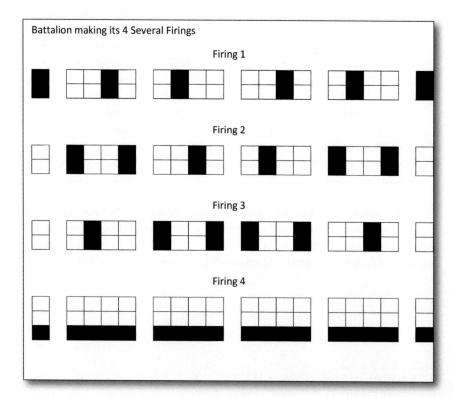

Details of the Dutch system of firing by platoon 1690, copied from Add MS 41141 Townsend Papers. (Author's photograph)

by Captain J. Storey, stated that there were four distances in use.[3] According to this treaty the distances between the rank and file were the same, these were:

Close Order	One foot and a half
Order	Three foot
Open Order	Six foot
Double Distance	Twelve feet

This would give an average frontage for a 600-man infantry battalion which was in line and in four ranks as 450ft or 150 metres in close order, this distance increases to 675ft or 205 metres in order and rising to 2,025ft or 617 metres at double distance. The treaties

A salvo. (Drawing by Alan Turton © Helion & Company)

recommend open order or 6ft distance for countermarching and either double distance or double, double distance (12 or 24ft) for the prevention of cannon shot. These distances are consistent in all later editions of English drill manuals.

The rules for forming up of battalions are specified in the 1701 *Exercise of Foot* and stipulate that companies shall place themselves within the battalion according to the date of their officer's commission.[4]

The Colonel's Company on the Right Wing
The Second or Lieutenant Colonel's Company on the Left Wing
The Major's or Third Company on the Right Wing next to the Colonel's Company
The Fourth or Eldest Captain's Company on the Left Wing next to the Lt-Colonel's Company

All other companies must place themselves, until the youngest company which stands in the centre. This version of military drill states that 'when the companies are marching to the place where the battalion is to be formed … the pikemen must always be placed on the left hand of the musketeers of their company.' This would result in the battalion pike being split evenly throughout the battalion and not massed together within the battalion's centre company. This would result in an even spread of fire over the whole battalion frontage and give the whole battalion protection from horse, not just the middle companies.

If we look at the first of these two options with a centre pike block, we need to look at just how much of a battalion would have been protected.

3   Storey, *Military Discipline*, p.2.
4   R. Thornton, *The Exercise of the Foot: With The Evolution, According to the Words of Command* (Dublin: M. Gunne, 1701), pp.139–40.

If we take an infantry battalion made up of companies of foot and one of grenadiers each of 60 men and 14 pikes per musketeer company as our starting point. In three lines this would give a central pike block of 56 men covering 252ft or 78 metres in open order, this is meant to protect a battalion's line that would be 1,170ft or 356 metres in open order, even in close order the distances covered by pike would only be 168ft or 51 metres out of a total battalion length of 780ft or 237 metres. With less than a quarter of any battalion protected by a central pike block, most of the battalion would be without the protection of their own pike. With the pike split between

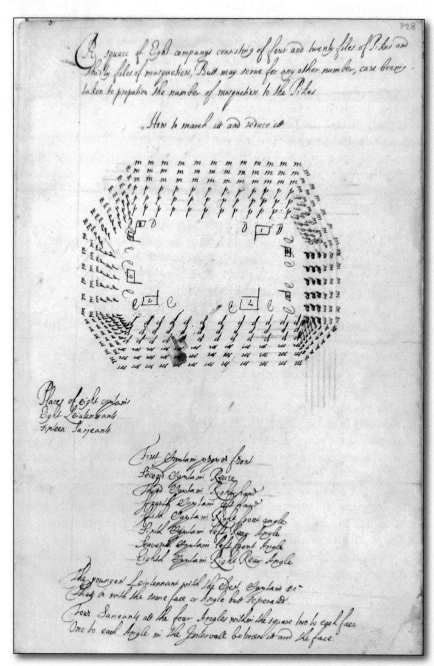

Infantry Square for 8 companies c.1685. (Author's collection, courtesy of the British Library)

the individual companies, the whole of the battalion would benefit from protection, although not a dense block.

Platoon Fire

There has ever since the introduction of large bodies of soldiers armed with muskets, there has been a debate relation to weight of firepower vs continuous fire. During the Thirty Years' War and the English Civil War, bodies of musketeers were generally formed six ranks deep and utilised firing by rank as their primary tactic. In this formation there were a number of variations possible, each with its own challenges and advantages; there were fire by single rank, fire by double rank, and fire by three ranks. The generally accepted form for firing by individual rank at this time was for the first five ranks to kneel, with the sixth rank standing, after they had fired the fifth rank would stand and fire. This practice would continue with each rank standing to fire in sequence, reloading after they had discharged their muskets. The idea being that by the time the front rank had fired, the rear rank would be loaded and ready to fire again. A variation of this used a 'caracole' system where all six ranks remained standing, after the first rank had fired, they wheeled and walked between the files of the other ranks and in essence became the 'new' rear rank. This system had generally fallen out of favour by the 1670s as it required the distance between infantry files to be 6ft (open order) and produced a slower rate of fire, as the second rank could not fire until the rank in front had turned passed them. When firing with two ranks, the first stooped and the second stood, with three ranks, the first rank knelt, the second stooped, and the third stood. Generally, either the first or last rank had their fire reserved for emergencies, this practice was still in use by the Dutch in the 1690s (see illustration 15a).

Infantry Formations

This section of the book is intended to provide details information on how battalions formed in the field and a brief description of each of the main formations that were possible.

Battalion Formation

When a battalion formed up there was a specific order in which the companies were placed, generally the odd-numbered companies were formed to the left of centre and the even- numbered companies to the right of the centre. Under normal conditions the grenadier company would be split into two sections and would form up on the extreme left and right of the battalion. If the battalion pikes were concentrated at the centre of the battalion the grenadier company could be formed into three sections, with the third section placed in front of the centre of the pikes. The following examples are for a battalion of 10 and 13 companies forming up without a centre block of pike:

Ten Companies	Thirteen Companies (inc. Grenadiers)
1,3,5,7,9,10,8,6,4,2	G,1,3,5,7,9,11,12,10,8,6,4,2,G

The Square or Hollow Square

The hollow square was certainly in use within the English army from the early 1680s, it would however, mistake this for the same type of tactical formation in use during the Napoleonic Wars. This formation was not a defence against the sudden appearance of horse, but a tactic to protect the infantry battalion against the possibility of being attacked by enemy horse when they would otherwise be exposed. The use of this formation required planning and time, so would be only useful in certain circumstances, such as unopposed river or bridge crossings. The following instruction on how to form a hollow square appeared in the 1686 *An Abridgement of the English Military Discipline* and state the following:

> Directions How to form Hollow Square
>
> The Battalion being drawn up, with muskets shouldered, and the pike advanced. You must first [advance] of all command and the colours, drums and ho-boys to the centre of the pikes: which done you are to make the ranks close forward to three large feet distance: then you must make [the] three outward files of pike on the left and the right, to double into the three files of pikes which are next to them on their right and left. After which you are to make the rear half-files of musketeers to double their front to the right or left; which being done, you must make all the body close order, and after having faced them again to the proper front. You are to make the pike face square, and close forward to cover order, as they then faced every way.
>
> Which done, you must make the pikes face again to their proper front. The you command the left wing of shot to face the right about.
>
> Which being done, both wings of shot are to march till clear of the front and rear of [the] pike.
>
> After you have made the musketeers to halt, both wings are to face to the left, and are to be led by the sergeants cross the front of the front and rear of the pikes.
>
> That is to say, the right wing of shot is to be led (as near the pikes as they can march) round, till the head of the shot comes even with the left rear angle of the pikes.
>
> And the left wing of shot is to be led in the manner round the rear of the pikes, till the head of the shot comes even with the front right angle of the pikes.
>
> Then you must command them all to face to the proper front. The officers are to move with the musketeers as they move.
>
> By which they will naturally fall into the posts where they are to be, viz. The lieutenants divided equally into the four angles, as also the sergeants.
>
> The Captains are to be divided in the following manner;
> First captain   To the proper front

Company of 1680 in line.
(Drawing by Alan Turton ©
Helion & Company)

Second captain	To the rear
Third captain	To the right flank
Fourth captain	To the left flank
Fifth captain	To the right front angle
Sixth captain	To the left front angle
Seventh captain	To the left rear angle
Eighth captain	To the right rear angle

The officers are to take care that every front of soldier do their duty, and the captains that are in the centre of each front are to retire into the first rank when the musketeers make ready.

When you have done this, you place your company of grenadiers (being divided into four equal parts) into the four angles, and if there not be room enough for them to stand in the angle without, you must take some of the files and place them within the angles, with their daggers in their firelocks, keeping the rest of the angles without, three deep, the last two ranks to fire their muskets, the first rank making ready their granados.

Logistics

One of the important areas that is overlooked within the study of armies of the late seventeenth century is the subject of logistics. Everyone I am sure is aware of the phrase, 'an army marches on its stomach'; a more realistic analogy would be a army cannot march without horses. Taking the example of a contract between Cornelius and Peter Draack (army contractors) and the English army to supply horses for the 1702 campaign season. This contract is to supply transport horses, so does not cover personal horses belonging to individual officers or for the horse or dragoons.

Siege of Limerick 1690,
possibly by Pieter Pickaert.
(Courtesy of the Rijksmuseum,
Netherlands)

Requirement for Horses to Transport Supplies	
80 Battalions of foot at 10 horses per battalion	800
100 Squadrons of Cavalry at 2 horses per squadron	200
My Lord, The Duke of Marlborough	40
4 Generals of Foot at 5 horses each	20
Lieutenant-Generals at 5 horses each	10
Major-Generals	10
Brigadiers	4
Total	1,084

An estimate of what horses are required to draw the cannon and ammunition to Faur-Lewis:

For 80 Cannon there is required	2,100
For 50,000 24lb ball at 300 per horse	4,000
For Powder	2,000
For 10 Great Mortars	170
For 10 Small Mortars	90
For 300 rounds for the Great Mortars	1,300
For 300 rounds for the Small Mortars	600
For 200,000lbs more of Powder for the Bombs and Infantry	700
For Working Tools	100

THE EVOLUTION OF INFANTRY TACTICS

Siege of Sligo 1690, possibly by Pieter Pickaert. (Courtesy of the Rijksmuseum, Netherlands)

For Timber and Iron for making Platforms	300
For 10,000 Bales [presumably horse feed]	200
For Small Shot and Grenades for the Infantry	300
Total	11,860

There is a note attached that states that 300 24lb balls is to muck for the horse to draw. Considering the horse and country we must load 250 and then must add 1,000 horses.

Cornelius and Peter Draack contract states a cost per horse of 80 gilders, which amounts to a cost of 86,720 gilders for supply horses for the army and a staggering 1,028,800 for the revised numbers for the artillery train. Additional comments suggest that the numbers of horses could be reduced to 3,000 if the train was split into four trips, each taking 12 days for round trip.

Stores

The amount of stores that even one regiment needs to keep it supplied during a time of war is considerable. The following supplies were requested to be delivered out of the stores to the regiment of guards, 2,400 pounds of match and 1,200 pounds of powder. A further four regiments of foot required 1,100 pounds of match and 500 pounds of powder. The disparity between the figures for the guards and the other regiments of foot is due to the guards having two battalions instead of a normal one.[5] Even during times of peace, each regiment was issued on average one barrel of powder per company and approximately three barrels of musket shot per regiment every three months.[6]

In preparation for the English army to congregate on Hounslow Heath during the summer of 1689, the following supplies were requested by Lord Shrewsbury on behalf of King William. The Board of Ordnance was instructed to send:[7]

Horse Tents	100
French Tents	1,378
Stand Poles	4,000
Ridge Poles	2,000
Tent Pins	42,000
Mallets	165
Spikes	1,000
Spades	200
Shovels	150
Pickaxes	200

Powder and Ball

A quick note should be given to the quantities of black powder and musket balls that a regiment would be expected to be supplied with. For a force of 1,000 musketeers and 200 cavalry, the average quantities noted are 40 barrels of powder and a proportionate amount of musket ball.[8]

First Day cover celebrating the tercentenary of the Royal Welch Fuziliers, originally raised by Henry, Lord Herbert for The Prince of Orange on 16 March 1689. (Author's collection)

Henry 4th Lord Herbert of Chirbury
Founder of the Regiment 16 March 1689

Brigadier A. C. Vivian CBE
Colonel of the Regiment

---

5   NA, WO55/336, f.76.
6   NA WO24/8 part 4, English Army Establishment, 29 June 1686, f.17.
7   NA WO55/336 Lord Shrewsbury to King William 10 August 1689, f.192.
8   WO55/336 King William to Lord Shrewsbury 23 May 1689, f.113.

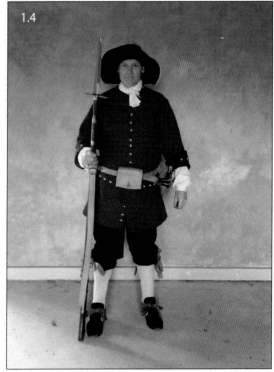

Plate 1: Drill for Plug Bayonet taken from *An Abridgement of the English Military Discipline.*
Images courtesy of Alan Larsen and Stuart Makin © author's photograph.
See Colour Plate Commentaries for further information.

Plate 2: Drill for Plug Bayonet taken from *An Abridgement of the English Military Discipline.*
Images courtesy of Alan Larsen and Stuart Makin © author's photograph.
See Colour Plate Commentaries for further information.

Plate 3.1, 3.2: Drill for Plug Bayonet taken from *An Abridgement of the English Military Discipline*. Images courtesy of Alan Larsen and Stuart Makin © author's photograph. See Colour Plate Commentaries for further information.

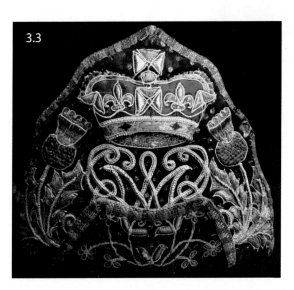

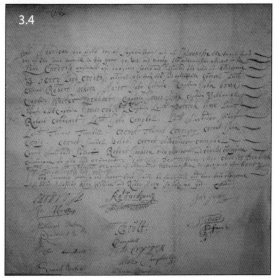

For captions to images 3.3 and 3.4 see Colour Plate Commentaries.

Plate 4: Harley's Regiment of Foot, Dunkirk 1662.
(Illustration by Patrice Courcelle © Helion & Company 2020)
See Colour Plate Commentaries for further information.

Plate 5: King's Own Royal Dragoons, 1685
(Illustration by Patrice Courcelle © Helion & Company 2020)
See Colour Plate Commentaries for further information.

Plate 6: Pikeman Viscount Kenmure's (Scottish) Regiment of Foot, 1689.
(Illustration by Patrice Courcelle © Helion & Company 2020)
See Colour Plate Commentaries for further information.

Plate 7: Grenadier, His Majesties First Regiment of Foot Guards, Flanders 1689.
(Illustration by Patrice Courcelle © Helion & Company 2020)
See Colour Plate Commentaries for further information.

Plate 8: Hamilton's Regiment of Foot, Portugal 1705
(Illustration by Patrice Courcelle © Helion & Company 2020)
See Colour Plate Commentaries for further information

6

The English Army

Introduction

As previously stated, the English army was in an almost constant state of expansion and contraction during the later half of the seventeenth century. England's and Parliament's abhorrence and distrust of a permanent standing army resulted in an establishment that had to constantly expand to meet any threat, with major expansion in 1685 and 1688. Without permanent army barracks, regiments were split down to the company level and quartered throughout England and the Channel Islands, as well as overseas garrisons. The English army expanded prior to the invasion by William of Orange in the latter half of 1688, and again following William's restructuring of the English army and its involvement in the war in Ireland and Flanders. From 1689 records show that as well as an expanded English army, Dutch and Danish regiments of both foot and horse were included on the rolls, with Parliament having to foot the bill. While records were kept separate up to 1692, the records from 1693 start to include regiments from all three countries.

The records have been transcribed *ad verbatim* with the following caveats, names and places have been replaced with there modern versions, there are a number of mathematical errors on the original documents, these have been corrected to stop any confusion regarding regimental strengths. Where servants have been listed, they have not been included in the regimental strength as they did not increase its fighting strength. All general staff and regimental staff have been included in the officer totals including chaplains, chirurgions, quartermasters, etcetera, with the exception of provosts, which have been recorded under men where they have been identified. Where regimental colonels have been included or identified, they have been included; however they have been left off where there is any doubt.

Although the establishment records provide useful information on both the size of the English army as well as on the structure of individual regiments of horse and foot, one must use them with a little care. The records show the maximum theoretical strengths of each regiment, not their actual strength, which would almost certainly be lower. The main area to be wary of is that these records show the establishment strength at one moment in time, the number of companies or troops or the size of each company or troop might and did change on a regular basis, so a document stating the strength of a particular regiment on 1 April 1689, might be incorrect by the end of that April. Two documents for the Holland Regiment in 1673 are a good example of this, the first document just dated 1673 gives the regiment's structure as 12 companies each of 50 men, while a second document dated November 1673 gives the structure as the colonel's company of 100 men and nine other companies each of 50 men.[1] Likewise, the Duke of York's Regiment goes from 12 companies, one of 80 men and 11 of 60 men, to 12 companies each of 60 men. The 1673 document contains an added memorandum for His Majesty's Scottish Regiment of Foot, which states that:

> If any of the lieutenants of the Scotch regiment should die or be displaced, their number should be reduced to one only in each company from the current two and if any sergeants should die or be displaced their number should be reduced to two in each company from the current three.

This change would bring the number of officers of each company to a captain, lieutenant, and ensign, only grenadier companies kept two lieutenants, the second in place of the ensign, as well as the number of sergeants from three down to the normal two.

Each summer the English army came together and camped on Hounslow Heath. This was the only time that the majority of the army was ever assembled together. This camp allowed for all regiments to receive training and to be able to work with other regiments in larger formations. The records of these camps give us a far more complete picture of the state and size of the English establishment and individual audits and regimental records. The other primary documents that are available are the yearly establishment of His Majesty's Guards, garrisons, and land forces within the Kingdom of England, Dominion of Wales and town of Berwick-upon-Tweed and the islands belonging. In addition to the details of the regiments of horse and foot, along with the independent troops and companies, they give the cost of the establishment and the daily pay for all members of the army.

Soldiers' Care

While a soldier's life has been correctly described as a hard life, efforts to improve this were undertaken by the four English monarchs that reigned during the time span covered by this book, King Charles II, King James II, King William III and Queen Mary II. King Charles II opened the Royal Chelsea Hospital English soldiers in 1682, the hospital was funded by the deduction of one day's pay every year out of the payments made to 'our guards, garrisons, and land-forces'.[2] Additional funds were obtained when Charles II in 1684 ordered that a charge or levy was to be taken from the

---

1   NA, WO24/6 War Office Establishment, 1673, f.5 and WO24/3 General Establishment of all His Majesties Forces, 1673, ff.6–7.
2   NA, WO24/14, War Office Establishment, Ireland 1690, f.8.

Chelsea Hospital, commissioned by King Charles II in 1682, print from 1755 by unknown artist. (Courtesy of the Rijksmuseum, Netherlands)

sale of all army officers' commissions.[3] Provisions for individual soldiers wounded or disabled in battle or by accident, were included in every warrant that covered the costs for the English establishment. The warrant fixed the amounts payable for soldiers lucky enough to be admitted to the Royal Hospital at Chelsea, these being:

To a Private Soldier	5d per day
To a Drummer	7d per day
To a Corporal	7d per day
To a Sergeant	11d per day
To a Trooper of the Guards	18d per day
To a Trooper of Light Horse	12d per day
To a Corporal of Horse	18d per day
To a Dragoon	6d per day
To a Corporal of Dragoons	9d per day
To a Master Gunner	14d per day
To a Gunner	7d per day

Entry into the Royal Hospital was on condition of being a soldier of non-commissioned officer who had served the crown for twenty years and 'are, or shall become, unfit for service'. The hospital was opened in February 1692 and by the end of that March had a full complement of pensioners of 492. The conditions of entry which were set by Charles II on the opening of the hospital, have not substantially changed to this day.[4] Today's main requirements are that pensioners are over the age of 65, in receipt of an army service pension (20 years' service) or war disability pension. In 1699, following

---

3   C. Walton, *History of the British Standing Army 1660 to 1700* (London: Harrison and Sons, 1894), pp.450–52.

4   NA, WO24/15, *War Office Establishment, 1692, Establishment and Regulations of Rewards to be made for Their Majesties Land-Forces*, f.19.

the end of the Nine Years' War (1668–97), there were 68 disabled officers and 600 disabled private men that were unable to be admitted to the Royal Hospital as it was already at maximum capacity.[5] These men were quartered at Windsor, Hampton Court, Chester, and Tinmouth (Teignmouth), where the officers received half pay and the private soldiers received five pence a day. In addition, the private soldiers still received new clothing every two years, which was the same for serving soldiers.

Soldiers' Pay

One of the draws of army life over the centuries has been the idea, if not the reality, of receiving regular pay and meals and the prospect of decent clothing. Unlike the navy, the army relied on volunteers, rather than recruitment by force via the press gang. Although the armies of James II and William III were technically an army of volunteers and operated without conscription, this must be viewed through a contemporary lense and not through rose-tinted glasses. The rank and file of regiments of foot would be filled with both willing and less-willing volunteers. Soldiers enlisted for a number of reasons, and while being careful not to over-generalise, less willing 'volunteers' enlisted due to poverty, starvation, to avoid prison, or just to find employment. Additionally, as so many regiments were raised in one location, often by the landed gentry, there were social and economic pressures to enlist into their landlord's regiment, both for the individual and their family. These caveats aside, the prospect of receiving a regular wage was an attraction. Due to the financial commitments of enlisting in a regiment of horse or dragoons, these pressures were absent. Cavalry and dragoon troopers were expected to bring their own horse and tack of sufficient standard, or when replacing an existing trooper to buy his horse and saddle.

Garrisons Towns, Forts, and Castles

In the following establishment lists, forts and castles have only been included where they have an independent garrison of soldiers in addition to any gunners or master gunners. Where a town, fort, or castle has not been included, it does not necessarily mean that it has been left unmanned, just that any garrison duties have been transferred to a part of a regiment (normally of foot) that is on the establishment roll. During the period in question the number of occupied forts and castles does vary, as does the number of master gunners and gunners posted within. The following list comprises all the locations which formed part of the defences of the realm and were financed by the war office. The list includes Berwick, Carlisle, Chepstow, Chester, Cinque Ports,[6] Clifford Port, Calshot Castle, Dartmouth, Guernsey, Gravesend and

---

5   NA, WO24/22 War Office Establishment of Our Guards, Garrisons and all Others, 26 March 1699, f.21.
6   The Cinque Ports are Sandwich, Dover, Hythe, New Romney, and Hastings.

Tilbury, Hull and its Block House, Holy Island, Hurst Castle, Jersey Island, Landguard Fort, St Maws, Pendennis Castle, Plymouth and St Nicholas Island, Portland Castle, Portsmouth, Sheerness, Scilly Island, Scarborough Castle, Tinmouth (Teignmouth) Castle, The Tower of London, Upnor Castle (including Cockhamwood fort, Gillingham, Windsor, North Yarmouth, Isle of Wight (including Sandown Fort, Yarmouth Castle, Carisbrooke Castle, Cowes Castle, and York and Clifford Tower).

Regimental Structure

Although the structure of each company or troop varies over the period in question, this section is intended to give a general guide for the most common structures and differences between regiments of horse, dragoons, guards and foot of both English, Danish and Dutch troops employed on the English Establishment. As a general guide English regiments of foot consisted of a greater number of companies than their Danish or Dutch equivalents, but with each company having fewer men. The regiments of foot guards tended to have both more and larger companies than line regiments.

Danish regiments of foot had a substantially different structure to that of their English counterparts. Danish regiments consisted of only six companies of between 94 and 100 private soldiers, compared to the more numerous but smaller English companies. Each company command consisted of a captain, two lieutenants, ensign, along with three sergeants and three corporals, in addition they also included a chirurgion, two carpenters and five servants. The regimental staff was similar to its English equivalent with the addition of an executioner.[7]

Although the size of English regiments of foot standardised in the later years of the seventeenth century at 12 companies of foot and one of grenadiers, this was not always the case. Both the number of companies and their size contracted and expanded due to perceived threats, financial considerations or changes in perceived best practice. The threat of invasion prior to the Monmouth Rebellion and the Glorious Revolution instigated a rapid expansion of the English army, with an equally abrupt contraction following the end of the Monmouth Rebellion. In June 1685 warrants are issued to increase the number of men in the troops belonging to the Royal Regiment of Horse and the Royal Regiment of Dragoons to 60 men.

In September 1688 King James II ordered that every troop of horse, dragoons, and company of foot to be expanded by an additional 10 men. Fifteen regiments were to recruit an extra company consisting of 60 private soldiers, three sergeants, three corporals and two drummers taking them up to 13 companies, with Lord Dumbarton's regiment to receive an extra five companies.[8] These changes added an extra 4,606 men to the English

---

7   NA, WO24/27 War Office Establishment of Her Majesties Foreign Forces in the Low Countries–1 June 1702, ff.14–39.

8   NA, WO55/400, Ordnance Warrants, ff.213–14.

establishment, and were almost immediately amended to add additional companies to several regiments:

Prince George of Denmark's Regiment	1 extra company
Colonel Cornwall's Regiment	2 extra companies
Earl of Bath's Regiment	2 extra companies
Lord Montgomery's Regiment	2 extra companies
Earl of Lichfield's Regiment	2 extra companies
Earl of Huntingdon's Regiment	2 extra companies
Sir John Hales' Regiment	2 extra companies
Colonel Tufton's Regiment	2 extra companies

In addition to the changes to existing regiments, James II ordered a number of new regiments and independent companies to be raised. These included two new regiments of horse (each of six troops), three independent troops of horse, three new regiments of foot under the command of Colonel Solomon Richards, Colonel Henry Gage, and the Duke of Newcastle, as well as 31 independent companies of foot and an additional company of pensioners.[9]

As previously stated, wherever possible multiple sources have been used to confirm the structure of the army, both in relation to the number of regiments, troops, and companies as well as the size of each of these structures. Despite the work carried out by historians including John Childs and Stephen Ede-Borrett, further research is needed especially in the area of the size and disposition of the English army between October and December 1688. Wherever possible regiments have been named in the following lists using original documents as well as using Dalton's army lists, although this does have some errors.

While non-commissioned officers and private soldiers were simply discarded in times of peace and contraction of the army, officers at various times could be placed on half pay. As an example of this practice on 28 March 1702, the following regiments had officers placed on half pay.[10]

Brigadier Wolsley's Regiment	23 officers
Colonel Echling's Regiment	6 officers
Colonel Cunningham's Regiment	8 officers
Earl of Drogheda's Regiment	10 officers
Colonel Mitchelburn's Regiment	29 officers
Colonel Thomas St John's Regiment	22 officers
Colonel Cheichton's Regiment	28 officers
Earl of Donegal's Regiment	12 officers
Lord Mountjoy's Regiment	10 officers
Sir George St George's Regiment	14 officers (3 officers seconded)
Colonel Villiers' Regiment	21 officers
Lord Charlemont's	21 officers (two seconded)

---

9   NA, WO55/400, Ordnance Warrants, f.223.
10 BL, Add MS 15897, J. Ellis Papers, ff.122–130.

In addition the following regiments had a smaller number of officers placed on half pay:

4 Officers: Tiffin's Regiment
3 Officers: Stanhope's, F. Hamilton's, Tidcomb's, Belasyse's, and Seymore's Regiment
2 Officers: Webb's, G. Hamilton's, and Jacob's Regiment.
1 Officer: Bridges', Brewer's, Howe's, and Ingoldsby's

English Army Establishments

English Establishment: For His Majesties Service in the Kingdom of Morocco, Sus, and Fez. 10 October 1661[11]

Name of Unit & Details	Officers	NCOs	Musicians	Men	Total
His Majesties Regiment of Foot Commanded by the Earl of Peterborough consisting of 10 Companies of Foot (each of 100 men)	44	60	24	1,000	1,128
His Majesties Regiment of Foot Commanded by Colonel Feralls consisting of 12 Companies (each of 50 men)	41	36	12	600	689
His Majesties Regiment of Foot Commanded by Colonel FitzGerald consisting of 12 Companies (each of 50 men)	41	36	12	600	689
His Majesties Regiment of Foot Commanded by Sir Robert Harley consisting of 10 Companies (each of 50 men)	37	30	10	500	577
Earl of Peterborough's Independent Troop of Horse	8	3	3	100	114
Staff belonging to the Train of Ordnance	11	N/A	N/A	21	32

English Establishment 1668

Name of Unit & Details	Officers	NCOs	Musicians	Men	Total
His Majesties Own Troops of Horse Guards Commanded by James Duke of Monmouth	7	4	5	100	218
His Royal Highness the Duke of York's Troop of Horse Guards	7	4	5	100	216
His Grace the Duke of Albemarle's Troop of Horse guards	7	4	5	200	216
His Majesties Regiment of Horse consisting of 8 troops of 50 men	35	24	17	400	476
His Majesties First Regiment of Foot Guards consisting of 24 Companies of Foot (1 of 80 men and 23 of 60 men)	79	121	48	1680	1,928
The Lord General's Regiment of Foot Guards consisting of 12 Companies of Foot and one of Grenadiers (each of 80 men)	43	61	24	960	1,088
The Lord High Admiral's Regiment of Foot consisting of 11 Companies (each of 60 men) and one Company quartered in Guernsey (of 100 men)	42	61	24	760	885

---

11 NA, WO24/1 *War Office Establishment 1661*, ff.1–10.

His Majesties Holland regiment of Foot consisting of 9 Companies (each of 60 men) and one Company quartered on Jersey (of 100 men)	42	61	12	640	755
His Royal Highness the Duke of York's Regiment of Foot consisting of one company at Sheerness (80 men) and 11 companies of Foot (50 men)	43	60	12	630	745
His Majesties Holland Regiment of Foot consisting of 12 Companies of Foot	37	60	12	600	715

Garrisons besides Regimental Garrisons 1668

Name of Garrison& Details	Officers	NCOs	Musicians	Gunners & Matross	Men	Total
Berwick On Tweed and Holy Island, 7 Companies (each of 60 men)	23	35	7	9	420	494
Carlisle, 3 Companies (each of 60 men)	9	15	3	4	180	211
Chepstow, 1 Company	3	5	1	1	60	70
Chester Castle, 1 company	2	3	1	N/A	60	66
Dover Castle, 1 Company	3	5	1	N/A	60	69
Deale, 1 Company	3	5	1	N/A	60	69
Gravesend Blockhouse and Tilbury Fort, 1 Company	3	5	1	2	60	71
Guernsey Island, 2 Companies (each of 100 men)	6	10	2	4	200	222
Hull and Blockhouse, 6 Companies (each of 60 men)	18	30	6	10	360	424
Harwich, 2 Companies of Foot (each of 60 men)	6	10	2	N/A	120	138
Jersey Island, 3 Companies of Foot (each of 100 men)	10	15	3	8	300	336
Landguard Fort, 1 Company of Foot	3	5	1	4	60	73
St Mawes Castle,	2	N/A	N/A	N/A	14	15
Pendennis Castle, 1 Company of Foot	3	5	1	4	60	73
Plymouth Fort and Island, 6 Companies of Foot (each of 60 men)	18	30	6	8	360	422
Portsmouth, 7 Companies of Foot (each of 60 men)	22	35	7	18	420	502
Sheerness, 1 Company of Foot	3	5	1	3	60	72
Scilly Islands, 2 Companies of Foot (each of 60 men)	8	10	2	5	120	145
Sandon Fort, Isle of Wight, 1 Company of foot	1	N/A	N/A	2	30	33
Scarborough Castle, 1 Company of Foot	3	5	1	4	60	73
Tinmouth Castle, 2 Companies of Foot (each of 60 men)	7	10	2	4	120	143
Tower of London, 3 Companies of Foot (each of 60 men)	9	15	3	N/A	180	207
Windsor Castle, 3 Companies of Foot (each of 60 men)	10	15	3	2	180	210
York and Clifford Tower, Three Companies of Foot (each of 60 men)	9	15	3	N/A	180	207
City of London and Westminster, Two Companies of Foot (each of 60 men)	6	10	2	N/A	120	138

English Establishment 15 November 1673[12]

Name of Unit & Details	Officers	NCOs	Musicians	Men	Total
General Staff	9	12	N/A	N/A	21
His Majesties Own Troops of Horse Guards Commanded by James Duke of Monmouth	7	4	5	200	216
Her Majesties Troop of Horse Guards	7	4	5	150	166
His Royal highness the Duke of York's Troop of Horse Guards	7	4	5	150	166
His Majesties Regiment of Horse consisting of 8 troops (each of 60 men)	35	24	17	480	556
His majesties Regiment of Dragoons consisting of 8 troops (each of 88 men)	42	55	22	968	1,087
His Majesties First Regiment of Foot Guards consisting of 24 Companies of Foot (each of 80 men)	79	121	48	1680	1,928
The Coldstream Regiment of Foot Guards consisting of 12 Companies of Foot and one of Grenadiers (each of 80 men)	43	61	24	960	1,088
His Royal Highness the Duke of York's Regiment of Foot consisting of 12 Companies (each of 60 men)	42	61	24	720	827
His Majesties Holland Regiment of Foot consisting of 10 companies (Colonel company of 100 men and nine companies each of 60 men)	36	50	20	640	746
His Majesties Regiment of Foot commanded by William, Lord Widdrington consisting of 10 Companies (each of 60 men)	36	50	10	600	686
His Majesties Regiment of Foot Commanded by Sir William Lockart consisting of 12 Companies (each of 60 men)	42	61	24	720	827
His Majesties Regiment of Foot Commanded by George, Duke of Buckingham consisting of 15 Companies (each of 60 men)[13]	52	75	31	900	1,058
His Majesties Regiment of Foot commanded by Richard Earl of Tyrone consisting of 12 companies (each of 50 men)[14]	42	61	25	720	828
His Majesties Regiment of Foot commanded by the Earl of Northampton consisting of 10 companies (each or 50 men)	36	50	20	600	706
His Majesties Regiment of Foot commanded by the Earl of Agyle consisting of 10 companies (each or 50 men)	36	50	20	600	706
His Majesties Regiment of Foot commanded by the Earl of Carlisle consisting of 10 companies (each or 50 men)	36	50	20	600	706
His Majesties Regiment of Foot commanded by Lord Marquess of Worcester consisting of 10 companies (each or 50 men)	36	50	20	600	706

12 NA, WO24/3 War Office Establishment, 1673.
13 Paid out of the revenue of the Kingdom of Ireland.
14 Paid for out of the revenue of the Kingdom of Ireland.

Name of Unit & Details	Officers	NCOs	Musicians	Men	Total
His Majesties Regiment of Foot commanded by the Earl of Moulgrave consisting of 10 companies (each or 50 men)	36	50	20	600	706
His Majesties Regiment of Foot commanded by the Duke of Albemarle's consisting of 10 companies (each or 50 men)	36	50	20	600	706
His Majesties Regiment of Foot commanded by Lord John Vaughan consisting of 10 companies (each or 50 men)	36	50	20	600	706
His Majesties Regiment of Foot commanded by Henry, Earl of Peterborough consisting of 10 companies (each or 50 men)	36	50	20	600	706

Garrisons besides Regimental Garrisons 1673

Name of Garrison & Details	Officers	NCOs	Musicians	Gunners & Matross	Men	Total
Berwick On Tweed and Holy Island, 1 Companies of Foot	4	5	1	4	60	74
Carlisle, 1 Companies of Foot	3	5	1	4	60	73
Chepstow, 1 Company of Foot	3	5	1	N/A	60	69
Chester Castle, 1 Company of Foot	2	3	1	N/A	60	66
Dartmouth	1	1	N/A	2	18	22
Guernsey, 2 Companies of Foot (each of 100 men)	7	10	2	5	200	224
Gravesend Blockhouse and Tilbury Fort, 1 Company	3	5	1	17	100	126
Guernsey Island, 2 Companies (each of 100 men)	6	10	2	4	200	222
Hull and Blockhouse, 6 Companies (each of 60 men)	7	10	2	8	120	147
Holy Island, 1 Companies of Foot	3	5	1	4	60	73
Jersey Island, 2 Companies of Foot (each of 100 men)	7	10	2	9	200	228
St Mawes Castle,	2	N/A	N/A	2	12	16
Pendennis Castle, 1 Company of Foot	3	5	1	9	60	78
Plymouth Fort and St Nicholas Island, 4 Companies of Foot (each of 60 men)	12	20	4	24	240	300
Portsmouth, 2 Companies of Foot (each of 60 men)	7	10	2	30	120	169
Scilly Islands, 2 Companies of Foot (each of 60 men)	8	10	2	11	120	151
Scarborough Castle, 1 Company of Foot	3	5	1	3	60	72
Tinmouth Castle, 1 Companies of Foot	4	5	1	5	60	75
Tower of London, 3 Companies of Foot (each of 60 men)	9	15	3	5	180	212
Upner Castle and the Two Batteries	1	1	N/A	7	30	39
Windsor Castle, 1 Company	4	6	2	7	90	109
Isle of Wight including Sandon fort, Yarmouth Castle, Carisbrooke Castle, and Cowes Castle, 3 companies (2 of 90 men and 1 of 30 men at Sandon Fort)	8	10	2	16	210	246
York and Clifford Tower, 3 Companies of Foot (each of 80 men)	9	15	3	5	240	272

English Establishment 15 November 1679[15]

Name of Unit & Details	Officers	NCOs	Musicians	Men	Total
General Staff	19	N/A	N/A	N/A	19
His Majesties Own Troops of Horse Guards Commanded by James Duke of Albemarle	9	4	5	200	218
Her Majesties Troop of Horse Guards Commanded by Sir Philip Howard	7	4	5	200	216
His Royal Highness the Duke of York's Troop of Horse Guards Commanded by Louis, Earl of Feversham	7	4	5	200	216
Three Troops of Horse Grenadiers (1 troop of 80 men and 2 companies each of 60 men)	9	18	9	200	236
His Majesties Regiment of Horse consisting of 8 troops (each of 60 men) Commanded by James, Duke of Monmouth	38	32	16	480	565
His Majesties Regiment of Horse consisting of 8 troops (each of 60 men) Commanded by the Earl of Peterborough	38	32	16	480	565
His Majesties Regiment of Horse consisting of 8 troops (each of 60 men) Commanded by Charles, Lord Gerard	38	32	16	480	565
His Majesties Regiment of Dragoons consisting of 8 troops (each of 80 men) Commanded by Louis, Earl of Feversham	42	55	22	640	1,087
His Majesties First Regiment of Foot Guards consisting of 24 Companies of Foot (each of 60 men)	79	121	48	1,440	1,688
The Coldstream Regiment of Foot Guards consisting of 12 Companies of Foot and one of Grenadiers (each of 60 men)	43	60	24	720	847
His Royal Highness the Duke of York's Regiment of Foot consisting of 12 Companies (Colonels company of 80 men each and 11 companies each of 50 men)	42	60	12	630	758
His Majesties Holland Regiment of Foot consisting of 12 companies (each of 50 men)	42	60	12	600	716
His Majesties Regiment of Foot consisting of 10 companies (each of 100 men)	37	60	20	1,000	1,117

Garrisons Besides Regimental Garrisons 1679

Name of Garrison & Details	Officers	NCOs	Musicians	Gunners & Matross	Men	Total
Berwick On Tweed and Holy Island, 1 Companies of Foot	4	5	1	4	60	74
Guernsey, 2 Companies of Foot (each of 100 men)	7	10	2	5	200	224
Gravesend Blockhouse and Tilbury Fort, 1 Company	3	5	1	17	100	126
Hull and Blockhouse, 6 Companies (each of 60 men)	7	10	2	8	120	147

---

15 NA, WO24, part 4 and 5 War Office Establishment of all our Guards, Garrisons and Land Forces 1673.

Name of Garrison& Details	Officers	NCOs	Musicians	Gunners & Matross	Men	Total
Jersey Island, 2 Companies of Foot (each of 100 men)	7	10	2	9	200	228
Pendennis Castle, 1 Company of Foot	3	5	1	9	60	78
Plymouth Fort and St Nicholas Island, 4 Companies of Foot (each of 60 men)	12	20	4	24	240	300
Portsmouth, 2 Companies of Foot (each of 60 men)	7	10	2	30	120	169
Tinmouth Castle, 1 Companies of Foot	4	5	1	5	60	75
Tower of London, 3 Companies of Foot (each of 60 men)	9	15	3	5	180	212
Upner Castle and the Two Batteries	1	1	N/A	7	30	39
Windsor Castle, 1 Company	4	6	2	7	90	109
Isle of Wight including Sandon fort, Yarmouth Castle, Carisbrooke Castle, and Cowes Castle, 3 companies (2 of 1,000 men and 1 of 30 men at Sandon Fort)	8	10	2	16	230	266
York and Clifford Tower, 3 Companies (each of 50 men)	9	15	3	1	180	208

English Establishment: Tangiers 7 July 1680[16]

Name of Unit & Details	Officers	NCOs	Musicians	Men	Total
Old Garrison				800	800
The Scotch Regiment when recruited with 680 from Scotland				1,680	1,680
The Battalion of Guards				600	600
Irish regiment including 200 recruits				400	400
New Regiment to be raised Commanded by the Earl of Plymouth's Regiment of Foot consisting of 16 companied	48			600	600

English Establishment: First Day of January 1684[17]

Name of Unit & Details	Officers	NCOs	Musicians	Men	Total
His Majesties Own Troops of Horse Guards Commanded by Christopher Duke of Albemarle	9	4	5	200	218
Her Majesties Troop of Horse Guards Commanded by Sir Philip Howard	7	4	5	200	216
His Royal Highness the Duke of York's Troop of Horse Guards Commanded by Louis, Earl of Feversham	7	4	5	200	216
Troop of Horse Grenadiers belonging to His Majesties Own Troop of Horse Guards	2	2	4	64	72
Troop of Horse Grenadiers belonging to Her Majesties Horse Guards	2	2	4	64	72
Troop of Horse Grenadiers belonging to the Duke of York's Horse Guards	2	2	4	64	72

16 BL Add MS 28938, J. Ellis Papers, ff.28–42. *Dalton's English Army List and Commission Registers 1661–1714*, Vol. 1 1661–1685 (London: Eyre & Spottiswoode, 1892), p.268, has six troops of horse under the command of Thomas, Earl of Ossory which do not appear in the Ellis Papers.

17 NA WO24/7 War Office Establishment 1684

Name of Unit & Details	Officers	NCOs	Musicians	Men	Total
His Majesties Regiment of Horse consisting of 8 troops of 50 men Commanded by Aubrey, Earl of Oxford	35	24	17	400	476
His Majesties First Regiment of Foot Guards consisting of 24 Companies of Foot and one of Grenadiers Commanded by Henry, Duke of Grafton	84	127	69	1,490	1,770
His Majesties Coldstream Regiment of Foot Guards consisting of 12 Companies of Foot and one of Grenadiers Commanded by William Earl of Craven	59	66	27	770	922
His Majesties Scottish Regiment of Foot consisting of 20 Companies of Foot and one of Grenadiers Commanded by Lt-Colonel Halket[18]	90	120	44	1,050	1,304
His Majesties Tangier regiment of Foot consisting of 10 Companies of Foot and one of Grenadiers Commanded by Colonel Percy Kirke	39	57	12	550	658
His Royal Highness the Duke of York's Regiment of Foot consisting of one company at Sheerness (80 men) and 11 companies of Foot (50 men) Commanded by Sir Charles Littleton	43	60	12	630	745
His Majesties Holland Regiment of Foot consisting of 12 Companies of Foot Commanded by Colonel John, Earl of Mulgrave	37	60	12	600	715
Colonel Charles Trelawny's Regiment of Foot consisting of 11 Companies of Foot and one of Grenadiers	37	61	12	600	716
His Majesties regiment of Dragoons consisting of 6 Troops commanded by John, Lord Churchill.	33	30	24	300	387
Independent Troop of Dragoons	4	3	1	60	68

Garrisons Besides Regimental Garrisons

Name of Garrison & Details	Officers	NCOs	Musicians	Gunners & Matross	Men	Total
Berwick On Tweed, one Company	6	5	1	4	50	66
Carlisle, one Company	3	5	1	4	50	63
Chepstow	2	1	1	1	18	23
Guernsey Island, two Companies	7	10	2	5	100	124
Gravesend and Tilbury, one Company	5	5	1	17	50	78
Hull and Blockhouse, two Companies	9	10	2	18	100	129
Jersey Island, two companies	6	10	2	9	100	127
Plymouth and St Nicholas Island, two Companies	6	10	2	22	100	140
Portsmouth, two Companies	7	10	2	21	100	140
Scilly Island, one Company	3	5	1	11	50	70
Tinmouth Castle, one Company	3	5	1	5	50	65
Tower of London, three Companies	9	15	3	5	150	182

18 No Colonel listed for this regiment at this time, although Lord George Douglass, Earl of Dumbarton appointed as colonel was backdated to the 21 October 1685.

Name of Garrison& Details	Officers	NCOs	Musicians	Gunners & Matross	Men	Total
Upner, Cockham Wood, and Gillingham Castle	1	1	N/A	17	30	49
Windsor Castle, one Company	3	5	1	7	50	66
Isle of Wight including Sandon Fort (30 soldiers), Yarmouth Fort, Carisbrooke Castle, and Cowes Castle, two Companies	7	10	2	16	130	165
York and Clifton Tower, three Companies	9	15	3	1	150	178

The following forts and castles were allocated master gunners and gunners, but no companies: Chester, Cinque Ports, Clifford Fort (near Tinmouth (Teignmouth)) Calshot Castle, Dartmouth, Holy Island, Hurst Island, Jamaica, Landguard Fort, St Maws, Sheerness, Scarborough Castle, Virginia, and North Yarmouth Fort.

English Establishment: 1 January 1685

Name of Unit & Details	Officers	NCOs	Musicians	Men	Total
General Staff including 3 Lieutenant Generals, 3 Major Generals, 4 Brigadiers in addition to Quartermasters, Adjutants, Chirurgeons, etc.	23				23
His Majesties Own Troops of Horse Guards Commanded by Christopher Duke of Albemarle	18	N/A	5	200	223
Her Majesties Troop of Horse Guards Commanded by George, Duke of Northumberland	16	N/A	5	200	221
His Royal Highness the Duke of York's Troop of Horse Guards Commanded by Lewis, Earl of Feversham	16	N/A	5	200	221
Troop of Horse Grenadiers belonging to His Majesties Own Troop of Horse Guards	3	2	4	64	73
Troop of Horse Grenadiers belonging to Her Majesties Horse Guards	2	2	4	64	72
Troop of Horse Grenadiers belonging to the Duke of York's Horse Guards	2	2	4	64	72
Total His Majesties Regiment of Horse consisting of 9 troops of 50 men Commanded by Aubrey, Earl of Oxford	42	27	19	450	538
Her Majesty the Queen Consort's Regiment of Horse consisting of 9 troops of 40 men Commanded by Sir John Lanier	42	27	19	360	448
Earl of Peterborough's Regiment of Horse consisting of 6 troops of 40 men	30	18	13	240	301
Earl of Plymouth's Regiment of Horse consisting of 6 troops of 40 men	30	18	13	240	301
Lord Dover's Regiment of Horse consisting of 6 troops of 40 men	30	18	13	240	301
Earl of Thanet's Regiment of Horse consisting of 6 troops of 40 men	30	18	13	240	301
Earl of Arran's Regiment of Horse consisting of 6 troops of 40 men	30	18	13	240	301
Earl of Shrewsbury's Regiment of Horse consisting of 6 troops of 40 men	30	18	13	240	301

Name of Unit & Details	Officers	NCOs	Musicians	Men	Total
Princess Anne of Denmark's Regiment of Horse consisting of 6 troops of 40 men Commanded by Robert, Earl of Scarsdale	30	18	13	240	301
The Queen Dowager's Regiment of Horse consisting of 6 troops of 40 men Commanded by Richard, Viscount Lumley	30	18	13	240	301
His Majesties First Regiment of Foot Guards consisting of 24 Companies of Foot and 2 of Grenadiers (each of 80 men) Commanded by Henry, Duke of Grafton	88	156	52	2,080	2,376
His Majesties Coldstream Regiment of Foot Guards consisting of 12 Companies of Foot and one of Grenadiers (each of 80 men) Commanded by William, Earl of Craven	59	66	27	1,040	922
His Majesties Scottish Regiment of Foot consisting of 20 Companies of Foot and one of Grenadiers (each of 50 men)	90	120	44	1,050	1,304
Her Majesty the Queen Dowager's Regiment of Foot consisting of 10 Companies of Foot and one of Grenadiers (each of 50 men) Colonel Percy Kirke	41	56	12	550	660
His Royal Highness Prince George of Denmark's Regiment of Foot consisting of 12 companies of Foot and one of Grenadiers (each of 50 men) Commanded by Sir Charles Littleton	47	66	14	650	776
His Majesties Holland Regiment of Foot consisting of 12 Companies of Foot and one of Grenadiers (each of 50 men) Commanded by John, Earl of Mulgrave	47	66	14	650	776
Her Majesty the Queen Consort's Regiment of Foot consisting of 10 Companies of Foot and one of Grenadiers (each of 50 men) Commanded by Colonel Charles Trelawney	41	56	12	550	659
His Majesty's Royal Regiment of Fusiliers consisting of 11 companies of Fusiliers (each of 50 men) and one of Miners (of 40 men) Commanded by George, Lord Dartmouth	40	63	21	590	714
Her Royal Highness the Princess Ann of Denmark's Regiment of Foot consisting of 10 companies of Foot (each of 50 men) Commanded by Robert, Lord Ferrers of Chartley	38	25	10	500	573
Colonel Henry Cornwall's Regiment of Foot consisting of 10 companies of Foot (each of 50 men)	38	25	10	500	573
Earl of Bath's Regiment of Foot consisting of 10 companies of Foot (each of 50 men)	38	25	10	500	573
Duke of Beaufort's Regiment of Foot consisting of 10 companies of Foot (each of 50 men)	38	25	10	500	573
Duke of Norfolk's Regiment of Foot consisting of 10 companies of Foot (each of 50 men)	38	25	10	500	573
Earl of Huntingdon's Regiment of Foot consisting of 10 companies of Foot (each of 50 men)	38	25	10	500	573
Sir Edward Hales's Regiment of Foot consisting of 10 companies of Foot (each of 50 men)	38	25	10	500	573

Name of Unit & Details	Officers	NCOs	Musicians	Men	Total
Sir William Clifton's Regiment of Foot consisting of 10 companies of Foot (each of 50 men)	38	25	10	500	573
14 Non-Regimental Companies of Grenadiers (each of 50 men)	42	70	14	700	826
1 Non-Regimental Company of Grenadiers	3	6	2	50	61
1 Non-Regimental Company of Foot	2	5	1	50	58
His Majesties Own Regiment of Dragoons consisting of 8 Troops (each of 50 men) Commanded by John, Lord Churchill	39	40	32	400	511
Her Majesty the Queen Consort's Regiment of Dragoons consisting of six troops (each of 50 men) Commanded by Charles, Duke of Somerset	31	30	24	300	405
Her Royal Highness the Princess of Ann of Denmark's Regiment of Dragoons Commanded by John, Viscount Fitzharding	31	30	24	300	405
Independent Troop of Dragoons	4	3	1	60	68

Garrisons besides Regimental Garrisons, 1 January 1685

Name of Garrison & Details	Officers	NCOs	Musicians	Gunners & Matross	Men	Total
Isle of Wight including Sandon Fort (30 soldiers), Yarmouth Fort, Carisbrooke Castle, and Cowes Castle, two Companies	1	N/A	N/A	15	30	165

King James' Army November 1688[19]

Horse with Colonels	Foot with Colonels
Lord Feversham's Regiment of Horse	First Regiment of Foot Guards – Duke of Grafton
Duke of Northumberland's regiment of Horse	Coldstream regiment of Foot Guards – Earl of Craven
Earl of Marlborough's Regiment of Horse	Major-General Kirke's Regiment of Foot
Lord Dover's Regiment of Horse – Disbanded	Sir Charles Littleton's regiment of Foot
Royal Regiment of Horse – Duke of Berwick	Holland Regiment of Foot – Sir Theophilus Oglethorpe
Queen's Regiment of Horse – Sir John Lanier's	Royal Regiment of Fuziliers – Lord Dartmouth
Earl of Peterborough's Regiment of Horse – Colonel Villiers	Princess Anne of Denmark's Regiment of Foot – Duke of Berwick
Sir John Fenwick's Regiment of Horse – Lord Colchester	Colonel Cornwall's Regiment of Foot
Earl of Thanet's Regiment of Horse Lt General Werden's – Disbanded	Lord Montgomery's Regiment of Foot
Earl of Arran's Regiment of Horse – Colonel Godfrey	Earl of Bath's Regiment of Foot
Colonel Hamilton's Regiment of Horse	Earl of Litchfield's Regiment of Foot – Colonel Brewer
Sir John Hamilton's Regiment of Horse	Earl of Huntingdon's Regiment of Foot – Colonel Hastings
Earl of Salisbury's Regiment of Horse – Disbanded	Sir Edward Hales's Regiment of Foot – Colonel William Beveridge
Marquis De Miremont's Regiment of Horse – Disbanded	Sir James Leslye's Regiment of Foot

---

19 NA WO24/6 Part I, List of King James Army in November 1688, f.1.

Horse with Colonels	Foot with Colonels
Colonel Henry Slingsby's Regiment of Horse – Disbanded	Colonel John Hales's Regiment of Foot
Lord Brandon's Regiment of Horse – Disbanded	Colonel Wachop's Regiment of Foot
Colonel George Holman's Regiment of Horse – Never Raised	Colonel McElligott's Regiment of Foot
Colonel Russell Regiment of Horse – Disbanded	Colonel Skelton's Regiment of Foot – Colonel Fitzpatrick
	Colonel Archibald Douglas' Regiment of Foot – Colonel Hodges
	Colonel Soloman Richard's Regiment of Foot – Colonel St George
Dragoons	Duke of Newcastle's Regiment of Foot – Disbanded
Royal Regiment of Dragoons – Lord Cornbury	Colonel Gage's Regiment of Foot – Disbanded
The Queen Consort's Regiment of Dragoons – Colonel Cannon	
Princess Anne of Denmark's Regiment of Dragoons – Lord Fitzharding	Lord Herbert's regiment of Foot – Disbanded prior to February 1689
	Sir John Carne's Regiment of Foot
Irish Regiments transferred onto the English Establishment	**Scottish Regiments transferred onto the English Establishment**
First Battalion Irish Foot Guards – 7 Companies (each of 80 men)	Troop of Scotch Horse Guards
Lord Forbes Regiment of Foot – 13 Companies (each of 50 men)	Royal Regiment of Scottish Horse – Viscount Dundee – 6 Troops (each of 49 men)
Colonel Anthony Hamilton's Regiment of Foot – 13 Companies (each of 50 men)	Royal Regiment of Scottish Dragoons – 6 Troops (each of 49 men)
Colonel Butler's Regiment of Dragoons – 10 Companies (each of 50 men)	Scottish Regiment of Foot Guards – Lt-General Douglass –
	Colonel Bockamirick's Regiment of Foot – 14 Companies (each of 50 men)

English Establishment: 1 May 1689[20]

Name of Unit & Details	Officers	NCOs	Musicians	Men	Total
General Staff including 3 Lieutenant Generals, 3 Major Generals, 4 Brigadiers in addition to Quartermasters, Adjutants, Chirurgeons, etc	18				18
His Majesties First Troop of Horse Guards	19	N/A	5	200	224
Her Majesties Third Troop of Horse Guards	19	N/A	5	200	224
Troop of Horse Grenadiers belonging to His Majesties First Troop of Horse Guards	3	4	4	60	71
Troop of Horse Grenadiers belonging to Her Majesties Third Troop of Horse Guards	2	4	4	60	70
Lord Colchester's Regiment of Horse consisting of 6 troops of 50 men	30	30	13	300	373
Colonel Godfrey's Regiment of Horse consisting of 6 troops of 50 men	30	30	13	300	373

---

20 NA WO24/9 War Office: Judge Advocate's Office 1689, ff.3–9 and BL Add MS 15897, Hyde Papers Pensions Army and Navy etc, 1664–1745, Vol, VI, f.88.

Name of Unit & Details	Officers	NCOs	Musicians	Men	Total
Colonel Langston's Regiment of Horse consisting of 6 troops of 40 men[21]	30	30	13	300	373
Their Majesties First Regiment of Foot Guards consisting of 24 Companies of Foot and 4 of Grenadiers (each of 80 men) One Battalion commanded by Colonel Selwyn	98	168	57	2,240	2,563
Colonel Trelawny's Regiment of Foot consisting of 12 companies of Foot and 1 of Grenadiers (each of 60 men)	46	78	26	780	930
Earl of Bath's Regiment of Foot consisting of 12 companies of Foot and 1 of Grenadiers (each of 60 men)	46	78	26	780	930
Colonel Beveridge's Regiment of Foot consisting of 12 companies of Foot and 1 of Grenadiers (each of 60 men)	46	78	26	780	930
Colonel St James Lesley's Regiment of Foot consisting of 12 companies of Foot and 1 of Grenadiers (each of 60 men)	46	78	26	780	930
Earl of Monmouth's Regiment of Foot consisting of 12 companies of Foot and 1 of Grenadiers (each of 60 men)	46	78	26	780	930
Sir John Guise's Regiment of Foot consisting of 12 companies of Foot and 1 of Grenadiers (each of 60 men)	46	78	26	780	930
Colonel Francis Luttrell's Regiment of Foot consisting of 12 companies of Foot and 1 of Grenadiers (each of 60 men)	46	78	26	780	930
Duke of Bolton's Regiment of Foot Commanded by Lt-Colonel Holt consisting of 12 companies of Foot and 1 of Grenadiers (each of 60 men)	46	78	26	780	930
Earl of Leven's Regiment of Foot consisting of 12 companies of Foot and 1 of Grenadiers (each of 60 men)	46	78	26	780	930
Colonel John Berkley's Regiment of Dragoons consisting of 6 Troops (each of 60 men)	25	30	24	360	439
Sir Thomas Levingston's Regiment of Dragoons consisting of 6 Troops (each of 60 men)	25	30	24	360	439
One Non-Regimented Company of Grenadiers at Windsor Commanded by Captain Minors	3	5	1	50	58
Their Majesties Troop of Scots Guards	11	N/A	5	118	134
Two Companies of Foot, New York (each of 60 men)	6	12	4	120	142
One Company of Foot, Leeward Islands	3	6	2	60	71
One Company of Foot, Sandown Fort, Isle of Wight	1	N/A	N/A	30	31

---

21 Colonel Langston's Regiment of Horse was transferred to Ireland on the 1 September 1689 WO24/10, William R to Lord Shrewsbury, 4 September 1689, f.33.

English Troops on the English Establishment for Service in Ireland: 1 July 1689[22]

Name of Unit & Details	Officers	NCOs	Musicians	Men	Total
General Staff including 3 Lieutenant Generals, 3 Major Generals, 4 Brigadiers in addition to Quartermasters, Adjutants, Chirurgeons, etc	42	N/A	N/A	24[23]	66
Sir John Lanier's Regiment of Horse consisting of 9 Troops (each of 50 men)	42	27	19	450	538
Colonel Edward Villiers' Regiment of Horse consisting of 6 Troops (each of 50 men)	30	18	13	300	361
Lord Delamier's Regiment of Horse consisting of 6 Troops (each of 50 men)	30	18	13	300	361
Colonel John Coy's Regiment of Horse consisting of 6 Troops (each of 50 men)[24]	30	18	13	300	361
Lord Hewitt's Regiment of Horse consisting of 6 Troops (each of 50 men)	30	18	13	300	361
Lord Cavendish's Regiment of Horse consisting of 6 Troops (each of 50 men)	30	18	13	300	361
The Marquis De Ruvigny's French Regiment of Horse consisting of 8 Troops (each of 50 men)	38	24	17	400	479
One Independent Troop of Horse	4	3	2	50	59
Lord Cornbury's Royal Regiment of Dragoons consisting of 8 Troops (each of 50 men)	39	40	32	480	591
Colonel Richard Leveson's Royal Regiment of Dragoons consisting of 6 Troops (each of 50 men)	31	30	24	360	445
Major-General Percy Kirke's Regiment of Foot Consisting of 12 companies of Foot and 1 of Grenadiers (each of 60 men)	46	78	26	780	930
Colonel John Beaumont's Regiment of Foot consisting of 12 companies of Foot and 1 of Grenadiers (each of 60 men)	46	78	26	780	930
Colonel William Stewart's Regiment of Foot consisting of 12 companies of Foot and 1 of Grenadiers (each of 60 men)	46	78	26	780	930
Sir John Hanmor's Regiment of Foot consisting of 12 companies of Foot and 1 of Grenadiers (each of 60 men)	46	78	26	780	930
Colonel Henry Wharton's Regiment of Foot consisting of 12 companies of Foot and 1 of Grenadiers (each of 60 men)	46	78	26	780	930
Colonel Ferdinando Hastings' Regiment of Foot consisting of 12 companies of Foot and 1 of Grenadiers (each of 60 men)	46	78	26	780	930
Sir George St George's Regiment of Foot consisting of 12 companies of Foot and 1 of Grenadiers (each of 60 men)	46	78	26	780	930

22 NA WO24/10, War Office Establishment Ireland 1689, ff.3–16 and BL Add MS 15897, *Hyde Papers Pensions Army and Navy etc, 1664–1745*, Vol, VI, f.88, this account from 1 April 1689 has 6 regiments of horse, with the French regiment and the independent troop missing, both dragoon regiments are shown, but only 8 infantry regiments are recorded, Kirke's, Beaumont's, Cunningham's, Hamners, Wharton's, Hastings, Edgworth's, and Richard's.

23 These are Provosts, attached to the Provost Marshall General.

24 Also spelt as Coyes regiment of horse.

Name of Unit & Details	Officers	NCOs	Musicians	Men	Total
Earl of Meath's Regiment of Foot consisting of 12 companies of Foot and 1 of Grenadiers (each of 60 men)	46	78	26	780	930
Colonel Gustavus Hamilton's Regiment of Foot consisting of 12 companies of Foot and 1 of Grenadiers (each of 60 men)	46	78	26	780	930
Duke of Norfolk's Regiment of Foot Consisting of 12 companies of Foot and 1 of Grenadiers (each of 60 men)	46	78	26	780	930
Duke of Bolton's Regiment of Foot consisting of 12 companies of Foot and 1 of Grenadiers (each of 60 men)	46	78	26	780	930
Earl of Kingston's Regiment of Foot consisting of 12 companies of Foot and 1 of Grenadiers (each of 60 men)	46	78	26	780	930
Earl of Droghedah's Regiment of Foot consisting of 12 companies of Foot and 1 of Grenadiers (each of 60 men)	46	78	26	780	930
Earl of Roscomin's Regiment of Foot consisting of 12 companies of Foot and 1 of Grenadiers (each of 60 men)	46	78	26	780	930
Viscount Lisburn's Regiment of Foot consisting of 12 companies of Foot and 1 of Grenadiers (each of 60 men)	46	78	26	780	930
Viscount Castleton's Regiment of Foot consisting of 12 companies of Foot and 1 of Grenadiers (each of 60 men)	46	78	26	780	930
Lord Lovelace's Regiment of Foot consisting of 12 companies of Foot and 1 of Grenadiers (each of 60 men)	46	78	26	780	930
Colonel Charles Herbert's of Foot consisting of 12 companies of Foot and 1 of Grenadiers (each of 60 men)	46	78	26	780	930
Sir Edward Derring's Regiment of Foot consisting of 12 companies of Foot and 1 of Grenadiers (each of 60 men)	46	78	26	780	930
Sir Henry Ingoldesby's Regiment of Foot consisting of 12 companies of Foot and 1 of Grenadiers (each of 60 men)	46	78	26	780	930
Sir Thomas Gower's Regiment of Foot consisting of 12 companies of Foot and 1 of Grenadiers (each of 60 men)	46	78	26	780	930
Colonel Thomas Earle's Regiment of Foot consisting of 12 companies of Foot and 1 of Grenadiers (each of 60 men)	46	78	26	780	930
Colonel Soloman Richard's Regiment of Foot consisting of 12 Companies of Foot and 1 of Grenadiers (each of 60 men)	46	78	26	780	930
Colonel de Cambon's Regiment of Foot consisting of 12 companies of Foot and 1 of Grenadiers (each of 60 men)	46	78	26	780	930
Colonel de La Caillemotte's Regiment of Foot of 12 companies of Foot and 1 of Grenadiers (each of 60 men)	46	78	26	780	930
One Company of Miners	2	2	2	50	56

	Chirurgeons & Chaplains	Clerks	Mates and Cooks	Nurses	Total
Hospital to Attend the Army into Ireland including Physician General, Chirurgeon General, and Apothecary General	10	5	20	12	47

English Establishment for Service in the Low Countries November 1689[25]

Name of Unit & Details	Officers	NCOs	Musicians	Men	Total
General Staff including 3 Lieutenant Generals, 3 Major Generals, 4 Brigadiers in addition to Quartermasters, Adjutants, Chirurgeons, etc	10	N/A	N/A	N/A	10
His Majesties Second Troop of Horse Guards	20	N/A	5	200	225
His Majesties Troop of Horse Grenadiers	2	4	4	60	70
His Majesties Royal Regiment of Horse consisting of 9 Troops (each of 50 men)	42	27	19	450	538
His Majesties Coldstream Regiment of Foot Guards consisting of 12 companies of foot and 2 company of grenadiers (each of 80 men)	52	84	28	1,120	1,284
His Majesties Regiment of Scots Guards consisting of 12 companies of Foot and 2 companies of grenadiers (each of 80 men)	52	84	28	1,120	1,284
His Majesties Royal Regiment of Foot consisting of 24 companies of foot and 2 companies of grenadiers (each of 60 men)	88	156	53	1,560	1,857
His Majesties Royal Regiment of Fuziliers consisting of 13 companies (each of 60 men)	47	78	26	780	931
Colonel Charles Churchill Regiment of Foot consisting of 12 companies of foot and 1 of grenadiers (each of 60 men)	46	78	26	780	930
Colonel John Hales Regiment of Foot consisting of 12 companies of foot and 1 of grenadiers (each of 60 men)	46	78	26	780	930
Sir David Collier's Regiment of Foot consisting of 12 companies of foot and 1 of grenadiers (each of 60 men)	46	78	26	780	930
Colonel Robert Hodges's Regiment of Foot consisting of 12 companies of foot and 1 of grenadiers (each of 60 men)	46	78	26	780	930
Colonel Edward Fitzpatrick's Regiment of Foot consisting of 12 companies of Foot and 1 of Grenadiers (each of 60 men)	46	78	26	780	930
Their Majesties Regiment of Foot Commanded by Colonel Fergus O'Farrell's consisting of 12 companies of Foot and 1 of Grenadiers (each of 60 men)	46	78	26	780	930

25 NA WO24/12 War Office Establishment: Low Countries, and BL Add MS 15897, Hyde Papers Pensions Army and Navy etc, 1664–1745, vol. VI, f.88.

Danish Troops on the English Establishment for Service in Ireland 4 November 1689[26]

Name of Unit & Details	Officers	NCOs	Musicians	Men	Total
General Staff including 1 Lieutenant Generals, 2 Major Generals, 1 Brigadier in addition to Quartermasters, Adjutants, Chirurgeons, and Executioner	18			3	21
The Baron Tuel's Regiment of Horse consisting of 6 Troops (each of 46 men)	33	18	12	276	339
Colonel Deneda's Regiment of Horse consisting of 6 Troops (each of 46 men)	33	18	12	276	339
Colonel Schested's Regiment if Horse consisting of 6 Troops (each of 46 men)	33	18	12	276	229
Battalion of Foot Guards consisting of 7 Companies (each of 100 men) commanded by Lt-General Ferdinand Wilhelm, Duke of Würtemberg-Neustadt	37	28	14	700	779
Queen Beatall's Battalion of Foot consisting of 6 Companies (each of 100 men) commanded by Colonel Johan Diderich von Haxthausen	33	36	12	600	669
Prince Frederick's Battalion of Foot consisting of 6 Companies (each of 100 men) commanded by Colonel Heinrich Wulf Kalneyn	33	36	12	600	669
Prince Christian's Battalion of Foot consisting of 6 Companies (each of 100 men) commanded by Brigadier Johan Anton Elnberger	33	36	12	600	669
The Zealand Battalion of Foot consisting of 6 Companies (each of 100 men) commanded by Major-General Julius Ernst von Tettau	33	36	12	600	669
Prince George Battalion of Foot consisting of 5 Companies (each of 100 men) commanded by Lt-Colonel von Ørtzen	28	30	10	500	568
Jutland Battalion of Foot consisting of 6 Companies (each of 100 men) Commanded by Lt-Colonel Hans Diderich	33	36	12	600	669
The Funish Battalion of Foot consisting of 6 Companies (each of 100 men) commanded by Lt-Colonel Hans von Erffa	33	36	12	600	669
The Oldenburg Battalion of Foot consisting of 5 Companies (each of 100 men) commanded by Colonel Otto von Vittinghof	28	30	12	500	568

English Establishment for Service in the Low Countries and Islands 1 June 1690

Name of Unit & Details	Officers	NCOs	Musicians	Men	Total
General Staff including 3 Lieutenant Generals, 3 Major Generals, 4 Brigadiers in addition to Quartermasters, Adjutants, Chirurgeons, etc	21	10	N/A	N/A	31
Their Majesties Second Troop of Horse Guards	20	N/A	5	200	225
Their Majesties Troop of Horse Grenadiers	2	4	4	60	70
Their Majesties Troop of Scott's Guards	11	N/A	5	118	134

---

26 NA, WO24/11, War Office, Danish Establishment, Nov 1689, ff.1–6.

Name of Unit & Details	Officers	NCOs	Musicians	Men	Total
Lord Colchester's Regiment of Horse consisting of 6 Troops (each of 50 men)	30	30	13	300	373
Colonel Charles Godfrey's Regiment of Horse consisting of 6 Troops (each of 50 men)	30	30	13	300	373
Colonel John Berley's Regiment of Dragoons consisting of 6 troops (each of 60 men)	30	30	24	300	384
Sir Thomas Levingston's Regiment of Dragoons consisting of 6 troops (each of 60 men)	30	30	24	300	384
Their Majesties First Regiment of Foot Guards consisting of 24 companies of foot and 4 company of grenadiers (each of 80 men)	97	168	56	2,240	2,561
Their Majesties Coldstream Regiment of Foot Guards consisting of 12 companies of foot and 2 company of grenadiers (each of 80 men)	52	84	24	1,120	1,280
His Majesties Regiment of Scots Guards consisting of 12 companies of Foot and 2 companies of grenadiers (each of 80 men)	52	84	28	1,120	1,284
His Majesties Royal Regiment of Foot consisting of 24 companies of foot and 2 companies of grenadiers (each of 60 men)	88	156	53	1560	1,857
Colonel Charles Churchill's Regiment of Foot commanded consisting of 12 companies of foot and 1 of grenadiers (each of 60 men)	46	78	26	780	930
Earl of Bath's Regiment of Foot consisting of 12 companies of foot and 1 of grenadiers (each of 60 men)	46	78	26	780	930
Colonel William Beveridge's Regiment of Foot consisting of 12 companies of foot and 1 of grenadiers (each of 60 men)	46	78	26	780	930
Sir James Lesley's Regiment of Foot commanded by Sir James Lesley consisting of 12 companies of foot and 1 of grenadiers (each of 60 men)	46	78	26	780	930
Colonel John Hales' Regiment of Foot consisting of 12 companies of Foot and 1 of Grenadiers (each of 60 men)	46	78	26	780	930
Sir David Collyear's Regiment of Foot consisting of 12 companies of Foot and 1 of Grenadiers (each of 60 men)[27]	46	78	26	780	930
Colonel Robert Hodges' Regiment of Foot consisting of 12 companies of Foot and 1 of Grenadiers (each of 60 men)	46	78	26	780	930
Colonel Fergus O'Farrell Regiment of Foot commanded by consisting of 12 companies of foot and 1 of grenadiers (each of 60 men)	46	78	26	780	930
Colonel Edward FitzPatrick's Regiment of Foot consisting of 12 companies of foot and 1 of grenadiers (each of 60 men)	46	78	26	780	930
Earl of Monmouth's Regiment of Foot consisting of 12 companies of foot and 1 of grenadiers (each of 60 men)	46	78	26	780	930

---

27   Also spelt Colyear.

Name of Unit & Details	Officers	NCOs	Musicians	Men	Total
Colonel Francis Luttrell's Regiment of Foot consisting of 12 companies of foot and 1 of grenadiers (each of 60 men)	46	78	26	780	930
Earl of Leven's Regiment of Foot consisting of 12 companies of Foot and 1 of Grenadiers (each of 60 men)	46	78	26	780	930
George, Viscount Regiment of Foot consisting of 12 companies of Foot and 1 of Grenadiers (each of 60 men)	46	78	26	780	930
Duke of Bolton's Regiment of Foot consisting of 12 companies of Foot and 1 of Grenadiers (each of 60 men)	46	78	26	780	930
Their Majesties Royal Regiment of Fuziliers consisting of 13 companies (each of 60 men)	47	78	26	780	930
Their Majesties Regiment of Foot commanding by the Duke of Bolton in the West Indies consisting of 11 companies of Foot and 1 of Grenadiers (each of 60 men)	43	72	24	720	859
One Company of Foot in the Leeward Islands	3	6	2	60	71
Two Companies of Foot in New York (each of 60 men)	6	12	2	120	142
One Non-Regimented Company of Grenadiers	2	5	1	50	58

War Office Establishment for Service in Ireland: 1 June 1690[28]

Name of Unit & Details	Officers	NCOs	Musicians	Men	Total
General Staff including 3 Lieutenant Generals, 3 Major Generals, 4 Brigadiers in addition to Quartermasters, Adjutants, Chirurgeons, etc	55	N/A	N/A	24[29]	66
Their Majesties First and Third Troop of Horse Guards (each of 200 men)	28	N/A	10	400	438
Two Troops of Horse Grenadiers (each of 60 men)	4	8	8	120	140
Their Majesties Royal Regiment of Horse consisting of 9 troops (each of 50 men)	42	27	19	450	538
Sir John Lanier's Regiment of Horse consisting of 9 Troops (each of 50 men)	42	27	19	450	538
His Grace the Duke of Schomberg's Regiment of Horse consisting of 9 Troops (each of 50 men)	42	27	19	450	538
Colonel Edward Villiers' Regiment of Horse consisting of 6 Troops (each of 50 men)	30	18	13	300	361
Colonel Theodore Rubell's Regiment of Horse consisting of 6 Troops (each of 50 men)	30	18	13	300	361
Colonel George John Coy's Regiment of Horse consisting of 6 Troops (each of 50 men)	30	18	13	300	361
Colonel Francis Langston's regiment of Horse consisting of 6 Troops (each of 50 men)	30	18	13	300	361
Colonel Robert Bryerley's Regiment of Horse consisting of 6 Troops (each of 50 men)	30	18	13	300	361

---

28 NA WO24/14, War Office Establishment Ireland 1689, ff.3–16. The establishment of the Londonderry and Inniskilling regiments of Horse, Foot, and Dragoons and of the Danish forces only excepted.

29 These are Provosts, attached to the Provost Marshall General.

Name of Unit & Details	Officers	NCOs	Musicians	Men	Total
Lord Cavendish's Regiment of Horse consisting of 6 Troops (each of 50 men)	30	18	13	300	361
One Independent Troop of Horse	4	3	2	50	59
His Majesties Royal Regiment of Dragoons consisting of 8 Troops (each of 60 men)	39	40	32	480	591
Colonel Richard Leverson's Regiment of Dragoons consisting of 6 Troops (each of 60 men)	31	30	24	360	445
Major-General Percy Kirke's Regiment of Foot Consisting of 12 companies of Foot and 1 of Grenadiers (each of 60 men)	46	78	26	780	930
Colonel Charles Trelawny's Regiment of Foot consisting of 12 companies of Foot and 1 of Grenadiers (each of 60 men)	46	78	26	780	930
Colonel John Beaumont's Regiment of Foot consisting of 12 companies of Foot and 1 of Grenadiers (each of 60 men)	46	78	26	780	930
Colonel William Stewart's Regiment of Foot consisting of 12 companies of Foot and 1 of Grenadiers (each of 60 men)	46	78	26	780	930
Sir John Hanmore's Regiment of Foot consisting of 12 companies of Foot and 1 of Grenadiers (each of 60 men)	46	78	26	780	930
Colonel Richard Brewer's Regiment of Foot consisting of 12 companies of Foot and 1 of Grenadiers (each of 60 men)	46	78	26	780	930
Colonel Ferdinando Hastings' Regiment of Foot consisting of 12 companies of Foot and 1 of Grenadiers (each of 60 men)	46	78	26	780	930
Earl of Meath's Regiment of Foot consisting of 12 companies of Foot and 1 of Grenadiers (each of 60 men)	46	78	26	780	930
Colonel Gustavus Hamilton's Regiment of Foot consisting of 12 companies of Foot and 1 of Grenadiers (each of 60 men)	46	78	26	780	930
Sir Henry Belasyse's Regiment of Foot Consisting of 12 companies of Foot and 1 of Grenadiers (each of 60 men)	46	78	26	780	930
Colonel Charles Herbert's Regiment of Foot consisting of 12 companies of Foot and 1 of Grenadiers (each of 60 men)	46	78	26	780	930
Lt-General Douglas's Regiment of Foot consisting of 12 companies of Foot and 1 of Grenadiers (each of 60 men)	46	78	26	780	930
Viscount Lisburn's Regiment of Foot consisting of 12 companies of Foot and 1 of Grenadiers (each of 60 men)	46	78	26	780	930
Colonel Daniel Deering's Regiment of Foot consisting of 12 companies of Foot and 1 of Grenadiers (each of 60 men)	46	78	26	780	930
Earl of Drogheda's Regiment of Foot consisting of 12 companies of Foot and 1 of Grenadiers (each of 60 men)	46	78	26	780	930

Name of Unit & Details	Officers	NCOs	Musicians	Men	Total
Colonel Thomas Earle's Regiment of Foot comprising 12 companies of Foot and 1 of Grenadiers (each of 60 men)	46	78	26	780	930
Colonel De La Meloniere's Regiment of Foot consisting of 12 companies of Foot and 1 of Grenadiers (each of 60 men)	46	78	26	780	930
Colonel du Cambon's Regiment of Foot consisting of 12 companies of Foot and 1 of Grenadiers (each of 60 men)	46	78	26	780	930
Colonel La Calimott's Regiment of Foot consisting of 12 companies of Foot and 1 of Grenadiers (each of 60 men)	46	78	26	780	930
Earl of Angus's Scottish Regiment of Foot consisting of 12 companies of Foot and 1 of Grenadiers (each of 60 men)	46	78	26	780	930
Their Majesties Scottish Regiment of Foot consisting of 12 companies of Foot and 1 of Grenadiers (each of 60 men)	46	78	26	780	930
Their Majesties Scottish Regiment of Foot consisting of 12 companies of Foot and 1 of Grenadiers (each of 60 men)	46	78	26	780	930
Their Majesties Scottish Regiment of Foot consisting of 12 companies of Foot and 1 of Grenadiers (each of 60 men)	46	78	26	780	930
One Company of Miners	2	4	2	50	58
One Non-Regimented Company of Fusiliers	3	6	2	60	71
Marching Hospital	12	N/A	N/A	20	32
Fixed Hospital	10	N/A	N/A	51	61

War Office English Establishment 1 April 1692[30]

Name of Unit & Details	Officers	NCOs	Musicians	Men	Total
General Staff including 3 Lieutenant Generals, 3 Major Generals, 4 Brigadiers in addition to Quartermasters, Adjutants, Chirurgeons, etc	31	N/A	N/A	N/A	
Their Majesties Three Troop of Horse Guards (each of 200 men)	63	N/A	15	600	678
There Majesties Three Troops of Horse Grenadiers	6	12	12	180	210
Their Majesties Troop of Scots Guards	11	N/A	5	118	134
Their Majesties Royal Regiment of Horse consisting of 6 troops (each of 50 men)	30	18	13	300	361
The Queen's Regiment of Horse consisting of 9 Troops (each of 50 men) Commanded by Colonel Henry Lumley	42	27	19	450	538
Colonel Edward Villiers' Regiment of Horse consisting of 6 Troops (each of 50 men)	30	18	13	300	361
Viscount Colchester's Regiment of Horse consisting of 6 Troops (each of 50 men)	30	18	13	300	361
Colonel Charles Godfrey's Regiment of Horse consisting of 6 Troops (each of 50 men)	30	18	13	300	361

---

30 NA WO24/15, War Office Establishment, Guards, Garrisons and land Forces, 1 April 1692.

Name of Unit & Details	Officers	NCOs	Musicians	Men	Total
Colonel John Coy's Regiment of Horse consisting of 6 Troops (each of 50 men)	30	18	13	300	361
The Princess Anne of Denmark's Regiment of Horse consisting of 6 Troops (each of 50 men)	30	18	13	300	361
Colonel Robert Brerley's Regiment of Horse consisting of 6 Troops (each of 50 men)	30	18	13	300	361
The Marquis de Ruvigny's French Regiment of Horse consisting of 6 Troops (each of 50 men)	30	18	13	300	361
Their Majesties Regiment of Horse consisting of 9 Troops (each of 50 men)	42	27	19	450	538
Their Majesties Royal Regiment of Dragoons consisting of 8 Troops (each of 60 men)	39	40	32	480	591
The Queen's Regiment of Dragoons consisting of 6 Troops (each of 60 men)	31	30	24	360	445
The Royal Regiment of Scots Dragoons consisting of 6 Troops (each of 60 men)	31	30	24	360	445
Princess Anne of Denmark's Regiment of Dragoons consisting of 6 Troops (each of 60 men)	31	30	24	360	445
Their Majesties First Regiment of Foot Guards consisting of 24 companies of Foot and 4 of Grenadiers (each of 80 men)	126	168	56	2,240	2,590
Their majesties Coldstream Regiment of foot Guards consisting of 12 companies of Foot and 2 of Grenadiers (each of 80 men)	52	84	28	1,120	1,284
Their Majesties Regiment of Scott's Guards consisting of 12 companies of Foot and 2 of Grenadiers (each of 80 men)	52	84	28	1,120	1,284
Their Majesties Royal Regiment of Foot consisting of 24 companies of Foot and 2 companies of Grenadiers (each of 60 men)	82	156	53	1,560	1,851
The Queen Dowager's Regiment of Foot consisting of 12 companies of Foot and 1 of Grenadiers (each of 60 men) commanded by Major-General Percy Kirke	46	78	26	780	930
Prince George of Denmark's Regiment of Foot consisting of 12 companies of Foot and 1 of Grenadiers (each of 60 men)	46	78	26	780	930
The Queen's Regiment of Foot consisting of 12 companies of Foot and 1 of Grenadiers (each of 60 men) Commanded by Henry Trelawny	46	78	26	780	930
Colonel Edward Lloyd's Regiment of Foot consisting of 12 companies of Foot and 1 of Grenadiers (each of 60 men)	46	78	26	780	930
The Prince of Hesse Darmstadt's Regiment of Foot consisting of 12 companies of Foot and 1 of Grenadiers (each of 60 men) commanded by Lt-Colonel Samuel Foxton	46	78	26	780	930
Lord Cutts's Regiment of Foot consisting of 12 companies of Foot and 1 of Grenadiers (each of 60 men)	46	78	26	780	930
The Princess Anne of Denmark's regiment of Foot consisting of 12 companies of Foot and 1 of Grenadiers (each of 60 men)	46	78	26	780	930

Name of Unit & Details	Officers	NCOs	Musicians	Men	Total
Colonel William Stewart's Regiment of Foot consisting of 12 companies of Foot and 1 of Grenadiers (each of 60 men)	46	78	26	780	930
Earl of Bath's Regiment of Foot consisting of 12 companies of Foot and 1 of Grenadiers (each of 60 men)	46	78	26	780	930
Sir John Hanmer's Regiment of Foot consisting of 12 companies of Foot and 1 of Grenadiers (each of 60 men)	46	78	26	780	930
Colonel Richard Brewer's Regiment of Foot consisting of 12 companies of Foot and 1 of Grenadiers (each of 60 men)	46	78	26	780	930
Colonel Ferdinand Hastings' Regiment of Foot consisting of 12 companies of Foot and 1 of Grenadiers (each of 60 men)	46	78	26	780	930
Colonel William Beveridge's Regiment of Foot consisting of 12 companies of Foot and 1 of Grenadiers (each of 60 men)	46	78	26	780	930
Sir James Lesley's Regiment of Foot consisting of 12 companies of Foot and 1 of Grenadiers (each of 60 men)	46	78	26	780	930
Colonel John Hales's Regiment of Foot consisting of 12 companies of Foot and 1 of Grenadiers (each of 60 men)	46	78	26	780	930
Colonel Robert Hodges's Regiment of Foot consisting of 12 companies of Foot and 1 of Grenadiers (each of 60 men)	46	78	26	780	930
Colonel Edward Fitzpatrick's Regiment of Foot consisting of 12 companies of Foot and 1 of Grenadiers (each of 60 men)	46	78	26	780	930
Sir George St. George's Regiment of Foot consisting of 12 companies of Foot and 1 of Grenadiers (each of 60 men)	46	78	26	780	930
Earl of Meath's Regiment of Foot consisting of 12 companies of Foot and 1 of Grenadiers (each of 60 men)	46	78	26	780	930
Sir David Collyear's Regiment of Foot consisting of 12 companies of Foot and 1 of Grenadiers (each of 60 men)	46	78	26	780	930
Earl of Monmouth's Regiment of Foot consisting of 12 companies of Foot and 1 of Grenadiers (each of 60 men)	46	78	26	780	930
Colonel John Foulkes Regiment of Foot consisting of 12 companies of Foot and 1 of Grenadiers (each of 60 men)	46	78	26	780	930
Colonel Thomas Earle's Regiment of Foot consisting of 12 companies of Foot and 1 of Grenadiers (each of 60 men)	46	78	26	780	930
Colonel Gustavus Hamilton's Regiment of Foot consisting of 12 companies of Foot and 1 of Grenadiers (each of 60 men)	46	78	26	780	930
Colonel O'Farrell's Regiment of Fusiliers consisting of 12 companies of Foot and 1 of Grenadiers (each of 60 men)	46	78	26	780	930

Name of Unit & Details	Officers	NCOs	Musicians	Men	Total
Duke of Bolton's [1st] Regiment of Foot consisting of 12 companies of Foot and 1 of Grenadiers (each of 60 men)	46	78	26	780	930
Duke of Bolton's [2nd] Regiment of Foot consisting of 12 companies of Foot and 1 of Grenadiers (each of 60 men)	46	78	26	780	930
Sir Henry Belasyse's Regiment of Foot consisting of 12 companies of Foot and 1 of Grenadiers (each of 60 men)	46	78	26	780	930
Colonel Toby Purcell's Regiment of Foot consisting of 12 companies of Foot and 1 of Grenadiers (each of 60 men)	46	78	26	780	930
Colonel Samuel Venner's Regiment of Foot consisting of 12 companies of Foot and 1 of Grenadiers (each of 60 men)	46	78	26	780	930
Viscount Castleton's Regiment of Foot consisting of 12 companies of Foot and 1 of Grenadiers (each of 60 men)	46	78	26	780	930
Viscount Lisburne's Regiment of Foot consisting of 12 companies of Foot and 1 of Grenadiers (each of 60 men)	46	78	26	780	930
Colonel De La Meloniere's Regiment of Foot consisting of 12 companies of Foot and 1 of Grenadiers (each of 60 men)	46	78	26	780	930
Their Majesties Royal Regiment of Fuziliers consisting of 13 companies of Foot commanded by Lord George Hamilton	47	78	26	780	931
One Company of Miners	2	4	2	50	58
One Company of Foot in the Leeward Islands	3	6	2	60	71
Two Companies of Foot in New York (each of 60 men)	3	12	4	120	139
One Non-Regimented Company of Grenadiers	2	5	1	50	58
One Company of Pensioners at Windsor Castle	4	12	2	150	168

Danish Troops on the English Establishment 1 April 1692[31]

Name of Unit & Details	Officers	NCOs	Musicians	Men	Total
General Staff including 1 Lieutenant Generals, 2 Major Generals, 1 Brigadier in addition to Quartermasters, Adjutants, Chirurgeons, and Executioner	18			3	21
The Baron Tuel's Regiment of Horse consisting of 6 Troops (each of 46 men)	33	18	12	276	339
Colonel Deneda's Regiment of Horse consisting of 6 Troops (each of 46 men)	33	18	12	276	339
Battalion of Foot Guards consisting of 7 Companies (each of 100 men) commanded by Lt-General Ferdinand Wilhelm, Duke of Württemberg-Neustadt	37	42	14	700	779
Queen Battalion of Foot consisting of 7 Companies (each of 98 men) commanded by Johan Diderich von Haxthansen	37	42	14	686	765

31 NA, WO24/18, War Office, Danish Establishment, April 1692, ff.1–7.

Name of Unit & Details	Officers	NCOs	Musicians	Men	Total
Prince Frederick's Battalion of Foot consisting of 6 Companies (each of 98 men) commanded by Colonel Heinrich Wulf Kalneyn	33	36	12	588	657
Prince Christian's Battalion of Foot consisting of 6 Companies (each of 98 men) commanded by Brigadier John Anton Elnberger	33	36	12	588	657
The Zealand Battalion of Foot consisting of 6 Companies (each of 98 men) commanded by Major-General Julius Ernst von Tettau	33	36	12	588	657
Prince George Battalion of Foot consisting of 6 Companies (each of 98 men) commanded by Lt-Colonel von Ørtzen	33	36	12	588	657
Jutland Battalion of Foot consisting of 6 Companies (each of 98 men) commanded by Lt-Colonel Hans Diderich	33	36	12	588	657
The Funen Battalion of Foot consisting of 6 Companies (each of 98 men) commanded by Lt-Colonel Hans von Erffa	33	36	12	588	657

War Office Establishment serving in the Kingdom of Ireland 1 January 1692[32]

Name of Unit & Details	Officers	NCOs	Musicians	Men	Total
General Staff including 3 Lieutenant Generals, 3 Major Generals, 4 Brigadiers in addition to Quartermasters, Adjutants, Chirurgeons, etc	14	N/A	N/A	N/A	66
His Majesties regiment of Horse consisting of 6 Troops (each of 50 men)	30	18	13	300	361
Colonel James Wynne's Regiment of Dragoons consisting of 8 Troops (each of 50 men)	39	40	32	480	591
His Majesties Inniskilling Regiment of Dragoons consisting of 6 Troops (each of 50 men)	31	30	24	360	445
Twelve reformed Captains	12	N/A	N/A	N/A	12
Colonel Abraham Creighton's Regiment of Foot consisting of 12 companies of Foot and 1 of Grenadiers (each of 60 men)	46	78	26	780	930
Colonel John Michelburne's Regiment of Foot consisting of 12 companies of Foot and 1 of Grenadiers (each of 60 men)	46	78	26	780	930
Earl of Drogheda's Regiment of Foot consisting of 12 companies of Foot and 1 of Grenadiers (each of 60 men)	46	78	26	780	930
Lt-General Douglas's Regiment of Foot consisting of 12 companies of Foot and 1 of Grenadiers (each of 60 men)	46	78	26	780	930
Colonel Zacharia Tiffin's Inniskilling Regiment of Foot consisting of 12 companies of Foot and 1 of Grenadiers (each of 60 men)	46	78	26	780	930
Their Majesties Regiment of Foot consisting of 12 companies of Foot and 1 of Grenadiers (each of 60 men)	46	78	26	780	930

---

32 NA, WO24/16 War Office Establishment Ireland 1692.

Name of Unit & Details	Officers	NCOs	Musicians	Men	Total
Their Majesties Regiment of Foot consisting of 12 companies of Foot and 1 of Grenadiers (each of 60 men)	46	78	26	780	930
Their Majesties Regiment of Foot consisting of 12 companies of Foot and 1 of Grenadiers (each of 60 men)	46	78	26	780	930
Their Majesties Regiment of Foot consisting of 12 companies of Foot and 1 of Grenadiers (each of 60 men)	46	78	26	780	930
Their Majesties Regiment of Foot consisting of 12 companies of Foot and 1 of Grenadiers (each of 60 men)	46	78	26	780	930
Their Majesties Regiment of Foot consisting of 12 companies of Foot and 1 of Grenadiers (each of 60 men)	46	78	26	780	930
Their Majesties Regiment of Foot consisting of 12 companies of Foot and 1 of Grenadiers (each of 60 men)	46	78	26	780	930
Their Majesties Regiment of Foot consisting of 12 companies of Foot and 1 of Grenadiers (each of 60 men)	46	78	26	780	930
Their Majesties Regiment of Foot consisting of 12 companies of Foot and 1 of Grenadiers (each of 60 men)	46	78	26	780	930
Their Majesties Regiment of Foot consisting of 12 companies of Foot and 1 of Grenadiers (each of 60 men)	46	78	26	780	930

Dutch Troops on the English Establishment 1 April 1692[33]

Name of Unit & Details	Officers	NCOs	Musicians	Men	Total
Garde du Corps commanded by Hendrick van Nassau-Ouwerkerk	19	N/A	5	200	224
Gardes te Paard Regiment of Horse Guards consisting of 6 Troops (each of 67 men) commanded by Hans Willem Bentinck	29	12	12	402	455
Matthias Hoeufft van Oyen's Regiment of Dutch Horse consisting of 3 Troops (each of 58 men)	24	9	6	174	213
Herr Van Ginkel's Regiment of Dutch Horse consisting of 3 Troops (each of 58 men)	24	9	6	174	213
Nassau-Zuylenstein's Regiment of Dutch Horse consisting of 3 Troops (each of 58 men)	24	9	6	174	213
Marquis de Montpouillan's Regiment of Dutch Horse consisting of 3 Troops (each of 58 men)	24	9	6	174	213
Robert van Ittersum's Regiment of Dutch Horse consisting of 3 Troops (each of 58 men)	24	9	6	174	213
Erik Gustaaf, Graaf van Steinbock's Regiment of Dutch Horse consisting of 3 Troops (each of 58 men)	24	9	6	174	213

---

33 NA, WO24/19, War Office, Dutch Troops on the English Establishment, April 1692, ff.1–5, and R. Hall, I. Stanford and Y. Roumegoux, *Flags and Uniforms of the Dutch Army 1685–1715, Vol.1: cavalry, Dragoons, Artillery, & Subsidy Regiments* (Romford: Pike and Shot Society, 2014).

Name of Unit & Details	Officers	NCOs	Musicians	Men	Total
Heer van Quadt-Soppenbroek's Regiment of Dutch Horse consisting of 3 Troops (each of 58 men)	24	9	6	174	213
Schack's Regiment of Horse consisting of 3 Troops (each of 60 men)	17	9	6	180	212
Heer van s'Gravemoer's Regiment of Horse consisting of 3 Troops (each of 60 men)	17	9	6	180	212
Gardes Dragonders (Eppinger) Regiment of Dragoons consisting of 10 Troops (each of 80 men)	47	50	40	800	937
Dutch Foot Guards Guarde te Voet consisting of 23 Companies of 91 men, 2 Companies of 101 men, and a Cadet Company of 86 men.	79	156	54	2,381	2,670
Prince of Brandenburg's Dutch Foot consisting of 12 companies (each of 54 men)	55	60	24	648	787
Count Nassau's Dutch Foot consisting of 12 companies (each of 54 men)	55	60	24	648	787
Van Graben's Dutch Foot consisting of 12 companies (each of 54 men)	55	60	24	648	787

War Office Establishment of Guards and Land Forces 1 April 1694[34]

Name of Unit & Details	Officers	NCOs	Musicians	Men	Total
General Staff including 2 Generals, 6 Lieutenant Generals, 8 Major Generals, 12 Brigadiers in addition to Quartermasters, Adjutants, Chirurgeons, etc	47	2	N/A	N/A	49
Their Majesties Horse Guards, 3 Troops (each of 200 men)	63	N/A	15	600	678
Their Majesties Troop of Horse Grenadiers[35]	11	12	8	180	210
Their Majesties Troop of Scott's Guards	11	N/A	5	118	134
Earl of Oxford's Regiment of Horse consisting of 9 Troops (each of 59 men)	42	27	19	531	619
The Queen's Regiment of Horse consisting of 9 Troops (each of 59 men)	42	27	19	531	619
Brigadier-General Leverson's Regiment of Horse consisting of 9 Troops (each of 59 men)	42	27	19	531	619
Colonel Cornelius Wood's Regiment of Horse consisting of 9 Troops (each of 59 men)	42	27	19	531	619
Colonel Fraser Langston's Regiment of Horse consisting of 9 Troops (each of 59 men)	42	27	19	531	619
Colonel Coy's Regiment of Horse consisting of 9 Troops (each of 59 men)	42	27	19	531	619
Colonel Hugh Wyndham's Regiment of Horse consisting of 9 Troops (each of 59 men)	42	27	19	531	619
The Duke of Schomberg's Regiment of Horse consisting of 9 Troops (each of 59 men)	42	27	19	531	619
Earl of Macclesfield's Regiment of Horse consisting of 6 Troops (each of 59 men)	30	18	13	354	415

34 NA, WO24/21, War Office Establishment of Guards, Garrisons, and Land Forces, 1 April 1694.

35 NA, WO24/21, Land Forces, 1 April 1694, f.4, states a total of one hundred & eight troopers in written form but 180 troopers in numeric form, the 180 is the correct figure.

Name of Unit & Details	Officers	NCOs	Musicians	Men	Total
Earl of Arran's Regiment of Horse consisting of 6 troops (each of 59 men)	30	18	13	354	415
Colonel Thomas Windsor's Regiment of Horse consisting of 6 troops (each of 59 men)	30	18	13	354	415
Their Majesties Regiment of Horse consisting of 9 troops (each of 59 men)[36]	115	27	19	531	692
Their Majesties Royal Regiment of Dragoons consisting of 8 Troops (each of 60 men)	39	40	32	480	591
Their Majesties Royal Scot's Regiment of Dragoons consisting of 8 Troops (each of 60 men)	39	40	32	480	591
The Queen's Regiment of Dragoons consisting of 8 Troops (each of 60 men)	39	40	32	480	591
Earl of Essex's Regiment of Dragoons consisting of 8 Troops (each of 60 men)	39	40	32	480	591
Earl pf Denbigh's Regiment of Dragoons consisting of 8 Troops (each of 60 men)	39	40	32	480	591
Colonel Edward Leigh's Regiment of Dragoons consisting of 8 Troops (each of 60 men)	39	40	32	480	591
Their Majesties Regiment of Dragoons consisting of 8 Troops (each of 60 men)	39	40	32	480	591
Their Majesties Regiment of Dragoons consisting of 8 Troops (each of 60 men)	39	40	32	480	591
Their Majesties First Regiment of Foot Guards consisting of 24 companies of Foot and 4 Companies of Grenadiers (each of 80 men)	98	168	56	2,240	2,562
Their Majesties Coldstream Regiment of Foot Guards consisting of 12 Companies of Foot and 2 Companies of Grenadiers (each of 80 men)	52	84	28	1,120	1,284
Their Majesties Regiment of Scott's Guards consisting of 14 Companies of Foot and 2 Companies of Grenadiers (each of 80 men)	58	96	32	1,280	1,466
Their Majesties Royal Regiment of Foot consisting of 24 Companies of Foot and 2 Companies of Grenadiers (each of 60 men)	88	156	53	1,560	1,857
The Queen Dowager's Regiment of Foot consisting of 12 Companies of Foot and 1 of Grenadiers	46	78	26	780	930
Prince George of Denmark's Regiment of Foot consisting of 12 Companies of Foot and 1 of Grenadiers	46	78	26	780	930
The Queen's Regiment of Foot consisting of 12 Companies of Foot and 1 of Grenadiers	46	78	26	780	930
Colonel Edward Lloyd's Regiment of Foot consisting of 12 Companies of Foot and 1 of Grenadiers	46	78	26	780	930
The Prince of Hesse Darmstadt's Regiment of Foot consisting of 12 Companies of Foot and 1 of Grenadiers commanded by Henry du Caumont, Marquis de Rada	46	78	26	780	930

36 This regiment's increase in officers consists of one reformed major in the regimental staff and two reformed captains, three reformed lieutenants and three reformed cornets in each of the nine companies.

Name of Unit & Details	Officers	NCOs	Musicians	Men	Total
Lord Cutts's Regiment of Foot consisting of 12 Companies of Foot and 1 of Grenadiers	46	78	26	780	930
Princes Anne of Denmark's Regiment of Foot consisting of 12 Companies of Foot and 1 of Grenadiers	46	78	26	780	930
Sir Bevil Grenville's Regiment of Foot consisting of 12 Companies of Foot and 1 of Grenadiers	46	78	26	780	930
Colonel Richard Brewer's Regiment of Foot consisting of 12 Companies of Foot and 1 of Grenadiers	46	78	26	780	930
Sir John Hanmer's Regiment of Foot consisting of 12 Companies of Foot and 1 of Grenadiers	46	78	26	780	930
Brigadier-General Ferdinand Hastings's Regiment of Foot consisting of 12 Companies of Foot and 1 of Grenadiers	46	78	26	780	930
Sir John Tidcomb's Regiment of Foot consisting of 12 Companies of Foot and 1 of Grenadiers	46	78	26	780	930
Sir James Lesley's Regiment of Foot consisting of 12 Companies of Foot and 1 of Grenadiers	46	78	26	780	930
Colonel J. Stanley's Regiment of Foot consisting of 12 Companies of Foot and 1 of Grenadiers	46	78	26	780	930
Colonel Fraser Collingwood's Regiment of Foot consisting of 12 Companies of Foot and 1 of Grenadiers	46	78	26	780	930
Sir George St George's Regiment of Foot consisting of 12 Companies of Foot and 1 of Grenadiers	46	78	26	780	930
Colonel Frederick Hamilton's Regiment of Foot consisting of 12 Companies of Foot and 1 of Grenadiers	46	78	26	780	930
Sir David Collyear's Regiment of Foot consisting of 12 Companies of Foot and 1 of Grenadiers	46	78	26	780	930
Earl of Monmouth's Regiment of Foot consisting of 12 Companies of Foot and 1 of Grenadiers	46	78	26	780	930
Colonel Luke Lillingston's Regiment of Foot consisting of 12 Companies of Foot and 1 of Grenadiers	46	78	26	780	930
Brigadier-General Thomas Earle's Regiment of Foot consisting of 12 Companies of Foot and 1 of Grenadiers	46	78	26	780	930
Colonel Gustavus Hamilton's Regiment of Foot consisting of 12 Companies of Foot and 1 of Grenadiers	46	78	26	780	930
Brigadier-General O'Farrell's Regiment of Fusiliers consisting of 12 Companies of Foot and 1 of Grenadiers	46	78	26	780	930
Colonel Richard Ingoldsby's Regiment of Foot consisting of 12 Companies of Foot and 1 of Grenadiers	46	78	26	780	930
Duke of Bolton's Regiment of Foot consisting of 12 Companies of Foot and 1 of Grenadiers	46	78	26	780	930
Colonel Samuel Venner's Regiment of Foot consisting of 12 Companies of Foot and 1 of Grenadiers	46	78	26	780	930

Name of Unit & Details	Officers	NCOs	Musicians	Men	Total
Colonel Henry Rowe's Regiment of Foot consisting of 12 Companies of Foot and 1 of Grenadiers	46	78	26	780	930
Viscount Castleton's Regiment of Foot consisting of 12 Companies of Foot and 1 of Grenadiers	46	78	26	780	930
Major-General Isaac De La Meloniere's Regiment of Foot consisting of 12 Companies of Foot and 1 of Grenadiers	46	78	26	780	930
Colonel Peter de Belcastel's Regiment of Foot consisting of 12 Companies of Foot and 1 of Grenadiers	46	78	26	780	930
Earl of Leven's Regiment of Foot consisting of 12 Companies of Foot and 1 of Grenadiers	46	78	26	780	930
Colonel Zacharia Tiffin's Inniskilling Regiment of Foot consisting of 12 Companies of Foot and 1 of Grenadiers	46	78	26	780	930
Earl of Argyle's Regiment of Foot consisting of 12 Companies of Foot and 1 of Grenadiers	46	78	26	780	930
Colonel John Buchan's Regiment of Foot consisting of 12 Companies of Foot and 1 of Grenadiers	46	78	26	780	930
Colonel George Hamilton's Regiment of Foot consisting of 12 Companies of Foot and 1 of Grenadiers	46	78	26	780	930
Earl of Donegal's Regiment of Foot consisting of 12 Companies of Foot and 1 of Grenadiers	46	78	26	780	930
Lord Strathnaver's Regiment of Foot consisting of 12 Companies of Foot and 1 of Grenadiers	46	78	26	780	930
Sir John Gibson's Regiment of Foot consisting of 12 Companies of Foot and 1 of Grenadiers	46	78	26	780	930
Colonel Thomas Farrington's Regiment of Foot consisting of 12 Companies of Foot and 1 of Grenadiers	46	78	26	780	930
Colonel William Northcote's Regiment of Foot consisting of 12 Companies of Foot and 1 of Grenadiers	46	78	26	780	930
Their Majesties Regiment of Foot consisting of 12 Companies of Foot and 1 of Grenadiers	46	78	26	780	930
Their Majesties Regiment of Foot consisting of 12 Companies of Foot and 1 of Grenadiers	46	78	26	780	930
Their Majesties Regiment of Foot consisting of 12 Companies of Foot and 1 of Grenadiers	46	78	26	780	930
Their Majesties Regiment of Foot consisting of 12 Companies of Foot and 1 of Grenadiers	46	78	26	780	930
Their Majesties First Marine Regiment of Foot consisting of 12 Companies of Foot and 1 of Grenadiers	46	78	26	780	930
Their Majesties Second Marine Regiment of Foot consisting of 12 Companies of Foot and 1 of Grenadiers	46	78	26	780	930
Their Majesties Royal Regiment of Fuziliers consisting of 13 Companies (each of 60 men)	47	78	26	780	931

Name of Unit & Details	Officers	NCOs	Musicians	Men	Total
Their Majesties Regiment of Foot consisting of 12 Companies of Foot and 1 Company of Grenadiers (each of 60 men)[37]	85	78	28	780	971
Their Majesties regiment of Foot for service in Barbados consisting of 5 Companies (each of 100 men) commanded by Colonel Francis Russell	20	30	10	500	560
One Company of Miners	2	4	2	50	58
One Non-Regimented Company of Grenadiers at Upnor castle	3	5	1	50	59
One Company of Foot in the Leeward Islands	3	6	2	60	71
One Company of foot in Jamaica[38]	3	6	2	100	111
Four Companies of Foot in New York (each of 100 men)	13	24	8	400	445
One Company of Pensioners at Windsor Castle	4	12	2	150	168
Three Companies of Pensioners at Tinmouth, Chester, and Hampton Court (each of 80 men)	9	21	6	240	276

War Office Establishment of Guards and land Forces 26 March 1699[39]

Name of Unit & Details	Officers	NCOs	Musicians	Men	Total
General Staff	9	7	N/A	N/A	16
His Majesties Horse Guards consisting of 3 Troops (each of 160 men)	48	N/A	15	480	543
His majesties Troop of Horse Grenadiers	11	12	24	145	192
His Majesties Royal Regiment of Horse consisting of 9 Troops (each of 36 men)	41	18	10	324	393
Her Majesty the Queen's Regiment of Horse consisting of 9 Troops (each of 36 men)	41	18	10	324	393
Major-General Leveson's Regiment of Horse consisting of six troops (each of 34 men)	28	12	7	204	251
Colonel Cornelius wood's Regiment of Horse consisting of six troops (each of 34 men)	28	12	7	204	251
Brigadier-General' Francis Langston's Regiment of Horse consisting of six troops (each of 34 men)	28	12	7	204	251
Duke of Schomberg's Regiment of Horse consisting of six troops (each of 34 men)	28	12	7	204	251
Earl of Macclesfield's Regiment of Horse consisting of six troops (each of 34 men)	28	12	7	204	251
His Majesties Royal Regiment of Dragoons consisting of 6 Troops (each of 38 men)	28	24	12	228	292
The Princess Anne of Denmark's Regiment of Dragoons consisting of 6 Troops (each of 38 men)	28	24	12	228	292

---

37 The extra officers for this regiment are one reformed captain, lieutenant, and ensign per company.

38 With the addition of one chirurgion's mate.

39 NA, WO24/22, *Establishment of His Majesties Guards, Garrisons and other Charles relating thereunto commencing the 26th March 1699*. Dalton's *English Army Lists and Commission Register, 1661–1714*, vol.4, p.220, has an additional regiment, the Earl of Galway's Regiment of French Horse.

Name of Unit & Details	Officers	NCOs	Musicians	Men	Total
The Inniskilling Regiment of Dragoons consisting of 6 Troops (each of 38 men)	28	24	12	228	292
His Majesties First Regiment of Foot Guards consisting of 24 Companies of Foot and 4 Companies of Grenadiers (each of 40 men)	96	140	56	1,120	1,412
His Majesties Coldstream Regiment of Foot Guards consisting of 12 Companies of Foot and 2 Companies of Grenadiers (each of 40 men)	51	56	28	560	695
The Queen Dowager's Regiment of Foot consisting of 9 Companies of Foot and 1 Company of Grenadiers (each of 36 men)	37	40	10	360	447
Prince George of Denmark's Regiment of Foot consisting of 9 Companies of Foot and 1 Company of Grenadiers (each of 36 men)	37	40	10	360	447
The Queen's Regiment of Foot consisting of 9 Companies of Foot and 1 Company of Grenadiers (each of 36 men)[40]	37	40	10	360	447
His Majesties Royal Regiment of Fuziliers in Jersey and Guernsey consisting of 13 companies (each of 40 men)	44	52	13	520	629
Colonel Francis Collingwood's Regiment of Foot in the West Indies consisting of 12 Companies of Foot and 1 Company of Grenadiers (each of 40 men)	44	54	13	520	631
Four Companies of Foot in New York (each of 50 men)	12	20	8	200	240
One Company of Foot in the Leeward Islands	3	6	2	60	71
One Company of Foot in Newfoundland	2	6	2	43	53

War Office Establishment of Guards and land Forces 25 April 1700[41]

Name of Unit & Details	Officers	NCOs	Musicians	Men	Total
General Staff	9	7	N/A	N/A	16
His Majesties Horse Guards consisting of 3 Troops (each of 160 men)	48	N/A	15	480	543
His Majesties Troop of Horse Grenadiers	11	12	8	145	176
His Majesties Royal Regiment of Horse consisting of 9 Troops (each of 30 men)	42	18	10	270	340

---

40 Dalton's *Army Lists, 1661–1714*, vol.4, p.220, has the following additional regiments, Brigadier-General Thomas Fairfax's, Colonel Ventris Columbine's, Princess Anne of Denmark's, Major-General William Stewart's, Sir John Hanmer's, Colonel John Tidcomb's, Colonel Emanuel Howe's, Colonel James Stanley's, Sir Matthew Bridges', Major General Thomas Erle's, Colonel Gustavus Hamilton's, Sir Henry Belasyse's, Brigadier-General Richard Ingoldsby's, Marquis de Puizar's, and Colonel Zachariah Tiffin's Regiment.

41 NA, WO24/23 *War Office Establishment of Guards, Garrisons, and Land Forces, 25 April 1700*. Dalton's *Army Lists*, vol. 4, has an additional regiment of horse commanded by Brigadier General Hugh Wyndham and the following regiments of foot, Brigadier General Thomas Fairfax's, Colonel Ventris Columbine's, Sir Bevil Granville's, Sir John Hanmer's, Colonel Emanuel Howe's, Colonel James Stanley's, Colonel Edward Fox's, Sir Matthew Bridges', Sir Henry Belasyse's, Colonel Richard Ingoldsby's, Marquis De Puizar's, Colonel Zacharia Tiffin's, and Colonel James Ferguson's regiments.

Name of Unit & Details	Officers	NCOs	Musicians	Men	Total
The Queens Regiment of Horse consisting of 9 troops (each of 30 men)	40	18	10	270	338
Colonel Daniel Harvey's Regiment of Horse consisting of 6 Troops (each of 30 men)	27	12	7	180	226
Earl of Arran's Regiment of Horse consisting of 6 Troops (each of 30 men)	27	12	7	180	226
Earl of Macclesfield's Regiment of Horse consisting of 6 Troops (each of 30 men)	27	12	7	180	226
His Majesties Royal Regiment of Dragoons consisting of 6 Troops (each of 40 men)	27	18	12	240	297
The Inniskilling Regiment of Dragoons consisting of 6 Troops (each of 40 men)	27	18	12	240	297
His Majesties First Regiment of Foot Guards consisting of 24 Companies of Foot (1 of 80 men and 23 of 50 men) and 4 Companies of Grenadiers (each of 60 men)	96	120	56	1,700	1,972
His Majesties Coldstream Regiment of Foot Guards consisting of 12 Companies of Foot (each of 50 men) and 2 Companies of Grenadiers (each of 60 men)	52	60	28	720	860
The Queen Dowager's Regiment of Foot consisting of 9 companies of Foot and 1 of Grenadiers (each of 50 men)	35	40	10	500	585
Prince George of Denmark's Regiment of Foot consisting of 9 companies of Foot and 1 of Grenadiers (each of 50 men)	35	40	10	500	585
The Queen's Regiment of Foot consisting of 9 companies of Foot and 1 of Grenadiers (each of 50 men)	35	40	10	500	585
His Majesties Royal Regiment of Fuziliers consisting of 9 Companies of Fuziliers and 1 Company of Grenadiers (each of 40 men)	35	42	11	400	488
Four Companies of Foot in New York (each of 100 men)	16	24	8	400	448
One Company of Foot in the Leeward Islands	3	6	2	60	71
One Company of Foot in Newfoundland	2	6	2	43	53

War Office Establishment of 12 Foot battalions for Holland, 1 June 1701[42]

Name of Unit & Details	Officers	NCOs	Musicians	Men	Total
General Staff	20	N/A	N/A	N/A	20
His Majesties Royal Regiment of Foot consisting of 22 companies of Foot and 2 of Grenadiers (each of 59 men)	82	122	49	1416	1,669
Princess Anne of Denmark's Regiment of Foot consisting of 11 companies of Foot and 1 of Grenadiers (each of 59 men)	43	61	14	708	826
His Majesties Regiment of Foot consisting of 11 companies of Foot and 1 of Grenadiers (each of 59 men)	43	61	14	708	826

---

42 NA, WO24/24 War Office Establishment of 12 Battalions of Foot for Holland, being sent from Ireland to Flanders, 1 June 1701, ff.1–4.

Name of Unit & Details	Officers	NCOs	Musicians	Men	Total
His Majesties Regiment of Foot consisting of 11 companies of Foot and 1 of Grenadiers (each of 59 men)	43	61	14	708	826
His Majesties Regiment of Foot consisting of 11 companies of Foot and 1 of Grenadiers (each of 59 men)	43	61	14	708	826
His Majesties Regiment of Foot consisting of 11 companies of Foot and 1 of Grenadiers (each of 59 men)	43	61	14	708	826
His Majesties Regiment of Foot consisting of 11 companies of Foot and 1 of Grenadiers (each of 59 men)	43	61	14	708	826
His Majesties Regiment of Foot consisting of 11 companies of Foot and 1 of Grenadiers (each of 59 men)	43	61	14	708	826
His Majesties Regiment of Foot consisting of 11 companies of Foot and 1 of Grenadiers (each of 59 men)	43	61	14	708	826
His Majesties Regiment of Foot consisting of 11 companies of Foot and 1 of Grenadiers (each of 59 men)	43	61	14	708	826
His Majesties Regiment of Foot consisting of 11 companies of Foot and 1 of Grenadiers (each of 59 men)	43	61	14	708	826
His Majesties Royal Regiment of Fuziliers consisting of 9 Companies of Fuziliers and 1 Company of Grenadiers (each of 40 men)	35	42	11	400	488
Four Companies of Foot in New York (each of 100 men)	16	24	8	400	448
One Company of Foot in the Leeward Islands	3	6	2	60	71
One Company of Foot in Newfoundland	2	6	2	43	53

War Office Establishment of Guards and Land Forces 24 December 1701[43]

Name of Unit & Details	Officers	NCOs	Musicians	Men	Total
General Staff	18	N/A	N/A	N/A	18
His Majesties Horse Guards consisting of 3 Troops (each of 160 men)	48	N/A	15	480	543
His Majesties Troop of Horse Grenadiers	11	12	8	145	176
His Majesties Royal Regiment of Horse consisting of 9 Troops (each of 40 men)	42	18	10	360	430
His Majesties Royal Regiment of Dragoons consisting of 6 Troops (each of 54 men)	31	30	24	324	409
His Majesties Regiment of Dragoons consisting of 6 Troops (each of 40 men)	31	30	24	324	409
His Majesties First Regiment of Foot Guards consisting of 24 Companies of Foot and 4 Companies of Grenadiers (each of 60 men)	96	168	59	1,680	2,003
His Majesties Coldstream Regiment of Foot Guards consisting of 12 Companies of Foot and 2 Companies of Grenadiers (each of 60 men)	52	84	28	840	1,004

---

43 NA, WO24/26 War Office Establishment of Guards, Garrisons, and Land Forces, 24 December 1701–1 June 1702. ff.1–4.

Name of Unit & Details	Officers	NCOs	Musicians	Men	Total
His Majesties Regiment of Foot consisting of 12 Companies of Foot and 1 of Grenadiers (each of 59 men)	46	61	24	708	839
His Majesties Regiment of Foot consisting of 12 Companies of Foot and 1 of Grenadiers (each of 59 men)	46	61	24	708	839
His Majesties Royal Regiment of Fuziliers consisting of 9 Companies of Fuziliers and 1 Company of Grenadiers (each of 40 men)	35	42	11	400	488
Four Companies of Foot in New York (each of 100 men)	16	24	8	400	448
One Company of Foot in Bermuda	3	4	1	50	58
One Company of Foot in Newfoundland	2	6	2	43	53

War Office Establishment of Guards and Land Forces for the Upcoming Expedition 1 June 1702[44]

Name of Unit & Details	Officers	NCOs	Musicians	Men	Total
General Staff for Troops going onboard the Fleet	25	N/A	N/A	N/A	25
Colonel George Villiers' Regiment of Marines consisting of 11 Companies of Foot and 1 Company of Grenadiers (each of 59 men)	43	61	24	708	839
Colonel Edward Fox's Regiment of Marines consisting of 11 Companies of Foot and 1 Company of Grenadiers (each of 59 men)	43	61	24	708	839
Colonel Henry Mordaunt's Regiment of Marines consisting of 11 Companies of Foot and 1 Company of Grenadiers (each of 59 men)	43	61	24	708	839
Colonel Henry Holt's Regiment of Marines consisting of 11 Companies of Foot and 1 Company of Grenadiers (each of 59 men)	43	61	24	708	839
Viscount Shannon's Regiment of Marines consisting of 11 Companies of Foot and 1 Company of Grenadiers (each of 59 men)	43	61	24	708	839
His Majesties Regiment of Marines consisting of 11 Companies of Foot and 1 Company of Grenadiers (each of 59 men)	43	61	24	708	839
Earl of Orkney's Regiment of Foot consisting of 12 Companies of Foot and 1 of Grenadiers (each of 59 men)	46	61	24	708	839
Princess Anne of Denmark's Regiment of Foot consisting of 12 Companies of Foot and 1 of Grenadiers (each of 59 men) commanded by colonel Webb	46	61	24	708	839
Sir Bevil Granville's Regiment of Foot consisting of 12 Companies of Foot and 1 of Grenadiers (each of 59 men)	46	61	24	708	839
Sir John Jacob's Regiment of Foot consisting of 12 Companies of Foot and 1 of Grenadiers (each of 59 men)	46	61	24	708	839

---

44 NA, WO24/26 War Office Establishment of Guards, Garrisons, and Land Forces, 24 December 1701–1 June 1702, ff.14–39.

Name of Unit & Details	Officers	NCOs	Musicians	Men	Total
Colonel Emanuel Howe's Regiment of Foot consisting of 12 Companies of Foot and 1 of Grenadiers (each of 59 men)	46	61	24	708	839
Colonel James Stanley's Regiment of Foot consisting of 12 Companies of Foot and 1 of Grenadiers (each of 59 men)	46	61	24	708	839
General Staff for the upcoming Expedition	16	N/A	N/A	N/A	16
The Queen's Regiment of Horse consisting of 9 Troops (each of 57 men)	41	27	10	518	596
His Majesties Regiment of Horse consisting of 9 Troops (each of 57 men)	41	27	10	518	596
His Majesties Regiment of Horse consisting of 6 Troops (each of 57 men)	30	18	13	342	403
His Majesties Regiment of Horse consisting of 6 Troops (each of 57 men)	30	18	13	342	403
His Majesties Royal Regiment of Dragoons consisting of 8 Troops (each of 54 men)	39	40	32	432	543
His Majesties Regiment of Dragoons consisting of 6 Troops (each of 54 men)	31	30	12	324	397
His Majesties Regiment of Dragoons consisting of 6 Troops (each of 54 men)	31	30	12	324	397
His Majesties Royal Regiment of Foot consisting of 24 Companies (each of 60 men) and 2 Companies of Grenadiers (each of 70 men)	88	156	49	1,580	1,873
Colonel Matthew Bridges' Regiment of Foot consisting of 12 Companies of Foot (each of 60 men) and 1 Company of Grenadiers (of 70 men)	43	78	24	790	935
Colonel Frederick Hamilton's Regiment of Foot consisting of 12 Companies of Foot (each of 60 men) and 1 Company of Grenadiers (of 70 men)	43	78	24	790	935
Earl of Huntingdon's Regiment of Foot consisting of 12 Companies of Foot (each of 60 men) and 1 Company of Grenadiers (of 70 men)	43	78	24	790	935
Lord Lucas's Regiment of Foot consisting of 12 Companies of Foot (each of 60 men) and 1 Company of Grenadiers (of 70 men)	43	78	24	790	935
Colonel Thomas Stringer's Regiment of Foot consisting of 12 Companies of Foot (each of 60 men) and 1 Company of Grenadiers (of 70 men)	43	78	24	790	935
Lord Mohun's Regiment of Foot consisting of 12 Companies of Foot (each of 60 men) and 1 Company of Grenadiers (of 70 men)	43	78	24	790	935
Sir Richard Temple's Regiment of Foot consisting of 12 Companies of Foot (each of 60 men) and 1 Company of Grenadiers (of 70 men)	43	78	24	790	935
Colonel Richard Coote's Regiment of Foot consisting of 12 Companies of Foot (each of 60 men) and 1 Company of Grenadiers (of 70 men)	43	78	24	790	935

Name of Unit & Details	Officers	NCOs	Musicians	Men	Total
His Majesties Regiment of Foot consisting of 12 Companies of Foot (each of 60 men) and 1 Company of Grenadiers (of 70 men)	43	78	24	790	935
His Majesties Regiment of Foot consisting of 12 Companies of Foot (each of 60 men) and 1 Company of Grenadiers (of 70 men)	43	78	24	790	935
His Majesties Regiment of Foot consisting of 12 Companies of Foot (each of 60 men) and 1 Company of Grenadiers (of 70 men)	43	78	24	790	935
His Majesties Regiment of Foot consisting of 12 Companies of Foot (each of 60 men) and 1 Company of Grenadiers (of 70 men)	43	78	24	790	935
His Majesties Regiment of Foot consisting of 12 Companies of Foot (each of 60 men) and 1 Company of Grenadiers (of 70 men)	43	78	24	790	935
His Majesties Regiment of Foot consisting of 12 Companies of Foot (each of 60 men) and 1 Company of Grenadiers (of 70 men)	43	78	24	790	935
General Staff for Home Service	15	N/A	N/A	N/A	15
Her Majesties Horse Guards consisting of 3 Troops (each of 160 men)	45	N/A	15	480	540
Her Majesties Troop of Horse Grenadiers	11	12	8	145	177
Her Majesties Royal Regiment of Horse consisting of 9 Troops (each of 40 men)	42	18	10	360	430
Her Majesties Regiment of Dragoons consisting of 6 Troops (each of 54 men)	31	30	12	324	397
Her Majesties Regiment of Dragoons consisting of 6 Troops (each of 54 men)	31	30	12	324	397
Her Majesties First Regiment of Foot Guards consisting of 24 Companies of Foot and 4 Companies of Grenadiers (each of 60 men)	96	168	56	1,680	2,000
Her Majesties Coldstream Guards consisting of 12 Companies of Foot and 2 Companies of Grenadiers (each of 60 men)	52	84	28	840	1,004
Her Majesties Regiment of Foot consisting of 11 Companies of Foot and 1 of Grenadiers (each of 59 men)	43	61	24	708	836
Her Majesties Regiment of Foot consisting of 11 Companies of Foot and 1 of Grenadiers (each of 59 men)	43	61	24	708	836
Her Majesties Royal Regiment of Fuziliers consisting of 9 Companies of Fuziliers and 1 Company of Grenadiers (each of 40 men)	37	42	11	400	490
Four Companies of Foot in New York (each of 100 men)	16	24	8	400	448
One Company of Foot in Bermuda	3	4	1	50	58
One Company of Foot in Newfoundland	4	6	2	80	92

War Office Establishment of Danish Forces in Majesties Service 1 June 1702[45]

Name of Unit & Details	Officers	NCOs	Musicians	Men	Total
Regiment of Danish Horse consisting of 6 Troops (each of 60 men)	45	18	13	360	436
Regiment of Danish Horse consisting of 6 Troops (each of 60 men)	45	18	13	360	436
Regiment of Danish Horse consisting of 6 Troops (each of 60 men)	45	18	13	360	436
Regiment of Danish Horse consisting of 6 Troops (each of 60 men)	45	18	13	360	436
Regiment of Danish Foot Commanded by the Duke of Wurtemberg consisting of 6 Companies (each of 94 men)	40	36	12	564	652
Regiment of Danish Foot consisting of 6 Companies of Foot (each of 94 men) and 1 Company of Grenadiers (of 100 men)	45	42	14	664	765

War Office Establishment of Prussian Forces in Her Majesties Service 1 January 1702[46]

Name of Unit & Details	Officers	NCOs	Musicians	Men	Total
General Staff, 2 Lieutenant General, 1 Adjutant General, & 1 Aide de Camp	4	N/A	N/A	N/A	4
Regiment of Prussian Horse consisting of 6 Troops (each of 55 men)	45	18	13	330	406
Regiment of Prussian Horse consisting of 6 Troops (each of 55 men)	45	18	13	330	406
Regiment of Prussian Foot consisting of 12 Companies (each of 54 men)	82	72	28	648	830
Regiment of Prussian Foot consisting of 12 Companies (each of 54 men)	82	72	28	648	830
Regiment of Prussian Foot consisting of 12 Companies (each of 54 men)	82	72	28	648	830
Regiment of Prussian Foot consisting of 12 Companies (each of 54 men)	82	72	28	648	830
Regiment of Prussian Foot consisting of 12 Companies (each of 54 men)	82	72	28	648	830
Spiegel Karabiniers Regiment of Hessian Horse consisting of 6 Troops (each of 50 men)	40	18	7	300	365
Prinz Philipp v. Hessen-Homburg Regiment of Hessian Dragoons consisting of 8 Troops (each of 68 men)	58	24	21	544	647
Gräfendorff, Erbprinz Friedrich Regiment of Hessian Dragoons consisting of 8 Troops (each of 68 men)	58	24	21	544	647
Regiment of Hessian Foot Guards consisting of 10 Companies (each of 71men)	71	50	26	710	857
Görtz, Löwenstein Regiment of Hessian Foot consisting of 10 Companies (each of 70 men)	70	50	26	700	846

---

45 NA, WO24/27 Her Majesties Foreign Forces in the Low Countries, 1 June 1702, ff.1–5.

46 WO24/27 Her Majesties Foreign Forces in the Low Countries, ff.6–10, and R. Hall, *The Armies of Hesse and the Upper Rhine Circle* (Farnham: Pike and Shot Society, 2007) pp.13–15.

Name of Unit & Details	Officers	NCOs	Musicians	Men	Total
Görtz, Löwenstein Regiment of Hessian Foot consisting of 10 Companies (each of 70 men)	70	50	26	700	846
Prinz Carl Regiment of Hessian Foot consisting of 10 Companies (each of 70 men)	70	50	26	700	846
Friedrich, Erbprinz von Hessen Regiment of Hessian Foot consisting of 10 Companies (each of 70 men)	70	50	26	700	846
Prinz Lebrecht von Anhalt Bernburg Regiment of Hessian Foot consisting of 10 Companies (each of 70 men)	39	18	13	276	346
Regiment of Hanover & Cell Horse consisting of 6 Troops (each of 46 men)	39	18	13	276	346
Regiment of Hanover & Cell Foot consisting of 7 Companies (each of 75 men)	59	35	19	525	638
Regiment of Hanover & Cell Foot consisting of 7 Companies (each of 75 men)	59	35	19	525	638
Regiment of Hanover & Cell Foot consisting of 7 Companies (each of 75 men)	59	35	19	525	638
Regiment of Hanover & Cell Foot consisting of 7 Companies (each of 75 men)	59	35	19	525	638
Regiment of Hanover & Cell Foot consisting of 7 Companies (each of 75 men)	59	35	19	525	638
Regiment of Hanover & Cell Foot consisting of 7 Companies (each of 75 men)	59	35	19	525	638
Regiment of Hanover & Cell Foot consisting of 7 Companies (each of 75 men)	59	35	19	525	638
Regiment of Hanover & Cell Foot consisting of 7 Companies (each of 75 men)	59	35	19	525	638
Regiment of Hanover & Cell Foot consisting of 7 Companies (each of 75 men)	59	35	19	525	638
Regiment of Hanover & Cell Foot consisting of 7 Companies (each of 75 men)	59	35	19	525	638
Regiment of Hanover & Cell Foot consisting of 7 Companies (each of 75 men)	59	35	19	525	638
Regiment of Hanover & Cell Foot consisting of 7 Companies (each of 75 men)	59	35	19	525	638

War Office Establishment of Guards and Garrisons, 1 January 1703[47]

Name of Unit & Details	Officers	NCOs	Musicians	Men	Total
General Staff,	16	N/A	N/A	N/A	16
Her Majesties Horse Guards consisting of 3 Troops (each of 160 men)	48	N/A	15	480	543
Her Majesties Troop of Horse Grenadiers	10	12	8	145	175
Her Majesties Royal Regiment of Horse Guards consisting of 9 Troops (each of 40 men)	42	18	10	360	430
The Queens Regiment of Dragoons consisting of 6 Troops (each of 54 men)	31	18	24	324	397
Her Majesties First regiment of Foot Guards consisting of 24 Companies of Foot and 4 Companies of Grenadiers (each of 60 men)	96	168	59	1,680	2,003

---

47   WO24/28 War Office Establishment for Guards and Garrisons 1 January 1703, ff.1–24.

Name of Unit & Details	Officers	NCOs	Musicians	Men	Total
Her Majesties Coldstream Regiment of Foot Guards consisting of 12 Companies of Foot and 2 Companies of Grenadiers	52	84	28	840	1,004
Her Majesties Regiment of Foot commanded by Sir Henry Belasyse consisting of 11 Companies of Foot and 1 Company of Grenadiers (each of 59 men)	43	61	24	708	836
The Queens Regiment of Foot commanded by Brigadier William Seymour consisting of 11 Companies of Foot and 1 Company of Grenadiers	43	61	24	708	836
Her Majesties Royal Regiment of Fuziliers consisting of 9 Companies of Fuziliers and 1 Company of Grenadiers (each of 40 men)	37	42	11	400	490
Four Companies of Foot in New York (each of 100 men)	16	24	8	400	448
One Company of Foot in Bermuda	3	4	1	50	58
One Company of Foot in Newfoundland	5	6	2	80	93
Colonel Henry Mordaunt's Regiment of Marines consisting of 11 Companies of Foot and 1 Company of Marines (each of 59 men)	43	61	24	708	836
Colonel Thomas Saunderson's Regiment of Marines consisting of 11 Companies of Foot and 1 Company of Marines (each of 59 men)	43	61	24	708	836
Colonel Henry Holt's Regiment of Marines consisting of 11 Companies of Foot and 1 Company of Marines (each of 59 men)	43	61	24	708	836
Colonel George Villiers Regiment of Marines consisting of 11 Companies of Foot and 1 Company of Marines (each of 59 men)	43	61	24	708	836
Colonel Edward Fox's Regiment of Marines consisting of 11 Companies of Foot and 1 Company of Marines (each of 59 men)	43	61	24	708	836
Lord Viscount Sharman's Regiment of Marines consisting of 11 Companies of Foot and 1 Company of Marines (each of 59 men)	43	61	24	708	836
Brigadier Ventris Colonbine's Regiment of Foot for Sea Service consisting of 11 Companies of Foot and 1 Company of Grenadiers (each of 59 men)	43	61	24	708	836
Major-General Erle's Regiment of Foot consisting of 11 Companies of Foot and 1 Company of Grenadiers (each of 59 men)	43	61	24	708	836
Brigadier Gustave Hamilton's Regiment of Foot consisting of 11 Companies of Foot and 1 Company of Grenadiers (each of 59 men)	43	61	24	708	836
Earl of Donnegal's Regiment of Foot consisting of 11 Companies of Foot and 1 Company of Grenadiers (each of 59 men)	43	61	24	708	836
Lord Charlemont's Regiment of Foot consisting of 11 Companies of Foot and 1 Company of Grenadiers (each of 59 men)	43	61	24	708	836
Lord Lucas' Regiment of Foot consisting of 11 Companies of Foot and 1 Company of Grenadiers (each of 59 men)	43	61	24	708	836

Name of Unit & Details	Officers	NCOs	Musicians	Men	Total
Her Majesties 4 Companies of Invalides (each of 75 men)	12	20	4	300	336

War Office Establishment of Her Majesties Forces in the Low Countries, 20 January 1703[48]

Name of Unit & Details	Officers	NCOs	Musicians	Men	Total
General Staff,	16	N/A	N/A	N/A	16
The Queens Regiment of Horse consisting of 9 Troops (each of 57 men)	42	27	19	513	601
Brigadier Wood's Regiment of Horse Wood consisting of 9 Troops (each of 57 men)	42	27	19	513	601
Major General Wyndham's Regiment if Horse consisting of 6 Troops (each of 57 men)	30	18	13	342	403
Duke of Schomberg's regiment of Horse consisting of 6 Troops (each of 57 men)	30	18	13	342	403
Her Majesties Royal Regiment of Dragoons consisting of 8 Troops (each of 54 men)	39	40	16	432	527
Lord Viscount Tiviot's Regiment of Dragoons consisting of 6 Troops (each of 54 m4n)	31	30	12	324	407
Brigadier Ross's Regiment of Dragoons consisting of 6troops (each of 54 men)	31	30	12	324	407
Her Majesties Royal Regiment of Foot consisting of 24 Companies of Foot (each of 60 men) and 2 Companies of Grenadiers (each of 70 men)	80	156	53	1580	1,869
Earl of Orkney's Regiment of Foot consisting of 12 Companies of Foot (each of 60 men) and 1 Company of Grenadiers (of 70 men)	46	78	26	790	940
His Royal Highness Prince George of Denmark's regiment of Foot commanded by Lieutenant-General Churchill consisting of 12 Companies of Foot (each of 60 men) and 1 Company of Grenadiers (of 70 men)	46	78	26	790	940
The Queens regiment of Foot commanded by Colonel Webb consisting of 12 Companies of Foot (each of 60 men) and 1 Company of Grenadiers (of 70 men)	46	78	26	790	940
Lt-General Stewart's Regiment of Foot consisting of 12 Companies of Foot (each of 60 men) and 1 Company of Grenadiers (of 70 men)	46	78	26	790	940
Lord North's Regiment of Foot consisting of 12 Companies of Foot (each of 60 men) and 1 Company of Grenadiers (of 70 men)	46	78	26	790	940
Earl of Barrymore's Regiment of Foot consisting of 12 Companies of Foot (each of 60 men) and 1 Company of Grenadiers (of 70 men)	46	78	26	790	940
Colonel How's Regiment of Foot consisting of 12 Companies of Foot (each of 60 men) and 1 Company of Grenadiers (of 70 men)	46	78	26	790	940

---

48   WO24/29 War Office Establishment for Forces in the Low Countries 20 January 1703, ff.1–8.

Name of Unit & Details	Officers	NCOs	Musicians	Men	Total
Earl of Darby's Regiment of Foot consisting of 12 Companies of Foot (each of 60 men) and 1 Company of Grenadiers (of 70 men)	46	78	26	790	940
Sir Matthew Bridges' Regiment of Foot consisting of 12 Companies of Foot (each of 60 men) and 1 Company of Grenadiers (of 70 men)	46	78	26	790	940
Brigadier Frederick Hamilton's Regiment of Foot consisting of 12 Companies of Foot (each of 60 men) and 1 Company of Grenadiers (of 70 men)	46	78	26	790	940
Major-General Ingoldsby's Regiment of Foot consisting of 12 Companies of Foot (each of 60 men) and 1 Company of Grenadiers (of 70 men)	46	78	26	790	940
Duke of Marlborough's Regiment of Foot consisting of 12 Companies of Foot (each of 60 men) and 1 Company of Grenadiers (of 70 men)	46	78	26	790	940
Earl of Huntingdon's Regiment of Foot consisting of 12 Companies of Foot (each of 60 men) and 1 Company of Grenadiers (of 70 men)	46	78	26	790	940
Colonel Ferguson's Regiment of Foot consisting of 12 Companies of Foot (each of 60 men) and 1 Company of Grenadiers (of 70 men)	46	78	26	790	940
Her Majesties Regiment of Scott's Fuziliers commanded by Colonel Archibald Row consisting of 12 Companies of Foot (each of 60 men) and 1 Company of Grenadiers (of 70 men)	46	78	26	790	940

War Office Establishment of Foreign Forces in Her Majesties Service, 20 January 1703[49]

Name of Unit & Details	Officers	NCOs	Musicians	Men	Total
General Staff, Danish, Prussian, and Hessian	22	N/A	N/A	5	27
Danish Regiment of Foot consisting of 6 troops (each of 60 men)	39	18	13	360	430
Danish Regiment of Foot consisting of 6 troops (each of 60 men)	39	18	13	360	430
Danish Regiment of Foot consisting of 6 troops (each of 60 men)	39	18	13	360	430
Danish Regiment of Foot consisting of 6 troops (each of 60 men)	39	18	13	360	430
Danish Regiment of Foot consisting of 6 troops (each of 60 men)	39	18	13	360	430
Danish Regiment of Foot consisting of 6 troops (each of 60 men)	39	18	13	360	430
Danish Regiment of Foot consisting of 6 troops (each of 60 men)	39	18	13	360	430

49   WO24/29 War Office Establishment for Forces in the Low Countries 20 January 1703, ff.9–15.

Name of Unit & Details	Officers	NCOs	Musicians	Men	Total
Danish Regiment of Foot consisting of 6 troops (each of 60 men)	39	18	13	360	430
Danish Battalion of Foot Guards consisting of 6 Companies (each of 100 men)	40	36	12	600	688
Danish Regiment of Foot consisting of 7 Companies of Foot (each of 100 men)	45	42	14	700	801
Danish Regiment of Foot consisting of 7 Companies of Foot (each of 100 men)	45	42	14	700	801
Danish Regiment of Foot consisting of 6 Companies of Foot (each of 94 men) and 1 Company of Grenadiers (of 100 men)	45	42	14	664	765
Danish Regiment of Foot consisting of 6 Companies of Foot (each of 94 men) and 1 Company of Grenadiers (of 100 men)	45	42	14	664	765
Danish Regiment of Foot consisting of 6 Companies of Foot (each of 94 men) and 1 Company of Grenadiers (of 100 men)	45	42	14	664	765
Danish Regiment of Foot consisting of 6 Companies of Foot (each of 94 men) and 1 Company of Grenadiers (of 100 men)	45	42	14	664	765
Danish Regiment of Foot consisting of 6 Companies of Foot (each of 100 men)	40	36	12	600	688
Danish Regiment of Foot consisting of 6 Companies of Foot (each of 94 men)	40	36	12	564	652
Danish Regiment of Foot consisting of 6 Companies of Foot (each of 94 men)	40	36	12	564	652
Danish Regiment of Foot consisting of 6 Companies of Foot (each of 94 men)	40	36	12	564	652
Prussian Regiment of Horse consisting of 6 Troops (each of 55 men)	45	18	13	330	406
Prussian Regiment of Horse consisting of 6 Troops (each of 55 men)	45	18	13	330	406
Prussian Regiment of Foot consisting of 12 Companies of Foot (each of 54 men)	60	36	24	648	768
Prussian Regiment of Foot consisting of 12 Companies of Foot (each of 54 men)	60	36	24	648	768
Prussian Regiment of Foot consisting of 12 Companies of Foot (each of 54 men)	60	36	24	648	768
Prussian Regiment of Foot consisting of 12 Companies of Foot (each of 54 men)	60	36	24	648	768
Prussian Regiment of Foot consisting of 12 Companies of Foot (each of 54 men)	60	36	24	648	768
Leibgarde zu Pferd: Regt. Spiegel zu Pferd Hessian Regiment of Horse consisting of 6 Troops (each of 50 men)	40	18	7	300	365
Spiegel Karabiniers Regiment of Hessian Horse consisting of 6 Troops (each of 50 men)	58	24	21	544	647
Prinz Philipp v. Hessen-Homburg Regiment of Hessian Dragoons consisting of 8 Troops (each of 68 men)	58	24	21	544	647
Gräfendorff, Erbprinz Friedrich Regiment of Hessian Dragoons consisting of 8 Troops (each of 68 men)	61	30	26	710	827

Name of Unit & Details	Officers	NCOs	Musicians	Men	Total
Regiment of Hessian Foot Guards consisting of 10 Companies (each of 71men)	61	30	26	700	817
Görtz, Löwenstein Regiment of Hessian Foot consisting of 10 Companies (each of 70 men)	61	30	26	700	817
Prinz Carl Regiment of Hessian Foot consisting of 10 Companies (each of 70 men)	61	30	26	700	817
Friedrich, Erbprinz von Hessen Regiment of Hessian Foot consisting of 10 Companies (each of 70 men)	61	30	26	700	817
Prinz Lebrecht von Anhalt Bernburg Regiment of Hessian Foot consisting of 10 Companies (each of 70 men)	39	18	13	276	346
Hanover & Cell Regiment of Horse consisting of 6 Troops (each of 46 men)	39	18	13	276	346
Hanover & Cell Regiment of Foot consisting of 7 Companies of Foot (each of 75 men)	38	133[50]	19	525	715
Hanover & Cell Regiment of Foot consisting of 7 Companies of Foot (each of 75 men)	38	133	19	525	715
Hanover & Cell Regiment of Foot consisting of 7 Companies of Foot (each of 75 men)	38	133	19	525	715
Hanover & Cell Regiment of Foot consisting of 7 Companies of Foot (each of 75 men)	38	133	19	525	715
Hanover & Cell Regiment of Foot consisting of 7 Companies of Foot (each of 75 men)	38	133	19	525	715
Hanover & Cell Regiment of Foot consisting of 7 Companies of Foot (each of 75 men)	38	133	19	525	715
Hanover & Cell Regiment of Foot consisting of 7 Companies of Foot (each of 75 men)	38	133	19	525	715
Hanover & Cell Regiment of Foot consisting of 7 Companies of Foot (each of 75 men)	38	133	19	525	715
Hanover & Cell Regiment of Foot consisting of 7 Companies of Foot (each of 75 men)	38	133	19	525	715
Hanover & Cell Regiment of Foot consisting of 7 Companies of Foot (each of 75 men)	38	133	19	525	715
Hanover & Cell Regiment of Foot consisting of 7 Companies of Foot (each of 75 men)	38	133	19	525	715
Hanover & Cell Regiment of Foot consisting of 7 Companies of Foot (each of 75 men)	38	133	19	525	715

Hounslow Heath Summer Camp, unknown artist c.1688. (Author's collection)

---

50 Including 16 under-corporals per company.

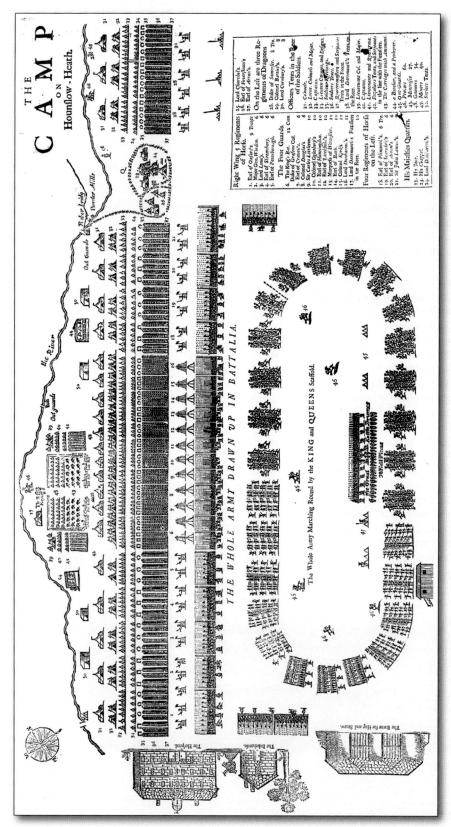

Print by George Croom, printed at the Blue-Ball, Thames Street, Baynard's Castle. (Author's collection)

Summer Camp

Hounslow Heath acted as the annual summer camp for the English army, this allowed the authorities to get an accurate picture of each of the regiments attending and gave both regimental commanders to exercise their whole regiment together, as they were normally billeted over a larger area. They also allowed larger formations to train and exercise together. Hounslow Heath took the appearance of a large town during this period and became a spectacle for the citizens of London to come onto the heath to watch.

The following troops were recorded at the summer camp in July 1686.[51]

	Troops / Companies	No of Men	Total inc. Officers
Earl of Oxford's Regiment of Horse	9	450	532
Queen Consort's Regiment of Horse	9	360	442
Earl of Peterborough's Regiment of Horse	6	240	294
Earl of Plymouth's Regiment of Horse	6	240	294
Major-General Werden's Regiment of Horse	6	240	294
Earl of Aran's Regiment of Horse	6	240	294
Earl of Shensbury's Regiment of Horse	6	240	294
Earl of Scarsdale's Regiment of Horse	6	240	294
First Regiment of Guards	12	1,040	1,183
Second Regiment of Guards	6.5	520	592
Scotch Regiment of Guards	7	560	644
Queen Dowager's Regiment of Foot	11	550	651
Prince George of Denmark's Regiment of Foot	13	650	769
Holland Regiment of Foot	13	650	769
Earl of Bath's Regiment of Foot	11	550	649
Duke of Norfolk's Regiment of Foot	10	500	590
Marquise of Worcester's Regiment of Foot	10	500	590
Earl of Huntingdon's Regiment of Foot	10	500	590
Sir Thomas Haggerston's Regiment of Foot	1	50	59
Captain Carter's Company of Foot	1	50	59
Earl of Plymouth's Regiment of Foot	1	50	59
Royal Regiment of Foot	11	550	671
Royal Regiment of Fuziliers	12	590	717
Royal Regiment of Dragoons	8	400	504
Queen Consort's Regiment of Dragoons	6	300	378
Princess Anne of Denmark's Regiment of Dragoons	6	300	378

This means that during the July of 1686 there were 12,884 soldiers billeted on the Heath.

The following records are from the summer camp of 1688 and were recorded in May and on 6 and 7 June for the regiments of foot and 20 June for the regiments of horse.[52]

---

51 BL, Add MS 15897, Hyde Papers, Pensions Army and Navy etc, 1664–1745, vol.1, f.86.
52 WO55/335 Hampstead Heath June 1688, f.31, and 19 May 1688, f.41.

Regiment of Foot	Sarg	Corp	Drummers	Privates
Two Battalions of the First Foot Guards	39	39	26	1,040
One Battalion Second Regiment of Foot Guards	21	21	14	560
One Battalion Scots Guards	17	24	20	632
Royal Regiment of Foot	33	33	24	540
Queen Dowager Regiment of Foot	27	39	14	638
Holland Regiment of Foot	27	39	12	638
Royal Regiment of Fuziliers	40	41	27	677
Earl of Litchfield's Regiment of Foot	23	33	12	539
Earl of Huntingdon's Regiment of Foot	23	33	12	539
Total Foot	250	302	162	5,803

Regiments of Horse	Corp	Trumpeters	Privates	
Royal Regiment	27	19	450	
Queen's Regiment of Horse	27	19	360	
Earl of Peterborough's Regiment of Horse	18	13	240	
Sir John Famoirt's Regiment of House	18	13	240	
Major General Wardoms' Regiment of Horse	18	13	240	
Earl of Arran's Regiment of Horse	18	13	240	
Colonel Hamilton's Regiment of Foot	18	13	240	
Princes Anne of Denmark's Regiment of Horse	18	13	240	
Queen Dowager's Regiment of Horse	18	13	240	
Total Horse	180	128	2,490	

Regiments of Dragoons	Sarg	Corp	Drummers	Privates
Royal Regiment of Dragoons	16	24	32	400
Queens Regiment of Dragoons	12	18	24	300
Princesses Regiment of Dragoons	12	18	24	300
Total	40	60	80	1,000

Quarters

Without permanent army barracks, the state was often forced to quarter regiments over a large area so that they did not place to great a strain on the local community. While it was possible for regiments to be quartered under canvas during the summer months, winter was another matter and more permanent accommodation had to be found. The first option was for a regiment or part thereof to be accommodated within a fortress and therefore also act as the garrison for that area, failing that, companies were quartered within local inns, with the landlords being paid a fixed amount to supply board and lodging. Soldiers were not supposed to be billeted on the local population without their consent. Previous occasions where soldiers were forcibly billeted in private houses, usually as a form of pacification or as retribution for the householder's previous loyalties or beliefs, provided some of the objections the English population held against the prospect of a standing army. One of the consequences of these regulations and the lack of regimental barracks was that winter quarters were dispersed over a large geographical area, the following examples from the winter of 1686 and April 1689 show just how widespread the army was. This had a serious effect on training, morale, and discipline within regiments, with training often being possible at the company level. Soldiers with trades were generally allowed to utilise them in order to supplement their wages.

Summer Quarters 1689[53]

First Troop of Guards	Bishop Stafford and Hockerell
Second Troop	Holland
Third Troop	Northampton and Wellingborough
Royal Regiment of Horse	Holland
Sir John Lanier's	Berwick
Colonel Villiers	Morpeth
Lord Colchester's	Newcastle
Colonel Godfrey	3 Troops Isle of Wight, 3 Troops Guildford, Dorking and Rygate
Colonel Coyes'	Newcastle
Colonel Langston's	Glasgow
Lord Hewitt	Penrith
Lord Cavendish	Newcastle
Lord Cornbury's	Newcastle
Colonel Leveson's	Kendall
Colonel Berkley's	Berwick
First Regiment Foot Guards	4 companies at Windsor, 4 companies at Winchester, 8 companies at Landguard Fort
Coldstream Regiment	Holland
Royal Regiment	Holland
Major General Kirke's	Ireland
Sir Charles Littleton's	Ireland
Lord Colonel Churchill's	Holland
Colonel Trelawney's	Plymouth, Scilly and Pendennis
Royal Regiment of Fusiliers	Holland
Colonel Beaumont's	Carlisle
Colonel Cunningham's	Ireland
Sir John Hanmor's	Ireland
Earl of Bath's	Jersey and Guernsey
Colonel Wharton's	10 Hull, York, Tinmouth & Scarbrough
Colonel Hastings	Berwick
Colonel Beveridge's	Kendall
Sir James Leslie's	10 Berwick, 3 Carlisle
Colonel John Hales'	Holland
Colonel Richards	Ireland
Colonel Hodges	Holland
Colonel Fitzpatrick	Holland
Colonel Luttrell's	Isle of Wight
Earl of Monmouth's	Portsmouth
Sir John Edgworth's	Chester
Sir John Guise's	Portsmouth
Sir Robert Peyton's	Exeter
Troop of Scott's Guards	Middlewich, Norwich
Sir Thomas Levingston's	Scotland

53 NA, WA55/336, Quarters of His Majesties Forces, 22 April 1689, ff.85–86.

Regiment of Scott's Guards	Holland
Sir David Collyear's	Holland
Colonel Dofferrell's	Holland
New Regiments	
Duke of Norfolk's	Reading and Norwich
Duke of Boulton's	1 regiment Bristol, the other at York
Earl of Kingston's	Litchfield and Coventry
Earl of Roscomon's	Salisbury, Wilton and Amberbury
Earl of Drogheda	Brecknock and Abergavenny
Lord Lovelace's	Oxford
Lord Castleton's	York
Lord Lisburn's	Huntingdon, Godman, Chester St Ives, St Neott's
Lord Herbert's	Bridgnorth, Shrewsbury
Sir Edward Dearing's	8 Worcester, 2 Evesham, 1 Droitwich, 1 Bromsgrove, 1 Pershore
Sir Henry Ingoldsby's	Birmingham
Sir Thomas Gorver's	Doncaster
Colonel Earle's	Bristol
Colonel Melonisie	Colchester, Cogshall, Manytree
Colonel Camboni	Ipswich, Woodbridge, Stow, Hadley, Needham
Colonel Cailemott's	Chatham, Stroud, Finsbury, Gillingham, Rochester, Milton, Sittingbourne and Maidstone
Dutch Forces	
Guarde de Corps	Westminster and Hampton Court
Blew Guard of Horse	Westminster
Marquise of Monpellion's	Towards Berwick
Major General Scravenmore's	Towards Berwick
Lt-General Ginkell's	Enfield, Cheston, Broxburn, Hoddesden, Anwell, Stanstes & St Margaretts
Colonel Von Oyen's	Towards Berwick
Colonel Lulerteini's	Towards Berwick
Colonel Sihack's	Towards Berwick
Grave Van Lippe's	Epping, Epping Street, and the two Angar
Colonel Boncour's	Towards Berwick
Blew Dragoons	Towards Berwick
Regiment of Foot Guards	Westminster and Hampton Court
Colonel Bubington's	Tower Hamlets
Colonel Tolmarsh	Tower Hamlets
Earl of Nasraus	Tower Hamlets
Colonel Cutt's	3 Sheerness, 4 Tilbury, 1 Landguard Fort, rest at Southwark
Prince of Brandenburg's	Paddington, Marylebone, Kilburn, Hampstead, Highgate Newington, Islington, Pomereys, Kentish Town, and Harleston Green.
Heer van Carolston's	Knightsbridge, Kennington, The Gravelpitts, Cheswick, Turnham Green, Hammersmith, Parsons Green, Fulham, Waltham Green and

Winter Quarters 1686[54]

Regiments	Number of Troops or Companies	Quarters
His Majesties Royal Regiment of Horse	Three Troops	Reading
	Two Troops	Newbury
	One Troop	Wallingford
	One Troop	Marlow
	One Troop	Wickham
	One Troop	Henley
The Queen's Regiment of Horse	Three Troops	Canterbury
	Two Troops	Maidstone
	One Troop	Sittingbourne
	One Troop	Faversham
	One Troop	Ashford
	One Troop	Lenham
Earl of Peterborough's Regiment of Horse	Three Troops	Oxford
	One Troop	Abingdon
	One Troop	Woodstock
	One Troop	Tame
Earl of Plymouth's Regiment of Horse	Three Troops	Cambridge
	Two troops	Huntingdon and Godmanchester
	One Troop	St Ives
Major-General Werden's Regiment of Horse	One Troop	Croydon
	Three troops	Epping, Bow, Stratford, and Romford
	Two Troops	Mitcham, Carshalton, Tooting, Streatham, and Bromley
Earl of Arran's Regiment of Horse	Three Troops	Leicester
	Three Troops	Ashby-de-la-Zouch, Loughborough, and Melton
Earl of Shrewsbury's Regiment of Horse	Two Troops	Buckingham
	One Troop	Wimslow
	Two Troops	Aylesbury
	One Troop	Wendover
The Princess Anne of Denmark's Regiment of Horse	Three Troops	Coventry
	Three Troops	Warwick
The Queen Dowager's Regiment of Horse	Three Troops	Bishop Stafford, Hockerel, Stansted, and Dunmow
	Three Troops	Saffron Walden, Littlebury, and Audley End
The Royal Regiment of Dragoons	Two Troops	Shrewsbury
	One Troop	Wrexham
	One Troop	Whitchurch
	One Troop	Oswestry
	One Troop	Ludlow

54 BL, Add MS 15897 Hyde Papers: Pensions Army and Navy etc., 1664–1745, vol.1, ff.78–80.

Regiments	Number of Troops or Companies	Quarters
	One Troop	Bridgnorth
	One Troop	Nanptwich
The Queens Regiment of Dragoon	Two troops	Pontefract and Ferrybridge
	One Troop	Wakefield
	Two Troops	Leeds
	One Troop	Halifax
The Princess's Regiment of Dragoons	Two Troops	Gloucester
	One Troop	?
	One Troop	Somerton
	One Troop	Evile
	One Troop	Bridgewater
First Battalion Foot Guards	Seven Companies	Rochester, Stroud, Chatham, and Gillingham
Royal Regiment of Foot	Ten Companies	Scotland
	Eight Companies	Yarmouth
	One Company	Landguard Ford
	Two Companies	Bungey
Queen Dowager's Regiment of Foot	Ten Companies	Bristol
	One Company	Chepstow
Prince George of Denmark's Regiment of Foot	Five Companies	Portsmouth
	Five Companies	Exeter
	Three Companies	Sheerness
The Holland Regiment of Foot	Nine companies	Hull
	Four Companies	York
The Queen's Regiment of Foot	Ten Companies	Plymouth
	One Company	Pendennis Castle
The Royal Regiment of Foot	Thirteen Companies	Tower of London and Tower Hamlets
The Princess's Regiment of Foot	Ten Companies	Berwick upon Tweed
Colonel Cornwall's Regiment of Foot	Ten Companies	Portsmouth
Earl of Bath's Regiment of Foot	Six Companies	Taunton
	Five Companies	Portsmouth
Marquis of Worcester's Regiment of Foot	Ten Companies	Chester
Earl of Litchfield's Regiment of Foot	Four Companies	Gravesend and Tilbury
	Two Companies	Guernsey
	Two Companies	Jersey
	Two Companies	Windsor
Sir Edward Hales Regiment of Foot	Ten Companies	Southwark
Colonel Herbert's Regiment of Foot	Three Companies	Tinmouth
	Seven Companies	Newcastle
Independent Companies	Sir Christopher Musgrave's	Carlisle
	Peter Shackerley's	Chester
	Lord Hatton's	Guernsey
	Sackville Tufton's	Gravesend
	Earl of Plymouth's	Hull
	Lord Jermin's	Jersey
	Earl of Gainsborough's	Portsmouth

Regiments	Number of Troops or Companies	Quarters
	Richard Carter's	Portsmouth
	Francis Godolphin's	Scilly Island
	Henry Villiers'	Tinmouth
	Thomas Cheeks	Tower of London
	Robert Minor's	Upton Castle
	Sir Robert Holmes'	Tower of London
	Sir John Reresby's	York

7

Conclusion

While there is a current trend in military history to encompass a wider political, socio-economic, or cultural context, research into the physical aspects of warfare is still an important and necessary addition to the available historiography. The intent of this manuscript is to add to the limited historiography and encourage debate into this neglected area of military technology, which was so eloquently stated by Black in the opening quotation.[1] As stated in the opening chapter, the primary intent is to rectify the lack of research and academic literature regarding the plug bayonet, by answering the primary research question – to what extent did the plug bayonet replace the pike during the second half of the seventeenth century?

The second chapter looked into the physical aspects of the plug bayonet utilising the reference collection at the Royal Armouries and the Broughton House collection. By detailed examination of the grips of 47 plug bayonets and the internal muzzle dimensions of 113 muskets this chapter addressed the pivotal issues and a general assumption regarding the plug bayonet – were plug bayonets a universal fit? The findings of the research are that Ordnance pattern bayonets were a universal fit, while all but four bayonets of non-Ordnance bayonets were also a universal fit. This equates to 92 percent of the bayonets from the research, encompassing 24 bayonet manufacturers fitting all the muskets sampled for this survey. These findings are the result of the first academic study in this area of research and can be extrapolated to say that the majority of plug bayonets were usable by all contemporary muskets.

The third chapter addressed the issues of weapons and supply, it looked at the standard weapons in use during the period in question, the musket (matchlock and flintlock), pike, and grenades. The chapter shows that both matchlock muskets and the pike were in use for longer than generally suggested, with matchlock muskets being ordered as late as the 1690s. evidence for the use of pikes into the 1700s by the English army is always going to be contentious, but on the basis of probability they were still being issued in 1704. All the evidence obtained from Board of Ordnance records

---

1 Black, *Rethinking Military History*, pp.123–124.

Battle of the Boyne, 1 July 1690, print by Dirk Mass, dated 1690. (Courtesy of the Rijksmuseum, Netherlands)

shows that weapons were not just issued on a speculative basis but issued in accordance with the number of men in the company or battalion requesting them. So, when the board issued 14 pikes per company, they requested the return of the corresponding muskets, the same goes for issues of flintlocks to replace matchlocks. When looking at the supply of plug bayonets; does the evidence support the hypothesis that bayonets were ordered in conjunction with muskets, or separately? And, is there evidence to show a simultaneous increase in bayonet requests with a similar decrease in requests for pikes. The primary source of information for this chapter is Board of Ordnance records that are part of the Dartmouth Papers. Even when taking the concerns raised by Chandler regarding reliability of government documents, these are an important and reliable source of historical records.[2] This manuscript is using the Ordnance records not just to show the physical manifestations of bayonet procurement, but also the change in the mindset of senior ordnance personnel, and a change in military theory regarding infantry weapons and tactics.

Documentary evidence shows large numbers of bayonets being ordered from 1672, with an order placed for 10,000 from Joseph Andley in 1678.[3] When this is combined with the evidence from 20 March 1678, this shows an intent to arm all musketeers with the bayonet, which changes our

2   Chandler, *Blenheim*, p.95.
3   SR, D(W)1778/V/13, Dartmouth Papers, folio 15.

understanding of the development of bayonets within the English army.[4] This confirms that there was both the resources and the intent at the Board of Ordnance to change infantry tactical theory, the reasons this change was never implemented is unclear, but one hypothesis is due to a lack of commitment from the regimental level. The evidence suggest that bayonets were considered suitable for units that historically were not issued with pikes to protect them against enemy horse – dragoons, grenadiers, and marine units until 1689. Bayonets were only generally issued to musketeers after 1689, but these were in addition to pike and not its replacement. Table 5 shows the numbers of bayonets and pikes in Ordnance stores, in 1684 there were two pikes in storage for every bayonet, by 1687 this was increased to five pikes for every bayonet, this could be due to pikes being returned to storage. Records show that as late as 1704 some troops were armed with a ratio of four muskets to one pike and one bayonet to every 10 muskets.[5] This contradicts the previously held view that all English troops were solely armed with muskets and bayonets by this time. The research shows that in 1687 the Board of Ordnance were in possession of 60 socket bayonets, but the data suggest these were never issues, as the stores held 60 socket bayonets for two years. Goldstein's interpretation that these were for 'some privately equipped regiment' and that the Board of Ordnance did not purchase socket bayonets until 1703, is not substantiated by the evidence.[6] The fact they these are held with Ordnance stores dictates they were purchased by the Ordnance and not privately. The data also confirms that during the seventeenth century bayonets were ordered separately from muskets and even scabbards, and there was not a single unified ordering system.

The evidence from English and Scottish battlefields reveals only two recorded archaeological remains for bayonets, these are both located in the Blake Museum, Somerset, although we know from records that 1,600 bayonets were issued prior to the Monmouth rebellion but only 538 returned. Due to the utilitarian nature of the plug bayonet, the remainder were either kept by individual regiments and soldiers or recovered by the civilian population. Further investigation and research is required at both the Sedgemoor and Killiecrankie battlefields to help fully understand the lack of archaeological records.

Chapter 4 incorporated research into contemporary drill manuals, the data from these has been used in a similar way to the Ordnance records in chapter three. The first mention of bayonets, dragoons, and grenadiers in English publications appear in 1678, the fact that these do not appear in their 1676 volume gives a transition date for the general inclusion of specific drills for dragoons, grenadiers, and bayonets.[7] The evidence from the drill manuals confirms the conclusion from Ordnance records in chapter three that until

---

4   SR, D(W)1778/V/71A, Folio 170, Armes and Amunicon Proposed for 12,978 foot, 20 March 1678.
5   BL, Add MS 61165 Blenheim Papers Vol. LXV pp.24–25, 15 June 1703.
6   E. Goldstein, *The Socket Bayonet*, p.8.
7   Anon., *Abridgement of the English Discipline*, 1678, p.141 and Anon., *Abridgement of the English Discipline*, 1676.

1689 bayonets were generally only available to dragoons and grenadiers etc. Only after 1690 do the drill manuals show bayonets issued to all musketeers, but in addition to troops armed with pikes. The drill manuals also confirm that bayonet drill was designed to combat enemy horse and not against enemy infantry, with a clubbed musket still being dictated for self-defence against foot.[8] Despite Chandlers concerns that drill manuals contained outdated information, the evidence from the *Exercise of Foot, Arm'd with Firelock-Muskets and Pikes* in illustration 7 confirms that these manuals were used over a period of time and updated to include new principles and theories of drill.

While further research into the records of later Master-Generals of Ordnance would hopefully expand on these results as would access to other collections of plug bayonets and documents, the evidence reported within this manuscript has produced conclusive results. While the plug bayonet was in use within the English army from 1662, with large numbers being ordered from 1677, the plug bayonet was apart from exceptional circumstances never intended as a replacement for the pike. The evidence has dismissed the general assumptions perpetuated by Norris that the swell was there to stop inexperienced troops getting the bayonet stuck in the musket barrel, and confirmed that plug bayonets were indeed a universal fit.[9]

The evidence presented confirms that the plug bayonet was intended as an ancillary protection against cavalry in conjunction with the pike and potentially could have been in general use from 1678. Therefore, General Hugh Mackay's explanation that the bayonet caused his defeat at Killiecrankie is at best down to his misuse of the weapon.

Chapters 5 and 6 look at developments in military discipline and corresponding evolution of infantry tactics. Historians have always taken the assumption that the use of the pike had not changed from pre-English Civil War days and remained confined to the middle of the battalion or regiment. Close examination of the records shows that although this could be the case, pikes were also deployed on a company. With each matching in a specific order, with their pike contingent, this would be the natural choice, giving great protection to the whole battalion. This method does produce a more even weight of fire over the whole battalion, but possibly without the befit of a solid central mass of pikes to act as a central point. Grenadiers are also shown in a new dimension, with a distinct role when the battalion closes with an enemy in the open as well as attacking fortifications. The information enclosed within various drill manuals, show that the grenade was used in both types of engagement and not just limited to siege warfare. Lastly, information provided from the records of the army's summer camps shows that battalions were issued with battalion guns certainly as early as 1685, which is years before the current historiography suggests.

Chapter 6 provides snapshots of the of the English establishment from 1661 to 1703, which shows how much the structure of battalions changed

---

8   Anon., *General Exercise*, 1689, pp.6–7. BL, Add MS 27892; *Treaties,* Douglas, pp.212–224, also J.S., *Military Discipline or the Art of War* (Cornhill: Robert Morton, 1689), pp.31–34.

9   Norris, *Fix Bayonets!*, pp.7–10.

until the battalion structure was fixed at 13 companies. We see how in times of peace the army's ranks contracted and independent companies were formed to garrison key towns, fortresses, and castles. These lists indicate the multi-national nature of the English establishment with troops from Hanover & Cell, Hess, Prussia, as well as Denmark and Holland.

In conclusion, the evidence shows that the development of the English army was intrinsically linked to the development of tactics and weapons. Furthermore, the evidence within this manuscript proves that the plug bayonet did not replace the pike during the second half of the seventeenth century but was used in conjunction alongside the pike. The plug bayonet was the correct weapon at the correct time and enabled the English army amongst others to eventually withdraw the pike and move eventually towards the successful socket bayonet.

Appendix I

Ordnance Pattern Plug Bayonet Dimensions (mm)

Royal Armouries Reference No:	Overall Length	Grip Length	Diameter Swell	Diameter Top	Diameter Middle	Diameter Base
10.741	480	125.0	30.5	24.7	19.1	15.9
10.289	857	137.9	29.9	26.1	23.3	18.2
10.1608	468	127.2	29.5	24.8	20.0	14.7
10.1606	422	103.5	29.0	27.1	21.4	17.5
10.1610	445	129.0	31.0	26.4	21.2	18.5
10.1611	357	111.2	30.2	25.9	21.1	14.7
10.1612	358	105.6	32.2	27.4	21.4	14.0
10.1609	476	154.5	33.3	27.1	22.6	18.3
10.1613	463	154.3	33.0	26.4	21.2	17.1
10.1615	464	133.8	33.5	33.1	22.6	17.9
10.1607	460	146.3	33.4	27.4	22.6	18.0
10.1614	373	117.9	31.6	29.6	22.1	17.6
10.4609	493	155.8	33.2	30.4	22.8	18.6
21.89	374	116.6	31.0	28.0	21.4	19.1
10.68	880	114.9	30.2	20.0	17.9	17.6
10.67	479	139.8	30.9	24.3	18.9	14.8
10.66	310	105.6	28.8	23.0	18.7	15.9
10.1592	478	151.8	31.5	28.4	20.7	18.4

Appendix II

Non-Ordnance Pattern Plug Bayonet Dimensions (mm)

Collection	Reference No:	Overall Length	Grip Length	Diameter Swell	Diameter Top	Diameter Middle	Diameter Base
Thomas Del Mar[1]	131/06 Dec 2017[2]	440	140	26.6	21.7		12.1
M. Shearwood	MS001	457	156	30.6	17.9	15.7	12.3
Hutchinson Scott[3]	206/25 May 2018	310	132	N/A	27.1	18.1	16.5
Boughton House Collection	N117	460	140	34	28	21.1	18
	N113	474	145	33	28	21.1	18
	N114	510	145	34	30.1	22	18
	No 6	N/A[4]	132	31	29	18	15
	No 10	N/A	138	25	20	18	17
	No Number	N/A	140	25	18	17	15
	No 116	N/A	140	26	20	18	17
	No 5	N/A	140	34	28	20	18
	NO 11	500	142	29	22	20	16
Royal Armouries	10.688	442	129.1	26.6	21.3	17.4	15.0
	10.235	460	100.7	19.7	18.1	17.6	16.1
	10.814	529	135.9	32.1	23.1	18.6	14.2
	10.64	557	152.5	36.9	30.3	18.8	16.8
	10.247	423	138.9	27.3	20.1	17.5	14.7
	10.207	303	104.3	25.3	21.9	15.1	11.4
	10.390	462	134.7	37.5	27.5	21.0	20.1
	X.71	460	152	28.1	21.5	17.9	13.9
	X.73	361	116	24.3	15.9	14.3	10.9

1   With thanks to Thomas Del Mar auction house.
2   References equates to the lot number and date of the auction.
3   With thanks to Hutchinson Scott auction house.
4   N/A bayonets were inside their original scabbards which could not be removed.

Collection	Reference No:	Overall Length	Grip Length	Diameter Swell	Diameter Top	Diameter Middle	Diameter Base
	X.381	508	146	32.9	18.6	14.5	14.5
	X.208	334	116	39.3	16.5	12.1	10.1
	X.368	662	136	19.8	15.0	12.0	10.0
	10.64	546	165	34.7	22.4	16.6	15.1
	X.207	292	112	24.1	16.8	14.9	11.1
	10.741	491	125	30.6	25.1	18.4	17.5
	10.69	850	153	40.5	26.3	18.2	16.4
	10.253	450	144	31.1	24.7	19.0	15.7

Appendix III

Royal Armoury Leeds (Reference Collection) Musket Dimensions (mm)

Musket Matchlock or Flintlock	Royal Armouries Ref No:	Overall length	Barrel Length	Flare Diameter	Internal Diameter	Flared Muzzle	Musket Description brief
Flintlock	XII.65	1,342	962	19.7	19.5	Yes	1690 Scottish
Flintlock	12.1573	1542	1,036	19.4	19.4	No	
Flintlock	12.3107	1585	1,172	19.8	19.8	No	
Flintlock	12.8523	1587	1,169	18.4	18.4	No	
Matchlock	12.38	1575	1,150	20.2	19.2	Yes	1690
Matchlock	12.37	1550	1,150	20.4	19.8	Yes	
Matchlock	12.25	1578	1,150	20.3	20.2	Yes	William III
Matchlock	12.28	1562	1,129	19.8	19.4	Yes	
Matchlock	12.32	1550	1,145	20.0	19.9	Yes	1690
Matchlock	12.8525	1586	1,166	19.3	19.1	Yes	1690
Matchlock	12.34	1538	1,135	20.9	20.4	Yes	1690
Matchlock	12.39	1562	1,150	19.3	19.3	No	1690
Flintlock / Matchlock	12.2648	1560	1,148	20.8	20.8	No	Dutch
Matchlock	12.41	1551	1,146	20.0	19.5	Yes	
Matchlock	12.8554	1554	1,150	19.8	19.8	No	
Matchlock	12.36	1545	1,130	20.7	20.0	Yes	
Matchlock	12.5559	1550	1,130	21.6	20.0	Yes	
Flintlock	12.74	1572	1,145	21.5	21.1	Yes	Brass fittings
Matchlock	12.1039	1555	1,156	20.2	20.0	Yes	

Colour Plate Commentaries

Commentary below refers to Plates 1, 2, 3.1 & 3.2

Drill for Plug Bayonet taken from *An Abridgement of the English Military Discipline: Reprinted by His Majesties Special Command* (London: John Bill, Henry Hill and Thomas Newcomb, 1685), but could have been taken from any drill manual up to 1700. The soldier in the image is wearing the uniform of the Royal Dragoons *c.*1670–80 and is equipped with a flintlock musket with sling, which was issued to all dragoon and grenadier units at this time. Although these could be slightly shorter that the standard muskets, dragoons were not always equipped with 'true carbines' until later in the period. The cartouche box holds a ready supply of cartridges, between 12 and 20 depending on the individual manufacturer.

While the following orders are for 'parade ground' drill, in times of need only the first four orders are required to use the bayonet for offence or defence.

Images courtesy of Alan Larsen and Stuart Makin, © author's photograph.

Plate 1

1.1 Calf about your Fire-Locks to [your] Left Side
1.2 Draw your Dagger
1.3 Screw your Daggers into the muzzle of your Fire-Locks [with the flat of the cross-guard towards you]
1.4 Recover your Arms

Plate 2

2.1 Charge to the Front [four times]
2.2 As you Were
2.3 Charge to the Left [four times, as you were, then to the right four times]
2.4 Recover your Arms

Plate 3

3.1 Calf Your Fire-Lock
3.2 Close up of how the plug bayonet fits the musket barrel, how the swell of the grip does not make contact with the musket barrel (see the conclusion of chapter 7 for detail)
3.3 Officer's genadier cap, Scottish regiment dated 1692 with the royal cypher of King William III and Queen Mary. National War Museum, Edinburgh Castle. (Photo author's collection)
3.4 Oath of Loyalty to King William III and Queen Mary signed by the officers of Lord Cardross's (Scottish) Regiment of Dragoons. National War Museum, Edinburgh Castle. (Photo author's collection)

Plate 4 – Harley's Regiment of Foot, Dunkirk 1662

Dunkirk was ceded to English control in 1658 under the Protectorate and continued to be an English garrison under Charles II until England's final withdrawal in 1662 (England gained Dunkirk briefly again in 1712 in part payment for its withdrawal from the Grand Alliance). The figure depicts a musketeer of Sir Robert Harley's Regiment of Foot prior to its transfer to Tangiers in January 1662 along with the Irish regiments belonging to Farrell and Fitzgerald. He is equipped with the typical matchlock musket still with the early type of trigger mechanism, bandolier, sword, and newly-issued plug bayonet (see chapter 1 for further information).

Plate 5 – King's Own Royal Dragoons, 1685

Known at various time as the King's Own, His Majesties Own Royal Regiment of Dragoons, or by its simpler title of the Royal Regiment of Dragoons was commanded in January 1685 by Lord John Churchill. The trooper shown is wearing what could become the traditional red coat, with brass buttons and blue lining. Cloth and the dyes to make them were sources locally, therefore there was not a standardised uniform colour during this period. He has been issued with a flintlock carbine, cartouche box, sword, and bayonet. He wears 'French' style dragoon boots with buckles at the ankle and lower calf, which were easier to wear when not riding.

Plate 6 – Pikeman, Viscount Kenmure's (Scottish) Regiment of Foot, 1689

Viscount Kenmure's Regiment of Foot raised in April 1689, which held the centre of the Government line at the Battle of Killiecrankie. There were recorded as being equipped with 450 bayonets and a mixture of matchlock and flintlocks muskets according to a privy council warrant prior to the battle. The were issued with one pike for every three muskets. The soldier is shown wearing a red coat with tin buttons, with red facings (there is some suggestion that the facings were white).

Plate 7 – Grenadier, His Majesties First Regiment of Foot Guards, Flanders 1689

In 1689 the First Regiment of Foot Guards consisted of 24 companies and four companies of grenadiers. Following the Glorious Revolution of 1688, William of Orange posted both battalions along with the Coldstream Guards to Flanders, with their duties in London being carried out by the Dutch Garde te Voet. The grenadier is shown wearing a red coat and waistcoat with yellow ribbons. His grenadier cap shows William's royal cypher *WR*. He is equipped with a flintlock musket with sling (only issued to grenadiers and dragoons at this time), cartouche box, grenade pouch and plug bayonet. The bayonet is of the style shown in image 9.

Plate 8 – Hamilton's Regiment of Foot, Portugal 1705

Hamilton's (later the 34th) Regiment of Foot was part of Peterborough's original force for the invasion of the Spanish Peninsula. When the Earl of Nottingham was involved in the planning for 1703 exhibition, he stipulated to the Board of Ordnance that one in four of the musketeers should have their muskets replaced with pikes. Ordnance records state that each company in Peterborough's Barcelona expedition of 1705 were to exchange fourteen muskets for pikes (and to return their muskets to the stores).

Bibliography

Primary Sources

Manuscripts: British Library
London, British Library, Add MS 61165 Blenheim Papers. Volume: LXV
London, British Library, Add MS 61285 Blenheim Papers. Vol. CLXXXV
London, British Library, Add MS 61287
NA Blenheim Papers. Vol. CLXXXVII
London, British Library, Add MS 61289 Blenheim Papers. Vol. CLXXXIX
London, British Library, Add MS 61295 Blenheim Papers. Vol. CXCV
London, British Library, Add MS 61298 Blenheim Papers. Vol. CXCVIII
London, British Library, Add MS 61331 Blenheim Papers. Vol. CCXXXI
London, British Library, Add MS 61332 Blenheim Papers. Vol. CCXXXII (ii+28)
London, British Library, Add MS 61335 Blenheim Papers. Vol. CCXXXV
London, British Library, Add MS 61346 Blenheim Papers. Vol. CCXLVI
London, British Library, Egerton MS 3336, Leeds Papers. Vol. XIII
London, British Library, Egerton MS 3344 Leeds Papers. Vol. XXI – Muster Rolls: 1688
London, British Library, Add MS 38848 Hodgkin Papers Vol. III
London, British Library, Add MS 15551 House of Commons Debates
London, British Library, Add MS 28877 John Ellis Papers
London, British Library, Add MS 41805 Middleton Papers. Vol. III
London, British Library, Add MS 41817 Middleton Papers. Vol. XV
London, British Library, Add MS 27892 Military Treaties of Gen. James Douglas

Manuscripts: National Archives
Kew, National Archives, ADM 106/445/85, 17 Oct 1694
Kew, National Archives, SP41 / 34 / 5, 6 July 1704, Estimate of Costs for 3,000 Firearms & 1,000 Bayonets & 1,000 tents
Kew, National Archives, SP41 / 3/ 7, 10 July 1704, Send arms, Bayonets and tents to Portsmouth
Kew, National Archives, SP41 / 41 / 11, 11 Nov 1704, Ordnance has 3,000 Muskets, 300 Bayonets but no Socket
Kew, National Archives, SP41 / 34 / 78, 16 Nov 1706, 500 Small arms for Nevis & St Christopher's, should Bayonets and Swords be sent
Kew, National Archives, CO323/4 Account of the Ordnance sent to the Plantations between the Restoration of Charles II and the Accession of King William in 1688
Kew, National Archives, WO47/9 Board of Ordnance minute book 1680
Kew, National Archives, WO47/12 Board of Ordnance minute book 1682
Kew, National Archives, WO47/13 Board of Ordnance minute book 1682–83
Kew, National Archives, WO47/17 Board of Ordnance minute book 1695–96
Kew, National Archives, WO47/18 Board of Ordnance minute book 1695–96
Kew, National Archives, WO47/33 Board of Ordnance minute book 1720

Master General & Board of Ordnance series 1

Kew, National Archives, WO55/334, 1685–1687, Entry Book of Warrants
Kew, National Archives, WO55/344, 1705–1709, Entry Book of Warrants
Kew, National Archives, WO55/345, 1709–1712, Entry Book of warrants,
NA WO55/401, Miscellaneous Entry Book, 1689–93
Kew, National Archives, WO55/470, 1682–1684, Entry Book of Warrants
Kew, National Archives, WO55/472,1682–1687, Entry Book of Warrants
Kew, National Archives, WO55/474, 1687–1689, Entry Book of Warrants
Kew, National Archives, WO55/475, 1688, Entry Book of Warrants
Kew, National Archives, WO55/476, 1689–1690,Entry Book of Warrants
Kew, National Archives, WO55/484, 1693–1702, Entry Book of Warrants
Kew, National Archives, WO55/485, 1693–1702, Entry Book of Warrants
Kew, National Archives, WO55/485, 1698–1702, Entry Book of Warrants

Manuscripts: Staffordshire Record Office

Stafford, Records Office, D(W)1778/V/2, Dartmouth Papers
Stafford, Records Office, D(W)1778/V/13, Dartmouth Papers
Stafford, Records Office, D(W)1778/V/20 Dartmouth Papers, Ordnance Papers
Stafford, Records Office, D(W)1778/V/39 Dartmouth Papers, Ordnance Papers
Stafford, Records Office, D(W)1778/V/44 Dartmouth Papers, Ordnance Papers E
Stafford, Records Office, D(W)1778/V/48 Dartmouth Papers, Ordnance Papers
Stafford, Records Office, D(W)1778/V/68 Dartmouth Papers, Ordnance Papers M
Stafford, Records Office, D(W)1778/V/70, Dartmouth Papers, Survey book Ireland
Stafford, Records Office, D(W)1778/V/71 A Dartmouth Papers, Ordnance Papers
Stafford, Records Office, D(W)177/V/1373, Dartmouth Papers. The General State of the Ordnance
    1679
Stafford, Records Office, D(W)1778/V/1374, Dartmouth Papers. A Survey and Remain of Northern
    Garrisons 1 May 1682
Stafford, Records Office, D(W)1778/V/1375A, Dartmouth Papers. The General State of the
    Ordnance 1684
Stafford, Records Office, D(W)1778/V/1375B, Dartmouth Papers. The General State of the
    Ordnance 1684
Stafford, Records Office, D(W)1778/V/1376, Dartmouth Papers. Ordnance: General State of Stores
    1686
Stafford, Records Office, D(W)1778/V/1377, Dartmouth Papers. Ordnance: State of Stores 1687
    Ireland
Stafford, Records Office, D(W)1778/V/1378, Dartmouth Papers. Ordnance: Ireland 13 March 1685
Stafford, Records Office, D(W)1778/V/1379, Dartmouth Papers. December 1677
Stafford, Records Office, D(W)1778/V/1380, Dartmouth Papers. Office of Ordnance 27 December
    1677
Stafford, Records Office, D(W)1778/V/1396, Dartmouth Papers, Tangiers State of Ordnance 1679
Stafford, Records Office, D(W)1778/V/194, Dartmouth Papers, 1688

Manuscripts: National Army Museum

London, National Army Museum, NAM:28900. Class No 355.332.'1706', Nutt, J., *Accomplished
    Officer.*
London, National Army Museum, NAM: 6807.211 *Letters from the Duke of Schomberg to the Board
    of Ordnance 1689*

Books

Anon., *The English Military Discipline 1660* (Newgate: John Overton, 1660)
Anon., *An Abridgement of the English Military Discipline: By His Majesties Permission* (London:
    John Bull and Christopher Barker, 1676)
Anon., *An Abridgement of the English Military Discipline: By His Majesties Permission* (London:
    John Bull and others, 1678)
Anon., *An Abridgement of the Military Discipline: Appointed by His Majesty, to be used by all His
    Forces in His Ancient Kingdom of Scotland* (Edinburgh: Andrew Anderson, 1680)
Anon., *English Military Discipline: or the Way and method of Exercising Horse & Foot* (London:
    Robert Harford, 1680)

Anon., *An Abridgement of the English Military Discipline: Reprinted by His Majesties Special Command.* (London: John Bull, Henry Hill and Thomas Newcomb, 1684)

Anon., *An Abridgement of the English Military Discipline: Reprinted by His Majesties Special Command.* (London: John Bill, Henry Hill and Thomas Newcomb, 1685)

Anon., *An Abridgement of the Military Discipline: Appointed by His Majesty, to be used by all His Forces in His Ancient Kingdom of Scotland, By His Majesties Special Command* (Edinburgh: Andrew Anderson, 1686)

Anon., *The General Exercise Ordered by His Highness the Prince of Orange, To be Punctually Observed of all the Infantry in the Service of the States General of The United Provences: Being a most Worthy Compendium, Very useful for all Persons Concerned in the Noble Exercise of Arms* (The Hague: Jacob Scheltus, 1688)

Anon., *The General Exercise Ordered by His Highness the Prince of Orange, To be Punctually Observed of all the Infantry in the Service of the States General of The United Provences: Being a most Worthy Compendium, Very useful for all Persons Concerned in the Noble Exercise of Arms* (London: William Marshall, 1689)

Anon., *Command for the Exercise of Foot, Arm'd with Firelock-Muskets and Pikes; with Evolutions* (London: Anon., 1690)

Anon., *The Exercise of the Foot with the Evolutions* (London: Charles Bill and Thomas Newcomb, 1690)

Anon., *The New Exercises of Firelocks & Bayonets; Appointed by His Grace The Duke of Marlborough to be used by all the British Forces: With Instructions to perform every Motion by Body Foot and Horse* (London: John Morphew, 1708)

Anon., *A Military Dictionary: Explaining All Difficult Terms in Martial Discipline, Fortifications, and Gunnery* (London: J Morphew, 1708)

Anon., *A Military and Sea Dictionary: Explaining All Difficult Terms in Martial Discipline, Fortification, and Gunnery, and all Terms of Navigation* (London: J Morphew, 1711)

Axe, T., *An Epitome of the Whole Art of War: in two parts; the First of Military Discipline. The Second of fortifications and Gunnery* (Warwick Lane: J Moxon, 1692)

Bailie, W., *A9 Dualling Programme Killiecrankie to Pitagowan: Archaeological Metal Detecting Survey at Killiecrankie Battlefield* (Glasgow: Guard Archaeology, 2015)

Barriffe, W., *Military Discipline or the Young Artillery-Man* (London: Gartrude Dawson, 1661, 6th Edition)

Bernier, M., *L'epave du Elizabeth and Mary (1690): Fouilles Archeologiques: Rapport d'activites 1997* (Ontario: Ontario Parks Canada, 1997)

Bill, C., Hill, H., & Newcomb, T., *An Abridgment of the English Military Discipline.* (London: Bill, Hill & Newcomb, 1686)

Blackwell, J., *A compendium of Military Discipline* (London: John Blackwell, 1726)

Boddington, N., *The Perfection of Military Discipline after the new methods, as practiced in England and Ireland etc.* (London: N. Boddington, 1690)

Boddington, N., *The Perfection of Military Discipline, after the Newest Method: As Practiced in England and Ireland, &c.* (London: W. Wild, 1691)

Boddington, N., *The Perfection of Military Discipline, after the Newest method: As Practiced in England and Ireland, &c.* (London: I. Dawk, 1702)

Darker, J., *A Breviary of Military Discipline. Compos'd and Published for the use of the Militia* (London: D. Brown, 1692)

Gent, W., *Militia Discipline: The Words of Command, and the Directions for Exercising the Musket, Bayonet and Cartridges: and the Exercise for the Soldier of Militia Horse*, 2nd Edition (London: R. Harbin, 1717)

Historical Manuscript Commission, *The Manuscripts of S.H.L.E. Flemming Esq of Rydal Hall* (London: HMSO, 1890)

J.H., *The Compleat Gentleman Soldier: Or, A Treatise of Military Discipline, Fortifications and Gunnery* (London: Thomas Ballard, 1702)

J.S., *Military Discipline or the Art of War* (Cornhill: Robert Morton, 1689)

Kane, R., *Campaigns of King William and Queen Anne from 1689–1712* (Whitehall: J. Millan)

Kane, R., *Campaigns of King William and Queen Anne: from 1689 to 1712: Also, A new System of Military Discipline, for a battalion of Foot in Action; with the Most Essential Exercise of the Cavalry. Adorn'd with a Map of the Seat of War and a Plan to the Exercise*, [Facsimile] (Uckfield: Navy and Military Press, 2014)

Mackay, H., *The Exercise of the Foot with the Evolutions According to the Words of Command as they are Explained: As also the Forming of Battalions, with Directions to be observed by all Colonels, Captains, and other Officers in Their Majesties Armies* (Edinburgh: John Reid, 1693)

—— *Memoirs of the War Carried on in Scotland and Ireland M.DC.LXXXIX–M.DC.XCI* (Edinburgh: Bannatyne Club, 1833)

Morden, R., *Fortification and Military Discipline: in Two parts* (London: Robert Morden,1688)

Morphew, J., *The New Exercise of Firelocks & Bayonets; Appointed by his Grace the Duke of Marlborough to be used by all the British Forces* (London: John Morphew, 1708)

Moxon, J., *An Epitome of the Whole Art of War: in Two Parts* (London: J. Moxon, 1692)

Richardson, T., & Rimer, G., *Littlecote: The English Civil War Armoury* (Leeds: Royal Armouries, 2012)

Stevens, J., *Fortification and Military Discipline 1688* [Facsimile] (London: Robert Morden. 1688)

Thornton. R., *The Exercise of Foot: With the Evolutions According to the Words of Command* (Dublin: M. Gunne, 1701)

Venn, T., *Military & Maritime Discipline in Three Books* (1672)

Whitmore, C., *A Treatise of the English Military Discipline: Both the Old Way, and the Shortest Way now in Use* (London: J. Grantham, 1682)

Secondary Sources

Books

Anderson, M., *War and Society in Europe of the Old regime 1618–1789* (Stroud: Sutton Publishing, 1998)

Arnold, D., *Everyday Technology: Machines and Making of India's Modernity* (Chicago: University of Chicago Press, 2013)

Baker, E., and others, *L'épave du Elizabeth and Mary (1690): Fouilles Archéologiques: Rapport d'Activités 1997* (Ontario: Service d'Archéologie, 2008)

Bapasola, J., *Threads of History: The Tapestries at Blenheim Palace* (Oxford: Adler Press, 2005)

Barnett, C., *Britain and Her Army: A Military, Political and Social History of the British Army 1509–1970* (London: Cassell & Co, 1970)

Black, J., *A Military Revolution? Military Changes and European Society 1550–1800* (Basingstoke: Macmillan Education, 1991)

—— *Rethinking Military History* (Abingdon: Routledge, 2004)

Blackmore, D., *Destructive & formidable: British Infantry Firepower 1642–1765* (London: Frontline Books, 2014)

Chandler, D., *The Art of Warfare in the Age of Marlborough* (London: B.T. Batsford, 1976)

—— *Blenheim Preparation: The English Army on the March to the Danube, Collected Essays* (Staplehurst: Spellmount Publishing, 2004)

—— *Sedgemoor 1685: From Monmouth's Invasion to the Bloody Assizes* (Staplehurst: Spellmount Books, 1995)

Childs, J., *The Army of Charles II* (London: Routledge & Kegan Paul, 1976)

—— *The Army, James II, and the Glorious Revolution* (Manchester: Manchester University Press, 1980)

—— *Armies and Warfare in Europe 1648–1789* (Manchester: Manchester University Press, 1982)

—— *The British Army of William III, 1689–1702* (Manchester: Manchester University Press, 1987)

—— *The Nine Years' War and the British Army 1688–97: The operations in the Low Countries* (Manchester: Manchester University Press, 1991)

—— *Warfare in the Seventeenth Century* (London: Cassell, 2001)

—— *The Williamite Wars in Ireland 1688–1691* (London: Hambledon Continuum, 2007)

—— *General Percy Kirke and the Later Stuart Army* (London: Bloomsbury, 2014)

Dalton, C., *English Army Lists and Commission Registers, 1661–1714*, Volume 2 (London: Eyre & Spottiswoode, 1894)

—— *The Scots Army: with memoirs of the Commanders-in-Chief* – Primary Source Edition [Facsimile] (Milton Keynes: Lightning Source, 2016)

Dorrell, N., *Marlborough's Other Army: The British Army and the campaigns of the First Peninsular War, 1702–1712* (Solihull: Helion & Co, 2015)

Ede-Borrett, S., *The Army of James II: Uniforms & Organisation* (Newthorpe: Partizan Press, 1987)

—— *The Army of James II 1685–1688: The Birth of the British Army* (Solihull: Helion & Company, 2017)

Evans, R., *The Plug Bayonet: An Identification Guide for Collectors* (Shipley: RDC Evans, 2002)

Falkner, J., *Marlborough's Sieges* (Stroud: Spellmount Ltd, 2007)

—— *Marlborough's War Machine 1702–1711* (Barnsley: Pen and Sword, 2014)

Flinn, M., *Men of Iron: The Crowleys in the Early Iron Industry* (Edinburgh: Edinburgh University Press, 1962)

Foard, G., & Morris, R., *The Archaeology of English Battlefields: Conflict in the Pre-Industrial Landscape* (York: Council for British Archaeology, 2012)

French, D., 'The Mechanization of the British Cavalry between the World Wars', *War in History,* 10.3 (2003) 296–320

Galster, K., *Danish Troops in the Williamite Army in Ireland, 1689–91* (Dublin: Four Courts Press, 2012)

Girton, T., *The Mark of the Sword: A narrative history of The Cutlers' Company 1189–1975* (London: Hutchinson Benham, 1975)

Goldman, E., & Eliason, L. (eds), *The Diffusion of Military Technology and Ideas* (Stanford: Stanford University Press, 2013)

Goldstein, E., *The Socket Bayonet: in the British Army 1687–1783* (Rhode Island: Andrew Mowbray publishing, 2000)

Hall, R., *The Armies of Hesse and the Upper Rhine Circle* (Farnham: Pike and Shot Society)

—— *Uniforms and Flags of the Armies of Hanover, Celle, and Brunswick 1670–1715* (Farnham: Pike and Shot Society, 2016)

Hall, R., Stanford, I., & Roumegoux, Y., *Flags and Uniforms of the Dutch Army 1685–1715*, 2 vols, (Romford: Pike and Shot Society, 2014)

Harding, D., *Small Arms of the East India Company 1600–1856*, Volume 2 (London: Foresight Books, 1997)

Hughes, M., 'Technology, Science and War' in *Palgrave Advances in Modern Military History*, ed. by M. Hughes and W. Philpott (Basingstoke: Palgrave Macmillan, 2006) pp.231–57

Jackson, S., *The History of the French Bayonet* (Toledo: Steve Jackson, 2017)

Kilpatrick, M., & Bailie, W., *A9 Dualling Programme Killiecrankie to Pitagowan: Archaeological Metal detecting Survey at Killiecrankie Battlefield* (Glasgow: Guard Archaeology, 2015)

King, S. (ed.), *Great Northern War Compendium: A Special Collection of Articles by International Authors on the Great Northern War 1700–1721,* 2 vols (St Louis: THGC Publishing, 2015)

Lawson, C., *A History of the Uniforms of the British Army: From the Beginnings to 1760,* vol. 2 (Littlehampton, Littlehampton Books Service)

Locicero, M., Mahoney, R., & Mitchell, S., *A Military Transformed? : Adaptation and Innovation in the British Military, 1792–1945* (Solihull: Helion and Co, 2014)

Louth, W., *The Arte Militaire: The Application of 17th Century Military Manuals to Conflict Archaeology* (Solihull: Helion & Co, 2016)

Morillo, S., *What is Military History?* (Cambridge: Polity Press, 2006)

Manning, R., *An Apprenticeship in Arms: The Origins of the British Army 1585–1702* (Oxford: Oxford University Press, 2006)

Megorsky, B., *The Russian Army in the Great Northern War 1700–21: Organisation, Material, Training and Combat Experience, Uniforms* (Warwick: Helion & Co, 2018)

Norris, J., *Fix Bayonets!* (Barnsley: Pen & Sword, 2015)

Nosworthy, B., *The Anatomy of Victory: Battle Tactics 1689–1763* (New York: Hippocrene Books, 1992)

Parker, ., *The Military Revolution: Military Innovation and the Rise of the West 1500–1800* (Cambridge: Cambridge University Press, 1988)

Pollard, T., & Oliver, N., *Two Men in a Trench: Uncovering the Secrets of British Battlefields* (London: Penguin, 2003)

—— 'Dissecting Seventeenth- and Eighteenth- Century Battlefields: Two Case Studies from the Jacobite Rebellion in Scotland', in *Historical Archaeology of Military Sites: Method and Topic.* Ed. by Geier, R., and others (Texas: Texas A&M University Press, 2011), pp.99–111.

Priest, G., *Socket Bayonets: A History and collector's Guide* (Stroud: Amberley Publishing, 2016)

Roberts, M., *The Military revolution, 1560–1660: an inaugural lecture delivered before the Queen's University of Belfast* (Belfast: Queen's University Press, 1956)

Reid, S., *The Flintlock Musket: Brown Bess and Charleville 1715–1865* (Oxford: Osprey Publishing, 2016)

—— *Battle of Killiecrankie 1689: The Last Act of the Killing Times* (Barnsley: Frontline Books, 2018)

Shaw, A., *Calendar of Treasury Books: 1689–1692*, Volume 2 (London: HMSO, 1931)

Scott, J., *The British Army: its Origin, Progress and Equipment* (London: Cassell, Petter, Galpin & Co, 2009)

Starkey, A., *War in the Age of Enlightenment, 1700–1789* (Westport: Praeger Publishers, 2003)

Speelman, P. (ed.), *War, Society and Enlightenment: The Works of General Lloyd* (Leiden: Brill, 2005)

Tallett, F., *War and Society in Early-Modern Europe 1495–1715* (Abingdon: Routledge, 2001)

Tallett, F., and Trim, D. (eds), *European Warfare 1350–1750* (Cambridge: Cambridge University Press, 2010)

Tincey, J., *Sedgemoor 1685: Marlborough's First Victory* (Barnsley: Pen & Sword Books, 2005)

Tomlinson, H., *Guns and Government: The Ordnance Office under the later Stuarts* (London: Royal Historical Society, 1979)

Wace, A., *The Marlborough tapestries at Blenheim Palace: and their Relationship to Other Military tapestries of the War of The Spanish Succession* (London: Phaidon Press, 1968)

Walton, C., *History of the British Standing Army 1660 to 1700* (London: Harrison and Sons, 1894)

Watts, J., and White, P., *The Bayonet Book* (Birmingham: G. Dams & Lock Ltd, 1975)

Urban, W., *Matchlocks to Flintlocks: Warfare in Europe and beyond 1500–1700* (London: Frontline Books, 2011)

Articles

Ballard, J, 'Statistical Analysis as an Adjunct to Historical Research: Identification of the Likely Manufacturers of British Pattern 1907 Bayonets Supplied by the Birmingham Small Arms Company to the Siamese Government in 1920', *Arms and Armour*, 15.1 (2018) <DOI 10.1080/17416124.2018.1436491>

Ede-Borrett, S., 'A Walk Around the Battle of Sedgemoor Museums' *Arquebusier: Journal of the Pike and Shot Society*, XXXV/V (2018), 15–19

Evans, R., 'The Early British Plug Bayonet: Early Iron Mount Pattern' *The Armourer (The Militaria Magazine)*, 5 (1994)

Hayes-McCoy, G., 'The Battle of Aughrim 1691', Journal of the Galway Archaeological and Historical Society, 20 (1942) pp.1–30 (p.8) <https://www.jstor.org/stable/25535220>

—— 'The Scottish Plug Bayonet', *The Armourer (The Militaria Magazine)*, 24 November/December (1997)

—— 'Plug Bayonets', *The New Zealand Antique Arms Gazette*. December (1999), 19–22

McLay, K., Book Review, *The Scottish Historical Review*, 90. 1, 148–149 (2001) < https://0-doi-org. wam.leeds.ac.uk/10.3366/shr.2011.0012> [accessed 25 January 2019]

Stone, John, 'The Point of the Bayonet', *Technology and Culture*, 53.4 (2012) <http://www.jstore.org/ stable/41682745> [accessed 19 February 2018]

Thesis

De Witt, B., *The Board of Ordnance and Small Arms Supply: The Ordnance System, 1714–1783*, unpublished Ph.D. thesis (London: King's College, 1988)